The New Testament
The Good News of Jesus Christ

TEACHER GUIDE
Living in Christ

Rita E. Cutarelli, EdD

Carrie J. Schroeder

To access the ancillary teaching resources for this course, go to http://www.smp.org/resourcecenter/books/

saint mary's press

The publishing team included Gloria Shahin, editorial director; Steven McGlaun and Jeanette Fast Redmond, development editors. Prepress and manufacturing coordinated by the production departments of Saint Mary's Press.

Cover Image: © The Crosiers / Gene Plaisted, OSC

Printed in the United States of America

1252

ISBN 978-1-59982-076-7, Print
ISBN 978-1-59982-456-7, Kno
ISBN 978-1-59982-121-4, Saint Mary's Press Online Learning Environment

Contents

      Article 32 – The Conventions of Apocalyptic Literature
      Article 33 – Symbolic Language in the Book of Revelation
      Article 34 – An Overview of Revelation
      Article 35 – Eternal Truths of Revelation
      Article 48 – Ephesians
      Article 49 – Colossians
      Article 50 – Second Thessalonians
      Article 51 – The Pastoral Letters
      Article 52 – Christ the High Priest
      Article 53 – Exhortations to Faithfulness
      Article 54 – The Letter of James
      Article 55 – The Letters of First and Second Peter, and Jude
      Article 56 – The Letters of John

Introducing the Living in Christ Series

The New Testament: The Good News of Jesus Christ is the twelfth-grade elective course in the Living in Christ series.

Saint Mary's Press developed the Living in Christ series in response to the needs of important stakeholders in the catechesis process. The courses follow the sequence and contain the material from the USCCB's Curriculum Framework. Each course also contains other material in the student book and teacher guide that students should know, understand, and be able to carry out. Each course responds to the varied needs that teachers have expressed, especially about limited time and the range of catechizing the young people in a high school religion class have had, offering wisdom from "secular" educational methods that can address both time limits and diversity in the classroom.

With the Living in Christ series, Catholic high school students will understand foundational concepts about the Bible, Jesus Christ as a member of the Trinity, the Paschal Mystery, the Church, the Sacraments, and morality. They will also have skills to learn more about their faith by studying Scripture, reading primary theological sources, consulting the Catholic faith community, doing self-reflection, and having conversations with their peers. With your guidance your graduates will possess a lived faith as they move into their future.

The Living in Christ Series

The Living in Christ series has a different look and feel from traditional high school theology textbooks and teaching manuals.

- **The teacher guide, rather than the student book, provides the scope and sequence for the course.** Teaching with the student book is more like teaching with *The Catholic Faith Handbook for Youth* (Saint Mary's Press, 2008) than a textbook. The sequence of a textbook is important because the content builds on what has come before. A handbook provides material in a sensible order, but because the content does not rely on what has come before in quite the same way, the material can be presented in several different sequences.

- **The teacher guide provides you with ideas about how to teach not only with the student book but also with the Bible, resources on the Saint Mary's Press Web site *(smp.org/LivinginChrist),* and other resources found on the Internet.** The teacher guide works as a command center for the course, providing ways for you to teach key concepts to the students by bringing in a wide variety of resources.

- **The Living in Christ series invites you as teacher to develop your abilities to facilitate learning.** This series asks you to become an expert about your own students, discern how they learn best, and then lead them to understand main concepts in a way that speaks to their lived experiences and the issues of the day.
- **The Living in Christ series invites the students to be more engaged in their own learning.** This series asks the students to take charge of their learning process and to practice what it will mean to be adult Catholics who must translate scriptural and Church teaching into their real world.

These changes will enable the students to consider the most important concepts in the course at a deeper level.

The Series Web Site: *smp.org/LivinginChrist*

In addition to the teacher guide and student book, the Living in Christ series provides an extensive collection of digital resources for each course to assist you in guiding the learning of your students. The digital resources are sorted on the Web site by course and unit. For each unit in a course, you will find the following resources at *smp.org/LivinginChrist*:

- **Handouts** All handouts for a unit are provided in multiple digital formats, including Word and rich text formats that you can revise.
- **Method articles** Method articles explain teaching methods introduced in a unit that might be unfamiliar to some teachers.
- **Theology articles** Theology articles provide an in-depth exploration of key theological concepts presented in a unit to assist you in explaining the concept and responding to student questions.
- **PowerPoint presentations** Student learning in each unit is enhanced with PowerPoint presentations. Beyond simply repeating student book content, these PowerPoint presentations engage students through reflection and discussion. All of the Living in Christ PowerPoint presentations are in a format that allows you to revise them.
- **Useful links** Links to other resources are provided so you can enhance your students' learning with additional resources. The links direct your students to Web sites you can trust, and are continually checked for appropriateness and to ensure that they are active.

At *smp.org/LivinginChrist* you will also have access to an online test bank, which provides hundreds of questions for each course, beyond what is provided in the units. You can use test questions as they are presented or modify them for your students' learning needs.

Introducing *The New Testament: The Good News of Jesus Christ*

This course leads the students toward a deeper understanding of the New Testament and the Catholic approach to Scripture. The course starts by examining the relationship between the Old Testament and the New, as well as the essential role of Scripture in the life of the Christian community. The students then explore three exegetical methods in the Catholic approach to Scripture and the development of the New Testament canon. Subsequent units delve into the history, Christology, and ecclesiology of the books of the New Testament, beginning with the synoptic Gospels and the Gospel of John, and then exploring the Acts of the Apostles, the Pauline and Deutero-Pauline Letters, the Book of Revelation, and the later first-century epistles.

The course has eight units centered on eight important concepts about the New Testament. Each unit builds on the knowledge, skills, and understanding of the previous one. Within each unit the knowledge, skills, and understanding also build as it progresses. The eight units are as follows:

- Unit 1: Introduction to the New Testament

- Unit 2: A Catholic Approach to Scripture: Exegetical and Interpretive Methods

- Unit 3: The Development of the Gospels and the Writing of Mark

- Unit 4: The Gospels of Matthew and Luke

- Unit 5: The Gospel of John

- Unit 6: The Acts of the Apostles

- Unit 7: The Pauline and Deutero-Pauline Letters

- Unit 8: Late First-Century Writings

The Structure of Each Unit in This Teacher Guide

This teacher guide offers the teacher one path through each unit, referring the students to the student book, the Bible, resources on the Saint Mary's Press Web site *(smp.org/LivinginChrist)*, and other Internet resources.

The path for each unit has the goal of leading all the students to comprehend four "understandings" with the related knowledge and skills. This curriculum model assumes that you will adjust your teaching according to the needs and capabilities of the students in your class. You do not have to complete every learning experience provided, and we hope you substitute your own ideas for those in the guide when needed.

Each unit has three basic parts: the Overview, the Learning Experiences, and handouts.

Overview

The Overview is a snapshot of the whole unit. It provides the following information:

- the concepts the students should understand by the end of the unit
- the questions the students should be able to answer by the end of the unit
- a brief description of the summary assessments (final performance tasks) offered, which will show that the students understand the most important concepts
- a list of articles from the student book covered in the unit
- a summary of the steps in the Learning Experiences section (Each step in the unit builds on the one before but must be adjusted to fit your schedule and the needs of the students. The use of *steps* is more flexible than is a structure based on 60-minute periods, for example.)
- a list of background material on content and methods that can be found on the Saint Mary's Press Web site *(smp.org/LivinginChrist)*
- a list of Scripture passages used
- a list of vocabulary that comes from the student book and from the learning experiences in the teacher guide

Learning Experiences

The instruction and learning occur in this section. Each unit contains a similar process for instruction.

Preassess Student Knowledge of the Concepts

Each unit opens with one or more options for preassessing what the students already know about a topic. It is useful to know this information as you prepare to present new material.

Preassessing the students' knowledge can help you to determine how to use your time effectively throughout the unit. It is not worth your time to teach the students what they already know or to teach above their heads. Students learn most effectively when new concepts build on what they already know. More often, you have a mixed group knowledge-wise, which is good, because the students can help one another.

Unit 1 offers a more comprehensive questionnaire to help you see where the students are coming from religiously and in terms of knowledge and belief. This preassessment will help you to make choices throughout the unit. Based on what you learn in your preassessment in unit 1, you may decide to spend more or less time on given topics.

Present the Final Performance Tasks to the Students

A final performance task is a type of summary assessment, which means that it is a means of determining what the students understand, know, and can do after a period of instruction such as a unit. (The unit test is also a summary assessment.)

In addition to providing a unit test, we encourage you to assess (determine) student understanding of the four most important concepts in each unit by assigning one of the short projects called final performance tasks. Through these projects the students can demonstrate their understanding of the main concepts. This assignment allows you to have another snapshot of what the students understand.

For example, the four understandings for unit 2 are:

- Various exegetical methods enable us to read and interpret Scripture contextually.
- Literary criticism enables us to analyze a scriptural text by examining its genre, plot, characters, and symbolism.
- Sociohistorical criticism enables us to understand the culture and world in which a scriptural text was written.
- Ideological criticism enables us to understand how our own worldview shapes our interpretation of Scripture.

The handout "Final Performance Task Options for Unit 2" (Document #: TX002217) in the teacher guide outlines the assignment options. Note that for all the options, the students must show their understanding of these concepts. The first final performance task option has them write a research paper on the Catholic approach to Scripture. The second asks them to develop a group presentation for a parish Bible study group using the three exegetical tools listed. A traditional unit test is also provided.

We suggest that you explain the performance task options early in the unit so the students can focus on the knowledge and skills they can use for the final performance task they choose. This also helps to decrease the number of "Are we learning anything today?" or "Why do we have to learn this?" questions by giving the students the big picture of where they are headed and how they will get there.

Provide Learning Experiences for the Students to Deepen Their Understanding of the Main Concepts

This teacher guide uses the term *learning experiences* rather than *activities* to emphasize that much of what goes on in the classroom should contribute to student learning, such as explaining assignments; presenting new material; asking the students to work individually, in pairs, or in groups; testing the students; and asking them to present material to their peers.

Each step in the teacher guide leads the students toward deeper understanding of the four key understandings of a unit. At times learning experiences are grouped into a single step because they work toward the same goal. At other times a step includes only one learning experience. If you have a better way of achieving a step goal, by all means use it. However, if new vocabulary or content is introduced in a step you have chosen to skip, you may want to go over that material in some way, or remove that material from the unit test.

Throughout the steps, references are made to student book articles, resources at *smp.org/LivinginChrist*, and other Internet resources. Often the teacher guide addresses the content in the student book early in the unit and then asks the students to uncover a deeper meaning with various learning experiences throughout. When applicable the book refers to *smp.org/LivinginChrist* for resources at your fingertips.

The goal of this course is for the students to gain a deeper understanding of the material. But what is understanding? The understanding we want the students to gain is multifaceted. Understanding encompasses several of the "facets of understanding," used by Jay McTighe and Grant Wiggins in their book *Understanding by Design*:

We have developed a multifaceted view of what makes up a mature understanding, a six-sided view of the concept. When we truly understand we

Explain

Can explain—via generalizations or principles, providing justified and systematic accounts of phenomena, facts, and data; make insightful connections and provide illuminating examples or illustrations.

Interpret

Can interpret—tell meaningful stories; offer apt translations; provide a revealing or personal historical dimension to ideas and events; make the object of understanding personal or accessible through images, anecdotes, analogies, and models.

Apply

Can apply—effectively use and adapt what we know in diverse and real contexts—we can "do" the subject.

Perceive

Have perspective—see and hear points of view through critical eyes and ears; see the big picture.

Empathize

Can empathize—find value in what others might find odd, alien, or implausible; perceive sensitively on the basis of prior direct experience.

Reflect

Have self-knowledge—show metacognitive awareness; perceive the personal style, prejudices, projections, and habits of mind that both shape and impede our own understanding; are aware of what we do not understand; reflect on the meaning of learning and experience.

(P. 84)

Understand

Note that Saint Mary's Press has created icons for each facet of understanding. When a majority of facets are present, there will be an "understand" icon. When relevant, all facets of understanding should be addressed in each unit. If you are used to Bloom's Taxonomy, see *smp.org/LivinginChrist* for a comparison of both models of understanding and learning.

Provide a Day or Partial Day for the Students to Work on the Final Performance Tasks

This guide encourages you to give the students time in class to work on their final performance tasks if you have assigned them. You do not, however, have to wait until the end of the unit. Not only does this day give the students time to work in groups if needed or to do some research, but it also gives you the opportunity to identify any students who may be having trouble with the assignment and allows you to work with them during class time.

Give the Students a Tool to Help Them Reflect on Their Learning

The handout "Learning about Learning" (Document #: TX001159; see Appendix) is a generic way to help the students think about what they have learned during the entire unit. This process, whether done this way or in another fashion, is valuable for several reasons:

- The students do not get much time to reflect while they are moving through each unit. Looking over the unit helps them to make connections, revisit any "aha!" moments, and identify which concepts remain difficult for them to understand.
- We give students a gift when we help them to learn how they learn best. Insights such as "I didn't get it until we saw the video" or "Putting together the presentation required that I really knew my stuff" can be applied to all the disciplines they are studying.

Feel free to have the students discuss the handout questions in pairs at times for variety.

Handouts

All the handouts in the teacher guide, as well as the unit tests, are available on the Saint Mary's Press Web site at *smp.org/LivinginChrist,* as PDFs, as Word documents, or in rich text format (RTFs), for downloading, customizing, and printing. The handouts found at the end of each unit in this guide are simply for teacher reference.

Appendix

The teacher guide has one appendix. In this appendix you will find frequently used handouts, resources on teaching methods used in several units, and a semester-long project for the students. All of these are also available at *smp.org/LivinginChrist* for downloading, customizing, and printing.

Thank You

We thank you for putting your confidence in us by adopting the Living in Christ series. Our goal is to graduate students who are in a relationship with Jesus Christ, are religiously literate, and understand their faith in terms of their real lives.

Please contact us and let us know how we are doing. We are eager to improve this curriculum, and we value your knowledge and expertise. You may e-mail us at *LivinginChrist@smp.org* to offer your feedback.

Unit 1   Introduction to the New Testament

Overview

This unit, which lays the groundwork for this course's exploration of the New Testament, will enable students to integrate their prior Scripture study with new material regarding a Catholic approach to Scripture.

Key Understandings and Questions

Upon completing this unit, the students will have a deeper understanding of the following key concepts:

- The New Testament continues the story of God's loving relationship with humanity through the life of Jesus Christ and the early Church.
- Scripture and Tradition are the means by which Divine Revelation is transmitted.
- Scripture informs the doctrine of the Church.
- Scripture plays an essential role in the life of the Christian community.

Upon completing the unit, the students will have answered the following questions:

- How does the New Testament continue the story of God's loving relationship with humanity?
- By what means is Divine Revelation transmitted?
- What is the relationship between Scripture and the doctrine of the Church?
- Why does Scripture play a significant role in the life of the Christian community?

How Will You Know the Students Understand?

The following resources will help you to assess the students' understanding of the key concepts covered in this unit:

- handout "Final Performance Task Options for Unit 1" (Document #: TX002194)
- handout "Rubric for Final Performance Tasks for Unit 1" (Document #: TX002195)
- handout "Unit 1 Test" (Document #: TX002206)

Student Book Articles

This unit draws on articles from *The New Testament: The Good News of Jesus Christ* student book and incorporates them into the unit instruction. Whenever the teaching steps for the unit require the students to refer to or read an article from the student book, the following symbol appears in the margin: (▣). The articles covered in the unit are from "Section 1: The Word of God," and are as follows:

- "Revelation and Inspiration" (article 1)
- "Covenants Old and New" (article 2)
- "An Overview of the New Testament Books" (article 3)
- "Jesus Christ, the Word of God" (article 8)
- "The Bible and the *Lectionary*" (article 9)
- "Scripture and the Eucharist" (article 10)

The Suggested Path to Understanding

This unit in the teacher guide provides you with one learning path to take with the students, to enable them to begin their study of the New Testament. It is not necessary to use all the learning experiences, but if you substitute other material from this course or your own material for some of the material offered here, check to see that you have covered all relevant facets of understanding and that you have not missed knowledge or skills required in later units.

Step 1: Preassess what the students already know about the New Testament through the "Meet Me in the Middle" exercise.

Step 2: Follow this assessment by presenting to the students the handouts "Final Performance Task Options for Unit 1" (Document #: TX002194) and "Rubric for Final Performance Tasks for Unit 1" (Document #: TX002195).

Step 3: Review basic Old Testament themes, events, and characters as preparation for study of the New Testament.

Step 4: Facilitate a close reading and discussion of Vatican Council II's *Dogmatic Constitution on Divine Revelation (Dei Verbum).*

Step 5: Guide the students in identifying the levels of authority in Church teachings and in exploring the use of Scripture in sample ecclesial documents at each level.

 **Step 6:** Help the students to understand how the New Testament continues the story of God's loving relationship with humanity by facilitating study of selected texts from the *Lectionary for Mass.*

 Step 7: Engage the students in reflecting on the ways in which regular contact with the Gospels, in the Sunday Eucharistic liturgy, plays an essential role in our individual and communal lives of faith.

 Step 8: Guide and support the students in writing and delivering homilies that demonstrate their understanding of the essential role of Scripture in the life of the Christian community.

 Step 9: Make sure the students are all on track with their final performance tasks, if you have assigned them.

 **Step 10:** Provide the students with an opportunity to engage in Scripture-based prayer through the Liturgy of the Hours.

 Step 11: Provide the students with a tool to use for reflecting on what they learned in the unit and how they learned.

Background for Teaching This Unit

Visit *smp.org/LivinginChrist* for additional information about these and other theological concepts taught in this unit:

- "Events at the Second Vatican Council" (Document #: TX002186)
- "Why the Second Vatican Council Really Is That Important" (Document #: TX002188)

The Web site also includes information on these and other teaching methods used in the unit:

- "Using the Jigsaw Process" (Document #: TX001020)
- "Informal Assessments" (Document #: TX002189)
- "Paired Verbal Fluency" (Document #: TX002190)
- "Writing Workshop" (Document #: TX002191)

Scripture Passages

Scripture is an important part of the Living in Christ series and is frequently used in the learning experiences for each unit. The Scripture passages featured in this unit are tied to the cycle of readings and are as follows:

- First Sunday of Advent, B:
    Isaiah 63:16–17,19; 64:2–7
    1 Corinthians 1:3–9
    Mark 13:33–37

- Third Sunday of the Year, A:
    Isaiah 8:23—9:3
    1 Corinthians 1:1–13,17
    Matthew 4:12–23

- Solemnity of Our Lord Jesus Christ, the King, C:
    2 Samuel 5:1–3
    Colossians 1:12–20
    Luke 23:35–43

- Sixth Sunday of the Year, B:
    Leviticus 13:1–2,44–46
    1 Corinthians 10:31—11:1
    Mark 1:40–45

- Eighth Sunday of the Year, C:
    Sirach 27:4–7
    1 Corinthians 15:54–58
    Luke 6:39–45

- Year A, Third through Seventh Sundays of the Year:
    Matthew 4:12–23
    Matthew 5:1–12
    Matthew 5:13–16
    Matthew 5:17–37
    Matthew 5:38–48

- Year B, Third through Seventh Sundays of the Year:
    Mark 1:14–20
    Mark 1:21–28
    Mark 1:29–39
    Mark 1:40–45
    Mark 2:1–12

- Year C, Third through Seventh Sundays of the Year:
  Luke 1:1–4,4,14–21
  Luke 4:21–30
  Luke 5:1–11
  Luke 6:17,20–26
  Luke 6:27–38

- Year A, Twentieth through Twenty-Fourth Sundays of the Year:
  Matthew 15:21–28
  Matthew 16:13–20
  Matthew 16:21–27
  Matthew 18:15–20
  Matthew 18:21–25

- Year C, Twentieth through Twenty-Fourth Sundays of the Year:
  Luke 12:49–53
  Luke 13:22–30
  Luke 14:1,7–14
  Luke 14:25–33
  Luke 15:1–32

Vocabulary

The student book and the teacher guide include the following key terms for this unit. To provide the students with a list of these terms and their definitions, download and print the handout "Vocabulary for Unit 1" (Document #: TX002196), one for each student.

Bible
biblical inerrancy
biblical inspiration
Church
codices
consecrate, consecration
covenant
Deposit of Faith
Divine Revelation
Eucharist, the
Gospels

Gentile
incarnate, Incarnation
Lectionary
liturgical year
Liturgy of the Hours
Magisterium
synoptic Gospels
Tradition
Vatican Council II
Word of God

Learning Experiences

Explain	**Step 1**

Preassess what the students already know about the New Testament through the "Meet Me in the Middle" exercise.

1. **Prepare** by moving all desks to one side to clear floor space in your classroom. Alternatively, you may wish to conduct this learning experience in a more open location like a gymnasium, a cafeteria, or outdoors. Download and make copies of the handout "'Meet Me in the Middle' Concepts" (Document #TX002193), one for each student.

> **Teacher Note**
>
> You may wish to arrange for a projector to display the concepts used in this unit, in addition to saying them aloud.

2. **Tell** the students that in preparing to begin this course together, it is important for you to get a sense of what they remember from prior courses about Scripture in general and the New Testament in particular. This will also help the students to gain confidence in what they already know and preview new material they will encounter in this course.

3. **Direct** the students to stand in a circle, facing the middle. Then explain how "Meet Me in the Middle" works. Tell the students that you will state or project a concept related to the first unit of this course. Students will walk toward the middle of the space, indicating the extent to which they believe they understand that concept *well enough to explain it to someone else.* In other words, students who are not at all familiar with the concept remain near the perimeter of the circle; students who feel 100-percent confident about explaining the concept walk all the way to the middle; and students whose understanding lies somewhere between these two extremes position themselves at an appropriate point between the perimeter and the middle.

4. **Demonstrate** the process with a simple example not related to the course, like basketball, French cooking, or subject-verb agreement. Before beginning, emphasize that this is simply a preassessment and self-assessment learning experience, not a formal test. It is acceptable for a student to remain at the perimeter for most or all of the time. Also reassure the students that even if they walk all the way to the middle, you will not at this time ask them to explain these concepts in front of the whole class.

5. **Lead** the learning experience, using this list of concepts from this unit:
   - the relationship between the Old Testament and the New Testament
   - similarities between the Old Testament and the New Testament
   - differences between the Old Testament and the New Testament
   - Tradition (with a capital *T*)
   - tradition (with a small *t*)
   - Revelation (not the Book of Revelation)
   - the *Lectionary*
   - doctrine
   - dogma
   - the relationship between Scripture and the teachings of the Church
   - the Gospels
   - Inspiration
   - Magisterium
   - *Dogmatic Constitution on Divine Revelation* (*Dei Verbum,* 1965)
   - Vatican Council II
   - the use of Scripture in Catholic liturgy
   - the use of Scripture in individual and communal prayer

6. **Move** the learning experience along quickly, noting for your own information which concepts draw a large number of students to the middle, which keep a large number of students on the perimeter, and which elicit mixed responses from the students. Invite the students to notice the diversity of knowledge and expertise among their classmates, but do not elicit commentary or discussion from the students at this time.

7. **Invite** the students, once the learning experience is completed, to be seated on the floor (or in their desks or chairs if feasible). The students will need pens. Distribute the handout "'Meet Me in the Middle' Concepts" (Document #: TX002193), which lists the concepts used in this learning experience.

8. **Invite** the students to review the list and to do the following:
   - Circle the three items they understand the best (i.e., the three items that brought them closest to the middle of the circle).
   - Place an *X* next to the three items they understand the least (i.e., the three items that made them stay near the perimeter of the circle).
   - Place a check mark next to the item they are most interested in learning about during this unit—this could be a circled item, an *X* item, or another item.

9. **Direct** the students to focus on the three items they marked with an *X*. Explain that although these concepts are the ones about which the students feel *least* confident, there is probably someone in the room who knows something about these concepts. Tell the students that they will now engage in a brief fact-finding mission. They will choose one concept they marked with an *X* and find another student who can tell them something about that concept. Ask the students to briefly interview that other student and write their newly discovered information on their handout. Allow about 5 minutes for the students to move around the room and complete this task.

10. **Draw** the class back together. Time permitting, invite several students to share something they learned about one of these concepts from a peer. Then review with all of the students what they have covered during this brief introductory learning experience:

   • They have been reminded of what they already know about Scripture (cite examples as appropriate).

   • They have previewed new concepts they will explore in the course of this first unit (cite examples as appropriate).

   • They have discovered that their peers can be great resources for their learning.

   Ask the students to keep the handout "'Meet Me in the Middle' Concepts" (Document #: TX002193) to refer to later. You may wish to have them write brief notes on this handout as they study each of these concepts throughout the unit.

Step 2

Follow this assessment by presenting to the students the handouts "Final Performance Task Options for Unit 1" (Document #: TX002194) and "Rubric for Final Performance Tasks for Unit 1" (Document #: TX002195).

This unit provides you with three ways to assess that the students have a deep understanding of the most important concepts in the unit: writing a pastoral letter to young people modeled on *Divine Revelation*, creating a visual representation of the Church's understanding of Scripture, or producing an educational video for middle school students. Refer to "Using Final Performance Tasks to Assess Understanding" (Document #: TX001011) and "Using Rubrics to Assess Work" (Document #: TX001012) at *smp.org/LivinginChrist* for background information.

Teacher Note

You may wish to preview sample educational videos available online so that you can better assist students who choose performance task option 3. A few options are available at *smp.org/ LivinginChrist.*

Teacher Note

You may wish to require that students vary their final performance tasks throughout the course. For example, you may require that students complete at least two individual and two partner or group final performance tasks. Or you may require that students choose different types of final performance tasks, such as written, multimedia, or artistic. If you have these requirements, share them with the students now so that they can choose their final performance tasks appropriately.

Teacher Note

You will want to assign due dates for the performance tasks.

If you have done these performance tasks, or very similar ones, with students before, place examples of this work in the classroom. During this introduction explain how each is a good example of what you are looking for, for different reasons. This allows the students to concretely understand what you are looking for and to understand that there is not only one way to succeed.

1. **Prepare** by downloading and printing the handouts "Final Performance Task Options for Unit 1" (Document #: TX002194) and "Rubric for Final Performance Tasks for Unit 1" (Document #: TX002195), one of each for each student.

2. **Distribute** the handouts. Give the students a choice as to which performance task to work on and add more options if you so choose.

3. **Review** the directions, expectations, and rubric in class, allowing the students to ask questions. You may want to say something to this effect:

   ➤ If you wish to work alone, you may choose option 1 or 2. If you wish to work with a partner, you may choose option 2 or 3. If you wish to work as part of a group of three or four students, you may choose option 3 only.

   ➤ Near the end of the unit, you will have one full class period to work on the final performance task. However, keep in mind that you should be working on, or at least thinking about, your chosen task throughout the unit, not just at the end.

4. **Explain** the types of tools and knowledge the students will gain throughout the unit so that they can successfully complete the final performance task.

5. **Answer** questions to clarify the end point toward which the unit is headed. Remind the students as the unit progresses that each learning experience builds the knowledge and skills they will need in order to show you that they understand these introductory concepts regarding the New Testament.

Explain	Apply

Step 3

Review basic Old Testament themes, events, and characters as preparation for study of the New Testament.

1. **Prepare** by downloading and printing one copy of the handout "Old and New Testament Passages" (Document #: TX002197). Cut apart the handout into separate slips of paper with one passage on each slip. If your class has fewer than thirty students, eliminate rows of passages as needed. If your class has an odd number of students, choose two students to work as a pair, with just one passage assigned to the two of them. Also download and make copies of the handout "Old Testament History: Major Time Periods" (Document #: TX002198), one for each pair of students.

    Gather the art supplies—such as crayons, markers, scissors, glue, and construction paper—needed for the students to create timeline symbols, or ask the students to bring in these items to share. If possible, provide a variety of fabric scraps, wallpaper samples, pipe cleaners, ribbons, cotton balls, and other artistic materials.

    Gather reference works such as the following to help the students do research for this learning experience:

    - Old Testament textbooks, either high school or college level
    - *Saint Mary's Press® Essential Bible Dictionary* (available at *smp.org/eSource/index.cfm*)
    - *Saint Mary's Press® Glossary of Theological Terms* (available at *smp.org/eSource/index.cfm*)
    - *Saint Mary's Press® Essential Guide to Biblical Life and Times*

2. **Comment** on the importance of understanding Scripture as a coherent whole. Because there are many connections and similarities between the Old and New Testaments, it is impossible to understand the New Testament without a solid background in the Old Testament. This learning experience will refresh the students' memories regarding key themes, events, and characters of the Old Testament to prepare them for their study of the New Testament.

> **Teacher Note**
>
> Based on your school's sequence of courses within the religious studies or theology curriculum, you may choose to do this entire learning experience or an abbreviated version of it. If your students have studied the Old Testament during the semester immediately before the current one, and if you are confident that they remember a great deal of that material, you may be able to skip this step entirely.

3. **Tell** the students that each will receive a brief Scripture passage from either the Old or New Testament. They must locate the person in the room who has the corresponding passage from the other testament. Explain that the passages correspond in one or more of the following ways: they may both mention the same person; the New Testament passage may quote from or allude to the Old Testament; or the passages may be similar in theme, focus, or genre. Once the pairs have found one another, they will briefly converse about the connections or correspondences between the two passages.

4. **Distribute** the slips of paper from the handout "Old and New Testament Passages" (Document #: TX002197). Allow about 10 minutes for the students to find their partners and engage in conversation.

5. **Draw** the class back together, asking the pairs to sit together. Invite four or five pairs of students to read their passages aloud and to comment on the connections between them. Engage the class in a brief conversation around the following questions:

   ➤ What similarities and correspondences between the Old and New Testaments have you discovered today? Are you surprised by these similarities? Why or why not?

   ➤ Based on what you have seen and heard during this learning experience, how would you describe the relationship between the Old and New Testaments?

   ➤ How does this brief learning experience help you to understand the importance of knowing the Old Testament well before studying the New Testament?

6. **Introduce** the next part of this learning experience by explaining that the students will work with their partners to create part of a timeline of Old Testament history, also known as the history of the ancient Israelites. Distribute the handout "Old Testament History: Major Time Periods" (Document #: TX002198). Review the handout with the students, indicating that these fifteen items represent major time periods in the history of ancient Israel, from the time of Abraham and Sarah until the lifetime of Jesus. Note that no dates are on the handout, because it is more important at this time for the students simply to familiarize themselves with the sequence of events.

7. **Assign** each pair one of the items from the handout "Old Testament History: Major Time Periods" (Document #: TX002198). If you have fewer than fifteen pairs of students, some items can be combined: for example, the wilderness years and the formation of the Sinai Covenant (items 4 and 5) or the Greek and Roman periods (items 14 and 15). Ask each pair to identify five key facts about their assigned time period, and then invite them to create a symbol of their assigned time period, drawing on what they know from prior Scripture study, from brief research they conduct during the time allotted for this process, or from both. The symbol should capture the main events, themes, and people of that time period *using few or no words*. Encourage student creativity in crafting a symbol of any size or material, in either two or three dimensions. (If you wish to set limits on the size or dimension of the symbols for practical purposes, share those expectations with the students now.) Provide art supplies for the pairs to use. Allow students a minimum of 45 minutes to research and create their symbols.

> **Teacher Note**
>
> Alternatively, you may allot some class time for initial planning and brainstorming and require that the students complete the symbol as homework. During the following class session, allow about 10 minutes for the pairs to reconvene and prepare to present their symbol to the class and share five key facts about their assigned time period.

8. **Invite** the students to present their completed symbols to the class, sharing their five key facts. Limit each presentation to 3 to 5 minutes to ensure that all pairs have time to present.

9. **Direct** students, as they listen to presentations, to write down three pieces of information (three total, not three from each presentation) about the history of ancient Israel that they did not know before. This type of focused note-taking not only helps to ensure that students are accountable for the material their classmates present but also helps them to differentiate between new material and material they have encountered before.

10. **Invite** several volunteers at the conclusion of the presentations to share something they learned that they did not know before.

11. **Conclude** by reminding the students that the story of God's loving relationship with humanity *begins* in the Old Testament and *continues* in the New Testament. Therefore, it is essential for the students to have some fluency in, or at least familiarity with, the themes, events, and characters of the Old Testament in order to study the New Testament productively. Note that you will post the timeline symbols in the classroom for ease of reference and review throughout the course.

> **Teacher Note**
>
> After assessing the students' timeline symbols, consider posting them in your classroom to provide a convenient reference, as needed, throughout the semester. If you teach multiple sections of this course, post the timelines parallel to one another, so that students can compare how their peers in other sections symbolized the various time periods.

Step 4

Facilitate a close reading and discussion of Vatican Council II's *Dogmatic Constitution on Divine Revelation (Dei Verbum).*

Articles
1, 8

1. **Prepare** by downloading Vatican Council II's *Dogmatic Constitution on Divine Revelation* (*Dei Verbum,* 1965) from the Vatican Web site (a link is available at *smp.org/LivinginChrist*). Make copies of the entire document, one for each student.

2. **Assign** the students to read article 1, "Revelation and Inspiration," and article 8, "Jesus Christ, the Word of God," in the student book as preparation for this learning experience. Download and print the handout "*Dogmatic Constitution on Divine Revelation* (*Dei Verbum,* 1965)" (Document #: TX002199), one copy for each student.

3. **Share** some basic background information about the Second Vatican Council. Direct the students to take notes. Include the following points:

   ➤ The Second Vatican Council, also known as Vatican Council II, was held from 1962 to 1965. It was the first Ecumenical Council, or meeting of all the world's bishops, in almost one hundred years. (Vatican Council I was held in 1870.)

   ➤ Vatican Council II was called and convened by Pope John XXIII and was completed by his successor, Pope Paul VI, after John XXIII died.

   ➤ The purpose of the Council was *aggiornamento,* an Italian word meaning "bringing up to date." Pope John XXIII recognized that the modern world was changing rapidly, bringing new challenges to people of faith in the areas of politics, economics, the workplace, and family life. He wanted the Church to articulate a relevant response to these many situations.

   ➤ In his opening speech to the Council on October 11, 1962, Pope John XXIII stated that "the substance of the ancient doctrine of the deposit of faith is one thing, and the way in which it is presented is another" (*Documents of Vatican II,* p. 715). In other words, the faith of the Church remains constant in every age; however, the way in which that faith is expressed must change as the world changes. The purpose of the Council was to give expression to Catholic Christian faith in a way that made sense to modern people.

Teacher Note

Further prepare for this learning experience by referring to the handout "Using the Jigsaw Process" (Document #: TX001020) as background information for this learning experience.

➤ The Council met annually for four years, concluding in 1965. It issued sixteen documents on various topics, such as the liturgy, religious life, the apostolate of lay people, and religious freedom. We will work with one of these documents today, the *Dogmatic Constitution on Divine Revelation,* sometimes referred to by its Latin name, *Dei Verbum.*

4. **Distribute** copies of *"Dogmatic Constitution on Divine Revelation (Dei Verbum,* 1965)" (Document #: TX002199). Instruct the students to count off by six to indicate which chapter of the document they will study in class (the first group will also read the prologue in addition to chapter 1). Ask the students to read the handout silently, so that they know what to look for as they study a section of this document.

5. **Direct** the students to meet in their numbered groups and to read their assigned chapters individually and silently for at least 10 minutes before beginning discussion and work on the handout. As most or all students finish reading, allow about 15 minutes for the groups to complete the handout.

6. **Use** the jigsaw process to reorganize the students into new groups. Have the members of the original groups count off by A, B, C, and so on. Then ask all group A students to meet together, all group B students, and so on. For example, if you have thirty students in your class, you will now have five groups with six people in each, one person from each of the original groups.

7. **Instruct** the students to report to these newly configured groups, summarizing their assigned section of the document and sharing several highlights from the handout. Have the other students in the group take notes on the back on their handouts, recording at least one or two points from each of the other people in the group. Just before reconvening the large group, direct the students' attention to item 5 of their handout, regarding the substantive questions. Invite the students to discuss these questions and to agree on the three that are most interesting or compelling. Invite one student from each group to write these three questions on the board.

8. **Reconvene** the large group. Because the students have shared their findings through the jigsaw process, it is not necessary to conduct an extensive debriefing with the whole class. However, you may wish to address any basic questions of clarification at this time (item 4 of the handout), as well as to state or reaffirm the following essential points:

➤ Divine Revelation is transmitted through both Scripture and Tradition, which together "make up a single sacred deposit of the Word of God" (*Divine Revelation,* 10).

➤ Because Scripture and Tradition both come from God, they do not contradict each other.

➤ Note that in this context, we are referring to Tradition with a capital *T.* Do not confuse this with tradition with a lowercase *t,* which refers to customs like lighting a candle in church while saying a prayer or singing "Silent Night" at a midnight Christmas Mass.

> ➤ Revelation is complete and closed: "No new public revelation is to be expected before the glorious manifestation of our Lord, Jesus Christ" (*Divine Revelation,* 4). However, the Church continues to grow in understanding Revelation more fully and in articulating it effectively to each new generation of believers.

> ➤ The Magisterium, the Church's living, official teaching authority, including all bishops in communion with the Pope, has been entrusted with the task of interpreting both Scripture and Tradition, in the name of Jesus Christ.

> ➤ Both the Old and New Testaments were written by human authors under the inspiration of the Holy Spirit.

> ➤ Interpreting Scripture accurately involves examining its literary forms and studying the sociocultural contexts in which its authors wrote.

> ➤ The Old and New Testaments are inextricably linked: the New is "hidden in the Old" and the Old is "made manifest in the New" (*Divine Revelation,* 16).

9. **Conclude** by drawing the students' attention to the questions written on the board. Erase any duplicate questions, as well as any that you deem too simplistic. For homework, instruct the students to write a substantive paragraph in response to any one of these questions. Their paragraph should integrate their growing knowledge about Scripture and Revelation with their own personal thoughts, reflections, and challenges regarding these topics.

Step 5

Guide the students in identifying the levels of authority in Church teachings and in exploring the use of Scripture in sample ecclesial documents at each level.

1. **Prepare** by downloading the PowerPoint presentation "Levels of Authority in Church Teaching" (Document #: TX002187) and arranging for the use of an LCD projector in your classroom. Download and make copies of the handout "The Use of Scripture in the Doctrine of the Church" (Document #: TX002200), one for each student. Gather dictionaries, including theological or biblical dictionaries, for the students to refer to during group work. Download the excerpts from the following ecclesial documents, which the students will examine during this learning experience, and make enough copies so that each student can work with one document. (Links to documents are available at *smp.org/LivinginChrist.*)

- Pope Pius XII's *Munificentissimus Deus* (November 1, 1950), defining the dogma of the Assumption, paragraphs 1–5, 24–30, and 44
- Vatican Council II's *Pastoral Constitution on the Church in the Modern World* (*Gaudium et Spes*, 1965), paragraphs 1–3 and 10–18
- Pope Leo XIII's *Rerum Novarum* (May 15, 1891), encyclical on capital and labor, paragraphs 1–3, 20–25, and 62–64
- Pope John Paul II's Bull of Indiction of the Great Jubilee of the Year 2000 (*Incarnationis Mysterium*, November 29, 1998), paragraphs 1–14 (entire document)
- United States Conference of Catholic Bishops' *Economic Justice for All: A Pastoral Letter on Catholic Social Teaching and the U.S. Economy* (November 18, 1986), paragraphs 30–52

2. **Begin** by reviewing some of the key concepts from the previous learning experience, especially the concept that Scripture and Tradition are the means by which Divine Revelation is transmitted. Tell the students that many Catholics, including adults, struggle to understand the relationship between Scripture and the teaching of the Church. Following are some common points of confusion; invite the students to consider whether any of these points has ever been problematic or difficult for them to understand.

   - The Church does not teach that everything in the Bible is literally true, for example, that God created the world in seven 24-hour days (see Genesis 1:1—2:4).
   - The Church also does not teach that everything in the Bible is to be obeyed literally, for example, the law that it is not only okay to have slaves but also okay to beat them as long as you do not kill them in the process (see Exodus 21:20–21).
   - On the other hand, the Church teaches some things that are not explicitly stated in the Bible, such as Mary's Assumption into Heaven.

   All of these examples, and many others, raise the broad question, What is the relationship between Scripture and the doctrine, or teachings, of the Church? Tell the students that today's learning experience will explore the many nuances of this question using examples of Church teachings.

3. **Present** the PowerPoint "Levels of Authority in Church Teaching" (Document #: TX002187). Direct the students to take notes. Supplement the material on the slides with your own explanations, taking care to include, minimally, the "notes" listed for each slide.

4. **Organize** the students into five groups. Assign each group one of the magisterial documents that you downloaded and indicate the assigned sections. Give each group member a copy of the group's assigned document, as well as a copy of the handout "The Use of Scripture in the Doctrine of the Church" (Document #: TX002200).

Allow 10 to 15 minutes for the students to read silently in their small groups before they begin discussing and working on the handout. As most or all of the students finish reading, allow an additional 10 to 15 minutes for the students to complete the handout in their small groups. Advise the students that each group will turn in one copy of the handout, but they may wish to make notes on another copy for their own review. Circulate among the groups to provide help and clarification as needed. You may also wish to have regular or theological dictionaries, or both, available as the students seek to understand these complex ecclesial documents.

> **Teacher Note**
>
> If limited time remains in the class period, you may wish to assign the reading and handout as homework and then during the following class session, have each group report on its work.

5. **Draw** the class back together, and invite each small group to share what its members learned from its assigned document, particularly the way in which the document uses Scripture. Comment as appropriate. It may be instructive to explore whether the students perceive any differences in the way documents with different levels of authority use Scripture. For example, does a pronouncement of dogma use Scripture differently than an encyclical or pastoral letter uses it?

6. **Conclude** by using the analogy of a plant to explain the relationship between Scripture and the doctrine of the Church:

   - Some doctrine is fully developed in Scripture—both roots and flower (such as the Resurrection of Jesus or the dignity of the human person).

   - Other doctrine is rooted in Scripture to a greater or lesser degree, but its full flower is outside Scripture (such as the Assumption of Mary).

Apply | Perceive | Step 6

Help the students to understand how the New Testament continues the story of God's loving relationship with humanity by facilitating study of selected texts from the *Lectionary for Mass.*

Articles
2, 3

1. **Prepare** by downloading and making copies of the handouts "Lectionary Word Splash" (Document #: TX002201) and "Sunday *Lectionary* Readings: God's Ongoing Story of Love for Humanity" (Document #: TX002202), one of each for each student. Gather five pieces of poster board or newsprint, as well as markers or crayons for making posters.

2. **Assign** the students to read article 2, "Covenants Old and New," and article 3, "An Overview of the New Testament Books," in the student book as preparation for this learning experience. Ask the students to bring their Bibles to class.

3. **Tell** the students that you will begin this learning experience by assessing what they already know about the *Lectionary for Mass.* Emphasize that this is simply an informal assessment, not a formal test.

4. **Organize** the students into groups of three. Distribute the handout "Lectionary Word Splash" (Document #: TX002201), one for each student. Explain that all the terms on the word splash have some connection with the word in the center, *Lectionary.* The students will have about 10 minutes to work in their groups to determine how each of the terms is related to the *Lectionary.* During this process, they will make notes on their handouts. Emphasize that if they are unsure, it is acceptable to make an educated guess, and reassure the students that some terms may be completely new to them. Allow the students to work in their groups for 5 to 10 minutes. Do not allow them to use their textbooks or other sources, because you are trying to determine what they already know and what they need to learn.

5. **Give** the students an additional 2 minutes to circulate around the classroom to ask other groups for any missing information once they have finished or have exhausted their present knowledge.

6. **Draw** the class back together, directing the students to return to their seats with their groups. As you review the word splash, direct the students to write additional information about each term on their handouts. Share the following points of clarification, as needed, based on gaps in your students' knowledge. If you have a *Lectionary,* pass it around for the students to examine.

   ➤ The *Lectionary for Mass* is the collection of Scripture readings assigned to the Eucharistic liturgy for each day of the year. This means that if you go to Mass on a particular day of the week anywhere in the world, you will hear the same readings.

   ➤ The *Lectionary* is not the Bible. Rather, it is an organized collection of readings from the Bible.

   ➤ In the *Constitution on the Sacred Liturgy (Sacrosanctum Concilium),* the bishops who were gathered at the Second Vatican Council asked that a lectionary be developed that would provide "more ample, more varied, and more suitable reading from sacred scripture" (35). Before Vatican Council II, there had been a lectionary, but it had offered a very limited selection of Scripture readings.

   ➤ At each Sunday Eucharistic liturgy, four readings are proclaimed, in this order: an Old Testament reading, a Psalm (which is usually sung), a New Testament reading (usually from the letters), and a Gospel reading.

   ➤ These Sunday readings are arranged in a three-year cycle: years A, B, and C. In Year A, the Gospel readings are primarily from Matthew; in Year B, from Mark; and in Year C, from Luke. John's Gospel is used on some Sundays of Year B (because Mark is the shortest Gospel) and on selected Sundays of the Lenten and Easter seasons.

➤ The Old Testament and Gospel readings were assigned to particular Sundays based on the principle of harmonious composition: the two readings for each Sunday are explicitly related by their theme, teaching, or events. The Gospel readings were selected first, and then Old Testament readings were selected to correspond to the Gospel readings.

➤ In contrast, the New Testament readings were assigned to particular Sundays based on the principle of semicontinuous reading. This means that for several weeks, the *Lectionary* may call for a reading of Paul's Letter to the Romans, for example, in a more or less continuous fashion (some selected verses or short passages may be skipped). These readings may be thematically related to the Old Testament reading or to the Gospel reading by coincidence but not by design.

➤ The exceptions to the principle of semicontinuous reading are the various liturgical seasons, such as Advent, Christmas, Lent, and Easter, in which all three readings may reflect the theological emphases of these seasons.

7. **Tell** the students that examining the Scripture readings that the *Lectionary* assigns to a particular Sunday can yield powerful insights into the relationship between the Old and New Testaments. In particular, such an examination can help us to understand how the New Testament continues the story of God's loving relationship with humanity, revealed in new ways through the life of Jesus Christ and the early Church.

8. **Direct** the word splash groups of three to merge to create groups of six students. Distribute the handout "Sunday *Lectionary* Readings: God's Ongoing Story of Love for Humanity" (Document #: TX002202), one for each student.

9. **Assign** each group one of the sets of readings listed on the handout "Sunday *Lectionary* Readings: God's Ongoing Story of Love for Humanity" (Document #: TX002202). Have the students work together in their groups to answer the questions on the handout and to create their posters. Although the handout is, in some ways, a means to an end (i.e., the poster), ensure that the students work carefully through all of the handout questions to gather the best ideas to include on their poster. Allow a minimum of 30 minutes for this entire process.

10. **Have** each group present its poster to the class. Alternatively, you may direct the students to hang up their posters and have the class take a "gallery tour," in which they observe the work of their classmates. If you choose the tour, you may wish to have the students write down for themselves at least one interesting point of information from each poster.

11. **Conclude** by reminding the students that the Old and New Testaments form a coherent whole. Both testaments recount the story of God's loving relationship with humanity. At each Eucharistic liturgy, the *Lectionary* ensures that we have an opportunity to hear and internalize various aspects of this story. This regular and prayerful exposure to Scripture is an essential aspect of our own growth in faith and understanding.

Articles
9, 10

Perceive **Step 7**

Engage the students in reflecting on the ways in which regular contact with the Gospels, in the Sunday Eucharistic liturgy, plays an essential role in our individual and communal lives of faith.

1. **Prepare** by downloading and printing one copy of the handout "Sunday Gospel Readings" (Document #: TX002203) and cutting it into slips of paper with one Gospel passage on each slip. If you have more than twenty-five students in your class, you will need to cut apart an additional copy of this handout (it is fine for some students to have duplicate passages). For your own reference, note the groupings of the Gospel passages (e.g., "Year A, Third through Seventh Sundays of the Year"), but do not give this information to the students. Also download and make copies of the handouts "Reflections on the Liturgical Year" (Document #: TX002204) and "Gospel Reflection Questions" (Document #: TX002205), one for each student.

2. **Assign** the students to read article 9, "The Bible and the *Lectionary*," and article 10, "Scripture and the Eucharist," in the student book as preparation for this learning experience. Ask the students to bring their Bibles to class.

3. **Begin** by reviewing key concepts from the previous learning experience and from the articles the students read as homework. In particular, remind the students that the Scripture readings the *Lectionary* assigns to any given Sunday in the liturgical year help us to understand how both testaments tell the story of God's loving relationship with humanity. Today's learning experience will examine the *Lectionary* in a slightly different way. Instead of looking at all the readings assigned to one Sunday, the students will study the Gospel readings assigned to consecutive Sundays.

4. **Distribute** copies of the handout "Reflections on the Liturgical Year" (Document #: TX002204). Invite several volunteers to read the excerpt aloud. Then direct the students to write brief answers to the questions at the bottom of the handout. When the students have finished writing, ask them to turn to someone near them and share their responses to the questions.

5. **Draw** the class back together, and briefly discuss the questions in the large group. Although there are many possible responses, be sure to draw out the following points in the conversation:
   - According to the handout, the purpose of the liturgical year is to make us more like Jesus: to immerse us so completely in his life, values, priorities, mission, and saving acts that we become like him.
   - The liturgical year seeks to accomplish this purpose through our sharing in the Eucharistic banquet and through the proclamation of Scripture, especially the Gospels.

6. **Tell** the students that the next part of this learning experience will invite them to reflect on and wrestle with this "continuing proclamation of the Scriptures, the centrality of the Gospels as the foundation of every liturgy, and the ongoing reflection on those readings in homilies" (Chittister, *Liturgical Year,* p. 13)—all of which are directed toward transforming us, more and more, into faithful disciples of Jesus, week after week and year after year.

7. **Distribute** the slips of paper you cut apart from the handout "Sunday Gospel Readings" (Document #: TX002203). Direct the students to organize themselves into five groups based on the Scripture passages they have been given. The students will find the other members of their group based on which Gospel, and which part of that Gospel, their reading is from.

> **Teacher Note**
>
> To make things easier, you may wish to tell the students that there is one Mark group, two Luke groups, and two Matthew groups. Instruct the students to find their groups.

Explain that each group has five Gospel readings that the *Lectionary* assigns to five consecutive Sundays of the liturgical year. In other words, if you went to Sunday liturgy for these five weeks in a row, these are the five Gospel readings you would hear. Tell the students that they will study these five readings and reflect on the cumulative effect these readings would have on someone who listens attentively and prayerfully to their proclamation over the course of five weeks. Distribute the handout "Gospel Reflection Questions" (Document #: TX002205).

8. **Direct** the students to work in their small groups to organize their readings into the order in which they are found in the Gospel and then to read each of those readings aloud together. Ask the students to take brief, informal notes on the handout "Gospel Reflection Questions" (Document #: TX002205) as they read and then complete the rest of the handout. Allow at least 15 minutes for this process.

9. **Explain** that each group is now going to use the information it recorded on the handout, as well as the other points that surfaced in conversation, to create an advertisement. This advertisement must have the following characteristics:

   - Must promote regular contact with Scripture—especially the Gospels, and especially in the context of the liturgy—as an essential means of growing in Christian discipleship.

   - Must incorporate specific references to at least two of the Gospel passages the group read.

   - May also incorporate part of the excerpt from the handout "Reflections on the Liturgical Year" (Document #: TX002204) if that is helpful.

   - May be written like a full-page newspaper or magazine ad or may be a TV ad that the students act out in front of the class.

   - Must be creative, eye-catching, intriguing, and appealing—like all effective ads.

   Allow at least 20 minutes for the groups to create their ads.

10. **Invite** the groups to present or perform their ads. In your comments on the students' work, or at the conclusion of the presentations, emphasize the following points:

➤ Our exposure to the person of Jesus, as presented in the Gospels, is meant to be an ongoing aspect of our formation as Christian disciples. We are meant to encounter the Gospels at least weekly, perhaps more often.

➤ This regular contact with the Gospels is essential, not optional, for Christian life. If we read the Gospels or hear them proclaimed only occasionally or sporadically, our efforts to become more like Jesus will be more difficult. We cannot become like Jesus if we do not continually learn about who he was, and is.

➤ On any given Sunday, we hear only a relatively brief excerpt from one of the Gospels. This may be a good thing, in that we probably wouldn't want liturgy to be two hours long. The challenge, then, becomes remembering that a given Gospel reading always has a larger context, which we will hear as the weeks go by if we go to Sunday liturgy faithfully. It is this constant telling and retelling of the stories of Jesus, month after month and year after year, that shapes us, more and more, into people worthy of the name we bear: Christian.

Understand

Step 8

Guide and support the students in writing and delivering homilies that demonstrate their understanding of the essential role of Scripture in the life of the Christian community.

1. **Prepare** by obtaining a copy of the *Lectionary* for students to use as a reference in this learning experience. Gather a variety of other references, including *Saint Mary's Press® Essential Bible Dictionary* and *Saint Mary's Press® Essential Guide to Biblical Life and Times*. Additionally, you will want to review the teaching method article "Writing Workshop" (Document #: TX002191) for this learning experience.

2. **Begin** by soliciting student responses to this question:

• What are the purposes of a homily, whether delivered at a Eucharistic liturgy or in another liturgical setting (such as a reconciliation service, a Liturgy of the Word, an evening prayer, and so on)?

Possible responses include the following:

- The homily may help us to understand the Scripture readings better.
- It may explicitly relate those readings to the joys and struggles of our lives today.
- It may inspire or move us to greater, more profound faith.
- It may motivate us to follow the example and teaching of Jesus in taking action on behalf of those in need.
- It may enable us to connect the readings with our sacramental life, for example, with our baptismal call or with our sharing in the Eucharistic banquet.

3. **Continue** the conversation with these or similar remarks:

  ➤ We know that Scripture is essential for our lives of discipleship. It is one of the key ways in which we learn of God's deep, abiding love for us, especially as that love is revealed in Jesus.

  ➤ As we learned in previous classes, regular and prayerful exposure to the Gospels is a primary means by which we can become more like Jesus.

  ➤ For many Catholics, the setting in which we most often hear and reflect on Scripture is the liturgy—this includes Sunday and weekday Eucharistic liturgies, as well as reconciliation services, Liturgies of the Word, weddings, Baptisms, funerals, and other occasions.

  ➤ Therefore, the homily is very important. The homily ideally should accomplish many or all of the points just listed, as the homilist breaks open the Word for those assembled, revealing how it both nourishes and strengthens us and calls us to conversion.

4. **Tell** the students that they will now have an opportunity to write and deliver a 3- to 4-minute sample homily. Explain that although someone who is ordained delivers the homily in the Mass, laypeople, including teenagers, can and do offer reflections on the Word during the Liturgy of the Hours, in retreat settings, and on other informal occasions.

Teacher Note

Although homilies are ordinarily written and delivered by one person, you may wish to offer students the option of working in a pair or a group of three for the purposes of this learning experience.

5. **Instruct** the students that each homily must incorporate at least two Scripture readings: an Old Testament reading and a Gospel reading. For the students' choice of readings on which to focus their homilies, you have several options:

  - You may use the readings with which the students worked in step 6, found on the handout "Sunday *Lectionary* Readings: God's Ongoing Story of Love for Humanity" (Document #: TX002202). In this case, they would have the advantage of some degree of familiarity with the readings.

- You may use the Gospel readings with which the students worked in step 7, using the handout "Sunday Gospel Readings" (Document #: TX002203). In this case, you or the students would use the *Lectionary* to look up the Old Testament readings that correspond to those Gospel readings.

- You may have the students choose a Gospel reading that is of interest to them and then help them to use the *Lectionary* to look up the Old Testament reading that corresponds to it.

- You may assign students to particular readings; for example, you may wish them to work with the readings that will be proclaimed at upcoming school liturgies or with the readings designated for the next several Sundays.

  Whichever option you choose, each student (or pair or group) should be working with different readings.

6. **Use** the "writing workshop" method to guide the students in writing their homilies. Allow the students at least 30 minutes to work on their homilies. Provide the resources you have gathered. Circulate among the students to provide help, ideas, and encouragement and to conduct brief one-on-one conferences with individual students or groups as needed. Maintain a quiet atmosphere in the room (even if some students are working in pairs or groups) so that all can reflect, think, concentrate, and write. Encourage the students to draw out the message of these readings in a way that will be meaningful to their classmates, who will hear their homily.

7. **Instruct** the students to finish their homilies as homework, coming to the next class session prepared to deliver them. Alternatively, you may offer them the option of recording themselves delivering the homily and bringing that recording to class in a format compatible with your classroom's audio-visual system.

8. **Have** the students deliver their homilies (either in person or via their recordings). Encourage and model prayerful, attentive listening, as well as enthusiastic support: in this context, applause after each homily is certainly appropriate.

9. **Instruct** the students to write a journal entry, after all of the homilies have been delivered, in response to this question:

   - What point (from any one of the homilies) was most meaningful to me? How did this point help me to understand Scripture or relate Scripture to my life in a new and powerful way?

10. **Conclude** by affirming the students' efforts and participation in interpreting Scripture, through a homily, for one another.

Step 9

Make sure the students are all on track with their final performance tasks, if you have assigned them.

If possible, devote 50 to 60 minutes for the students to ask questions about the tasks and to work individually or in their small groups.

1. **Remind** the students to bring to class any work they have already prepared so that they can work on it during the class period. If necessary, reserve the library or media center so the students can do any book or online research. Download and print extra copies of the handouts "Final Performance Task Options for Unit 1" (Document #: TX002194) and "Rubric for Final Performance Tasks for Unit 1" (Document #: TX002195). Review the final performance task options, answer questions, and ask the students to choose one if they have not already done so.

2. **Provide** some class time for the students to work on their performance tasks. This then allows you to work with the students who need additional guidance with the project.

Step 10

Provide the students with an opportunity to engage in Scripture-based prayer through the Liturgy of the Hours.

1. **Prepare** by downloading the PowerPoint "Liturgy of the Hours" (Document #: TX002192) and arranging for the use of an LCD projector in your classroom. If you will be praying the Liturgy of the Hours using a handout, create the handout and make copies of it, one for each student. Additionally, you will want to review the teaching method article "Paired Verbal Fluency" (Document #: TX002190) for this learning experience.

2. **Begin** by organizing the students into pairs. Tell them that they will engage in a structured conversation with their partners called "paired verbal fluency" (PVF). If necessary, teach this technique to your students or review it with them using the method article "Paired Verbal Fluency" (Document #: TX002190). Tell them that the question for the PVF conversation is as follows:

   • What do you know about the Liturgy of the Hours?

3. **Instruct** the students to talk with their partners, following the parameters of the PVF process. When the process is complete, draw the class back together, and invite the students to share their knowledge about the Liturgy of the Hours. Record this information on the board.

4. **Present** the PowerPoint "Liturgy of the Hours" (Document #: TX002192). Depending on the depth of your students' current knowledge, you may move quickly through the slides, using them primarily as review, or you may take more time and require the students to take notes.

5. **Invite** follow-up questions and comments from the students about the Liturgy of the Hours and then transition into an experience of this prayer together. Choose one of the following options, depending on what resources are readily available in your classroom:

   • If you have a class set of *The Catholic Youth Prayer Book,* from Saint Mary's Press, you may refer to chapter 13 for settings of morning and evening prayer for the entire four-week cycle of the Liturgy of the Hours.

   • Numerous Web sites contain the Liturgy of the Hours for each day. A link is provided at *smp.org/LivinginChrist.* You could either download that information onto a handout for the students or simply display the Web page on your LCD projector. In the latter case, the students would read the prayers directly from the screen.

6. **Divide** the class into two sections to facilitate praying the psalms and canticle choir-to-choir (or antiphonally). Attend to any other logistical considerations and then lead the class through the prayer. Be sure to allow the students the opportunity to voice their own prayers of petition following the set prayers given in the resource you are using.

7. **Invite** the students to offer any brief comments or reflections regarding this prayer experience. Conclude by encouraging the students to pray some version of the Liturgy of the Hours—using print or online resources—on their own. Explain that it is an excellent way for them to pray with Scripture, to grow in unity with the Church throughout the world, and to cultivate the discipline of daily prayer.

Reflect

Step 11

Provide the students with a tool to use for reflecting on what they learned in the unit and how they learned.

This learning experience will provide the students with an excellent opportunity to reflect on how their understanding of the New Testament as a whole has developed throughout the unit.

1. **Prepare** for this learning experience by downloading and printing the handout "Learning about Learning" (Document #: TX001159; see Appendix), one for each student. Ask the students to bring their preassessment handout, "'Meet Me in the Middle' Concepts" (Document #: TX002193).

2. **Distribute** the handouts and give the students about 15 minutes to answer the questions quietly. For the question "How did your understanding of the subject matter change throughout the unit?" direct the students to refer back to the handout "'Meet Me in the Middle' Concepts" (Document #: TX002193). Invite them to consider these questions:

   - Which concepts were familiar to you before the unit? How has your understanding of these concepts deepened or become more complete?

   - Which concepts were brand new to you? To what extent would you now feel confident in explaining these concepts to others?

   - Which concepts were you most interested in learning about when this unit began? To what extent has your curiosity been satisfied?

   - Which concept do you think you've learned the most about during this unit? What experience or experiences helped that learning to occur?

3. **Invite** the students to share any reflections they have about the content they learned as well as their insights into the way they learned.

4. **Direct** the students to keep this handout in a separate section of their folder or binder so that they can refer back to it at the conclusion of the course.

"Meet Me in the Middle" Concepts

the relationship between the Old Testament and the New Testament

similarities between the Old Testament and the New Testament

differences between the Old Testament and the New Testament

Tradition (with a capital *T*)

tradition (with a small *t*)

Revelation (not the Book of Revelation)

the *Lectionary*

doctrine

dogma

the relationship between Scripture and the teachings of the Church

the Gospels

Inspiration

Magisterium

Dei Verbum

Vatican Council II

the use of Scripture in Catholic liturgy

the use of Scripture in individual and communal prayer

Document #: TX002193

Final Performance Task Options for Unit 1

Important Information for All Three Options

The following are the main ideas that you are to understand from this unit. They should appear in this final performance task so that your teacher can assess whether you learned the most essential content.

- The New Testament continues the story of God's loving relationship with humanity through the life of Jesus Christ and the early Church.

- Scripture and Tradition are the means by which Divine Revelation is transmitted.

- Scripture informs the doctrine of the Church.

- Scripture plays an essential role in the life of the Christian community.

In addition to demonstrating understanding of these four main concepts of the unit, your final performance task must also contain or demonstrate the following:

- In-depth, substantial content appropriate for an upper-level high-school religious studies course

- Responsible and accurate use of Scripture

- Substantive content that creatively and accurately engages with and interprets the material of this unit

- Proper grammar, spelling, and diction

- A neat and well-organized presentation

Option 1: A Pastoral Letter to Young People Modeled on *Divine Revelation*

You have been asked by the Office of Youth Ministry in your diocese to write a pastoral letter to young people modeled on the Second Vatican Council's *Dogmatic Constitution on Divine Revelation* (*Dei Verbum,* 1965). This letter will be distributed to young people in Catholic high schools and parish religious education programs to help them grasp the Church's understanding of Scripture. Your pastoral letter must address the same topics as *Divine Revelation* but in language that is more accessible to young people. These topics are as follows:

- Divine Revelation

- the transmission of Divine Revelation

- Sacred Scripture: its divine Inspiration and its interpretation

- the Old Testament

- the New Testament

Document #: TX002194

- Sacred Scripture in the life of the Church

You must write *at least* one substantive paragraph on each of these topics, explaining the topic in a manner that is understandable for high school age youth.

It is not necessary to do outside research to complete this task; however, if you choose to do research to supplement what you have learned in class, be sure to include a bibliography.

Option 2: A Visual Representation of the Church's Understanding of Scripture

Create a visual and tactile display that clearly demonstrates the Church's understanding of Scripture. In particular, your visual aid must demonstrate the relationship between Scripture and each of the following:

- Tradition

- the doctrine of the Church

- prayer and liturgy

The visual aid may be a poster, display board, mobile, 3-D model, or some other object you design.

It is not necessary to do outside research to complete this task; however, if you choose to do research to supplement what you have learned in class, be sure to include a bibliography.

Option 3: An Educational Video for Middle School Students

The middle school religion teacher at the elementary school from which you graduated has asked for your help in teaching her students about the Church's understanding of Scripture. You have agreed to create a 5-minute (minimum) educational video to aid her students in grasping key concepts regarding Scripture. The video should address the following topics:

- Divine Revelation

- Scripture and Tradition as the means by which Divine Revelation is transmitted

- the way in which Scripture informs the doctrine of the Church

- the role of Scripture in the life of the Church

Your video must communicate this material in an age-appropriate way, preferably using music, animation, or other techniques appealing to younger students. Your teacher can refer you to some examples of videos available online that might help to spark your own creative thinking in completing this task.

It is not necessary to do outside research to complete this task; however, if you choose to do research to supplement what you have learned in class, be sure to include a bibliography.

Rubric for Final Performance Tasks for Unit 1

Criteria	4	3	2	1
Assignment includes all items requested in the instructions.	Assignment includes all items requested, and they are completed above expectations.	Assignment includes all items requested.	Assignment includes over half of the items requested.	Assignment includes less than half of the items requested.
Assignment shows understanding of the following concept: *The New Testament continues the story of God's loving relationship with humanity through the life of Jesus Christ and the early Church.*	Assignment shows unusually insightful understanding of this concept.	Assignment shows good understanding of this concept.	Assignment shows adequate understanding of this concept.	Assignment shows little understanding of this concept.
Assignment shows understanding of the following concept: *Scripture and Tradition are the means by which Divine Revelation is transmitted.*	Assignment shows unusually insightful understanding of this concept.	Assignment shows good understanding of this concept.	Assignment shows adequate understanding of this concept.	Assignment shows little understanding of this concept.
Assignment shows understanding of the following concept: *Scripture informs the doctrine of the Church.*	Assignment shows unusually insightful understanding of this concept.	Assignment shows good understanding of this concept.	Assignment shows adequate understanding of this concept.	Assignment shows little understanding of this concept.
Assignment shows understanding of the following concept: *Scripture plays an essential role in the life of the Christian community.*	Assignment shows unusually insightful understanding of this concept.	Assignment shows good understanding of this concept.	Assignment shows adequate understanding of this concept.	Assignment shows little understanding of this concept.
Assignment uses proper grammar, spelling, and diction.	Assignment has no grammar or spelling errors.	Assignment has one grammar or spelling error.	Assignment has two grammar or spelling errors.	Assignment has more than two grammar or spelling errors.
Assignment uses its assigned or chosen media effectively.	Assignment uses its assigned or chosen media in a way that greatly enhances it.	Assignment uses its assigned or chosen media effectively.	Assignment uses its assigned or chosen media somewhat effectively.	Assignment uses its assigned or chosen media ineffectively.
Assignment is neatly done.	Assignment not only is neat but is exceptionally creative.	Assignment is neatly done.	Assignment is neat for the most part.	Assignment is not neat.

Vocabulary for Unit 1

Bible: The collection of Christian sacred writings, or Scripture, accepted by the Church as inspired by God and composed of the Old and New Testaments.

biblical inerrancy: The doctrine that the books of Scripture are free from error regarding the truth God wishes to reveal through Scripture for the sake of our salvation.

biblical inspiration: The gift of the Holy Spirit, which assisted human beings to write biblical books, so they have God as their author and teach faithfully and without error the saving truth that God willed to give us.

Church: The term *Church* has three inseparable meanings: (1) the entire People of God throughout the world; (2) the diocese, which is also known as the local Church; (3) the assembly of believers gathered for the celebration of the liturgy, especially the Eucharist. In the Nicene Creed, the Church is recognized as One, Holy, Catholic, and Apostolic—traits that together are referred to as "marks of the Church."

codices: Book-like manuscripts that replaced scrolls.

consecrate, Consecration: To declare or set apart as sacred or to solemnly dedicate to God's service; to make holy. At Mass the Consecration occurs during the Eucharistic Prayer when the priest recites Jesus' words of institution, changing the bread and wine into the Body and Blood of Christ.

covenant: A solemn agreement between human beings or between God and a human being in which mutual commitments are made.

Deposit of Faith: The heritage of faith contained in Sacred Scripture and Sacred Tradition. It has been passed on from the time of the Apostles. The Magisterium takes from it all that it teaches as revealed truth.

Divine Revelation: God's self-communication through which he makes known the mystery of his divine plan. Divine Revelation is a gift accomplished by the Father, Son, and Holy Spirit through the words and deeds of salvation history. It is most fully realized in the Passion, death, Resurrection, and Ascension of Jesus Christ.

Eucharist, the: The celebration of the entire Mass. The term sometimes refers specifically to the consecrated bread and wine that have become the Body and Blood of Christ.

Gentile: A non-Jewish person. In Scripture, the Gentiles were those outside the covenant, those who did not know how to fulfill God's will. Without this knowledge, they could not be in right relationship with God, and so were considered "unholy" or "unclean." In the New Testament, Saint Paul and other evangelists reached out to the Gentiles, baptizing them into the family of God.

© 2012 by Saint Mary's Press
Living in Christ Series

Gospels: Translated from a Greek word meaning "good news," referring to the four books attributed to Matthew, Mark, Luke, and John, "the principal source for the life and teaching of the Incarnate Word"[1] (*CCC,* 125), Jesus Christ.

incarnate, Incarnation: From the Latin, meaning "to become flesh," referring to the mystery of Jesus Christ, the Divine Son of God, becoming man. In the Incarnation, Jesus Christ became truly man while remaining truly God.

Lectionary: The official liturgical book containing the readings of the Mass, the Gospels, the Responsorial Psalms, and the Gospel Acclamations.

liturgical year: The Church's annual cycle of religious feasts and seasons that celebrate the events and mysteries of Christ's birth, life, death, Resurrection, and Ascension, and that form the context for the Church's worship.

Liturgy of the Hours: Also known as the Divine Office, the official public, daily prayer of the Catholic Church. The Divine Office provides standard prayers, Scripture readings, and reflections at regular hours throughout the day.

Magisterium: The Church's living teaching office, which consists of all bishops, in communion with the Pope.

synoptic Gospels: From the Greek for "seeing the whole together," the name given to the Gospels of Matthew, Mark, and Luke because they are similar in style and content.

Tradition: From the Latin *tradere,* meaning "to hand on," referring to the process of passing on the Gospel message. Tradition, which began with the oral communication of the Gospel by the Apostles, was written down in Scripture, is handed down and lived out in the life of the Church, and is interpreted by the Magisterium under the guidance of the Holy Spirit.

Vatican Council II: The Ecumenical or general Council of the Roman Catholic Church that Pope John XXIII (1958–1963) convened in 1962 and that continued under Pope Paul VI (1963–1978) until 1965.

Word of God: The entire deposit of truth revealed by God throughout history and transmitted through Scripture and Tradition, under the guidance of the Holy Spirit. Through all the words of Sacred Scripture, God speaks of the Word, Jesus Christ, the fullness of Revelation and the Eternal Son of God. Jesus Christ became man (the Word incarnate) for the sake of our salvation.

Endnote Cited in a Quotation from the *Catechism of the Catholic Church,* Second Edition

1. *Dei Verbum* 18.

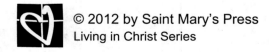

Old and New Testament Passages

Old Testament Passages	New Testament Passages
Genesis 38:27,29b–30 When the time of her delivery came, there were twins in her womb. . . . He was called Perez. Afterward his brother . . . came out; he was called Zerah.	Matthew 1:3a Judah became the father of Perez and Zerah, whose mother was Tamar.
Joshua 2:1b When the two reached Jericho, they went into the house of a prostitute named Rahab, where they lodged.	Hebrews 11:31 By faith Rahab the harlot did not perish with the disobedient, for she had received the spies in peace.

Document #: TX002197

Old Testament Passages	New Testament Passages

Amos 5:11–12
 	
Therefore, because you tax the destitute
 	
    and exact from them levies of grain,
 	
Though you have built houses of hewn
 	
    stone,
 	
    you shall not live in them;
 	
Though you have planted choice
 	
    vineyards,
 	
    you shall not drink their wine.
 	
Yes, I know how many are your crimes,
 	
    how grievous your sins:
 	
Oppressing the just, accepting bribes,
 	
    turning away the needy at the gate.
	James 5:1,4–5
	
	Come now, you rich, weep and wail over your impending miseries. . . . Behold, the wages you withheld from the workers who harvested your fields are crying aloud, and the cries of the harvesters have reached the ears of the Lord of hosts. You have lived on earth in luxury and pleasure; you have fattened your hearts for the day of slaughter.

Document #: TX002197

Old Testament Passages	New Testament Passages

Joel 3:1–2
 	
It shall come to pass
 	
    I will pour out my spirit upon all people.
 	
Your sons and daughters shall prophesy,
 	
    your old men will dream dreams,
 	
    your young men will see visions.
 	
Even upon your male and female servants,
 	
    in those days, I will pour out my spirit.
	Acts of the Apostles 2:14,16–17
	
	Then Peter stood up with the Eleven,
	
	raised his voice, and proclaimed to them,
	
	"You who are Jews, indeed all of you
	
	staying in Jerusalem. Let this be known to
	
	you, and listen to my words. . . . This is
	
	what was spoken through the prophet
	
	Joel:
	
	    'It will come to pass in the last days,'
	
	      God says,
	
	      'that I will pour out a portion of my
	
	        spirit upon all flesh.
	
	    Your sons and your daughters shall
	
	      prophesy,
	
	      your young men shall see
	
	      visions,
	
	      your old men shall dream
	
	      dreams.'"

Document #: TX002197

Old Testament Passages	New Testament Passages
Deuteronomy 6:13–14 The LORD, your God, shall you fear; him shall you serve, and by his name shall you swear. You shall not go after other gods, any of the gods of the surrounding peoples—	Luke 4:3a,7–8 The devil said to him, . . . "All this will be yours, if you worship me." Jesus said to him in reply, "It is written: 'You shall worship the Lord, your God, and him alone shall you serve.'"
Isaiah 40:3 A voice proclaims: In the wilderness prepare the way of the LORD! Make straight in the wasteland a highway for our God!	Mark 1:1–3 The beginning of the gospel of Jesus Christ [the Son of God]. As it is written in Isaiah the prophet: "Behold, I am sending my messenger ahead of you; he will prepare your way. A voice of one crying out in the desert: 'Prepare the way of the Lord, make straight his paths.'"
Genesis 1:1–2 When God created the heavens and the earth—and the earth was without form or shape, with darkness over the abyss and a mighty wind sweeping over the waters—	John 1:1–2 In the beginning was the Word, and the Word was with God, and the Word was God. He was in the beginning with God.

Document #: TX002197

Old Testament Passages	New Testament Passages

Isaiah 28:16a
 	
Therefore, thus says the Lord GOD:
 	
    See, I am laying a stone in Zion,
 	
    a stone that has been tested,
 	
A precious cornerstone as a sure
 	
    foundation.
	1 Peter 2:5–6
	
	Like living stones, let yourselves be built
	
	into a spiritual house to be a holy
	
	priesthood to offer spiritual sacrifices
	
	acceptable to God through Jesus Christ.
	
	For it says in scripture:
	
	    "Behold, I am laying a stone in Zion,
	
	    a cornerstone, chosen and
	
	    precious,
	
	    and whoever believes in it shall not be
	
	    put to shame."

Hosea 11:1 When Israel was a child, I loved him, out of Egypt I called my son.	Matthew 2:14–15 Joseph rose and took the child and his mother by night and departed for Egypt. He stayed there until the death of Herod, that what the Lord had said through the prophet might be fulfilled, "Out of Egypt I called my son."

Document #: TX002197

Old Testament Passages	New Testament Passages
1 Samuel 21:5a,7 The priest replied to David, "I have no ordinary bread on hand, only holy bread." . . . So the priest gave him holy bread, for no other bread was on hand except the showbread which had been removed from before the LORD and replaced by fresh bread when it was taken away.	Mark 2:25–26 [Jesus] said to them, "Have you never read what David did when he was in need and he and his companions were hungry? How he went into the house of God when Abiathar was high priest and ate the bread of offering that only the priests could lawfully eat, and shared it with his companions?"
2 Kings 4:43–44 But his servant objected, "How can I set this before a hundred?" Elisha again said, "Give it to the people to eat, for thus says the LORD: You will eat and have some left over."	John 6:10b–13 The men reclined, about five thousand in number. Then Jesus took the [five] loaves, gave thanks, and distributed them to those who were reclining, and also as much of the [two] fish as they wanted. When they had had their fill, he said to his disciples, "Gather the fragments left over, so that nothing will be wasted." So they collected them, and filled twelve wicker baskets with fragments from the five barley loaves that had been more than they could eat.

Old Testament Passages	New Testament Passages
1 Samuel 2:1–2 And Hannah prayed: "My heart exults in the LORD, my horn is exalted by my God. I have swallowed up my enemies; I rejoice in your victory. There is no Holy One like the LORD; there is no Rock like our God."	Luke 1:46–49 Mary said: "My soul proclaims the greatness of the Lord; my spirit rejoices in God my savior. For he has looked upon his handmaid's lowliness; behold, from now on will all ages call me blessed."
Genesis 12:1 The LORD said to Abram: Go forth from your land, your relatives, and from your father's house to a land that I will show you.	Acts of the Apostles 7:1–3 Then the high priest asked, "Is this so?" And [Stephen] replied, "My brothers and fathers, listen. The God of glory appeared to our father Abraham while he was in Mesopotamia, before he had settled in Haran, and said to him, 'Go forth from your land and [from] your kinsfolk to the land that I will show you.'"

Old Testament Passages	New Testament Passages
Exodus 2:1–2 Now a man of the house of Levi married a Levite woman, and the woman conceived and bore a son. Seeing what a fine child he was, she hid him for three months.	Hebrews 11:23–25 By faith Moses was hidden by his parents for three months after his birth, because they saw that he was a beautiful child, and they were not afraid of the king's edict. By faith Moses, when he had grown up, refused to be known as the son of Pharaoh's daughter; he chose to be ill-treated along with the people of God rather than enjoy the fleeting pleasure of sin.
Genesis 22:9 When they came to the place of which God had told him, Abraham built an altar there and arranged the wood on it. Next he bound his son Isaac, and put him on top of the wood on the altar.	James 2:21 Was not Abraham our father justified by works when he offered his son Isaac upon the altar?

Old Testament History: Major Time Periods

1. The era of the patriarchs and matriarchs

2. The Israelites enslaved in Egypt

3. The Exodus from Egypt

4. The wilderness years

5. The formation of the Sinai Covenant

6. Settlement in Canaan: The era of the judges

7. The rise of the monarchy: King Saul

8. The united nation of Israel: King David

9. The last king of the united nation: King Solomon

10. The split of the kingdom: The divided monarchy

11. The era of the prophets

12. The Babylonian Exile

13. The return from Exile: Restoration and rebuilding

14. The Greek period

15. The Roman period

Dogmatic Constitution on Divine Revelation (*Dei Verbum*, 1965)

Write all answers in complete sentences.

1. Circle the chapter of *Dei Verbum* that your group is discussing:

   Prologue and Chapter 1   Chapter 2   Chapter 3

   Chapter 4   Chapter 5   Chapter 6

2. What are three pieces of information in this chapter that are familiar to you, either from the textbook reading or from other sources?

3. What are three new pieces of information that you have discovered in this chapter or three pieces of information that you have come to understand more fully?

4. What are three basic questions that you have about this chapter—for example, concepts or terms that need clarification? (*Note:* You may list fewer than three questions if you believe you understand your chapter thoroughly.)

5. What are three substantive or theoretical questions you have about this chapter? (*Note:* These should be "why" questions that invite deep, thoughtful reflection.)

Document #: TX002199

The Use of Scripture in the Doctrine of the Church

1. Write the name of your document here, in Latin and English if both are given.

2. Who wrote or issued this document?

3. At what level of Church teaching was this document issued? (Refer to levels 1 through 5 from the PowerPoint presentation.)

4. What year was this document written? What do you know about world events at that time that may help you to better understand the themes and emphases of this document?

5. Summarize the Church doctrine this document presents.

6. List at least three biblical references found in your document. These may be direct quotes, paraphrases, or allusions. For each reference, explain how it is being used. For example, is it being used to support a doctrine of the Church? as evidence for the importance of the doctrine? as a potential defense against those who might dismiss the doctrine or not take it seriously?

Document #: TX002200

7. Does this document draw on the Old Testament, the New Testament, or both? Why do you think this is? If the document draws on both, what differences do you observe in how the document uses each testament?

8. Do you think reading this document would encourage someone to read Scripture? Why or why not?

9. How might the time period in which your document was written have affected the way it uses (or does not use) Scripture?

10. How does this document help you to better understand the complex relationship between Scripture and the doctrine of the Church?

Document #: TX002200

Lectionary Word Splash

Old Testament reading   Gospel reading

Psalm

harmonious composition

Lectionary

liturgical seasons

**Constitution on the Sacred Liturgy
(*Sacrosanctum Concilium*, 1963)**

New Testament reading

3-year cycle

semicontinuous reading

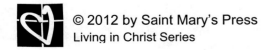

Sunday *Lectionary* Readings: God's Ongoing Story of Love for Humanity

Circle the set of readings that your group has been assigned:

First Sunday of Advent, B: Isaiah 63:16–17,19; 64:2–7

                                               1 Corinthians 1:3–9

                                             Mark 13:33–37

Third Sunday of the Year, A: Isaiah 8:23—9:3

                                    1 Corinthians 1:1–13,17

                                    Matthew 4:12–23

Solemnity of Our Lord Jesus Christ, the King, C: 2 Samuel 5:1–3

                                              Colossians 1:12–20

                                             Luke 23:35–43

Sixth Sunday of the Year, B: Leviticus 13:1–2,44–46

                                    1 Corinthians 10:13—11:1

                                    Mark 1:40–45

Ninth Sunday of the Year, C: Sirach (Ben Sira) 27:4–7

                                    1 Corinthians 15:54–58

                                    Luke 6:39–45

1. Write a two-sentence summary of each of your three readings.

2. What images or symbols do these readings (either two or all three) have in common?

Document #: TX002202

3. What themes or ideas do these readings (either two or all three) have in common?

4. How is God's loving relationship with humanity revealed in the Old Testament reading?

5. How is that loving relationship with humanity continued in the Gospel reading? in the New Testament reading?

6. What is the Church trying to teach us by intentionally assigning these three readings to one particular Sunday liturgy? Pay attention to any important message that may be conveyed by pairing the Old Testament reading and the Gospel reading.

Create a Poster

Use your answers to the questions above, and other points that have surfaced in your discussion, to create a poster about your three readings, including the following elements:

- It should be primarily visual (symbols and images), but it may contain some words.

- It must convey the content of your three readings, including the connections and commonalities among them.

- It must convey the idea of God's ongoing love for humanity, revealed through all three readings (that is, through both Testaments).

Document #: TX002202

Sunday Gospel Readings

Year A, Third through Seventh Sundays of the Year

✂ ───

Matthew 4:12–23

✂ ───

Matthew 5:1–12

✂ ───

Matthew 5:13–16

✂ ───

Matthew 5:17–37

✂ ───

Matthew 5:38–48

✂ ───

Year B, Third through Seventh Sundays of the Year

✂ ───

Mark 1:14–20

✂ ───

Mark 1:21–28

✂ ───

Mark 1:29–39

✂ ───

Document #: TX002203

✂ _____

Mark 1:40–45

✂ _____

Mark 2:1–12

✂ _____

Year C, Third through Seventh Sundays of the Year

✂ _____

Luke 1:1–4, 4:14–21

✂ _____

Luke 4:21–30

✂ _____

Luke 5:1–11

✂ _____

Luke 6:17,20–26

✂ _____

Luke 6:27–38

✂ _____

Year A, Twentieth through Twenty-Fourth Sundays of the Year

✂ _____

Matthew 15:21–28

✂ _____

Matthew 16:13–20

✂ _____

Matthew 16:21–27

✂ _____

Matthew 18:15–20

✂ _____

Matthew 18:21–35

✂ _____

Year C, Twentieth through Twenty-Fourth Sundays of the Year

✂ _____

Luke 12:49–53

✂ _____

Luke 13:22–30

✂ _____

Luke 14:1,7–14

✂ _____

Document #: TX002203

✂ _____

Luke 14:25–33

✂ _____

Luke 15:1–32

✂ _____

Reflections on the Liturgical Year

by Joan Chittister

The liturgical year is the year that sets out to attune the life of the Christian to the life of Jesus, the Christ. It proposes, year after year, to immerse us over and over again into the sense and substance of the Christian life until, eventually, we become what we say we are—followers of Jesus all the way to the heart of God. The liturgical year is an adventure in human growth, an exercise in spiritual ripening.

. . .

From the liturgy we learn both the faith and Scripture, both our ideals and our spiritual tradition. The cycle of Christian mysteries is wise teacher, clear model, and recurring and constant reminder of the Christ-life in our midst. Simply by being itself over and over again, simply by putting before our eyes and filtering into our hearts the living presence of the Jesus who walked from Galilee to Jerusalem doing good, it teaches us to do the same. As Jesus lived, despite either the restrictions or the regulations of His age, so, the liturgical year teaches us, must we.

In the liturgy, then, is the standard of what it means to live a Christian life both as the church and as individuals. The seasons and cycles and solemnities put before us in the liturgical year are more than representations of time past; they are an unending sign—a veritable sacrament of life. It is through them that the Christ-life becomes present in our own lives in the here and now.

It is in the liturgy that we meet the Jesus of history and come to understand the Christ of faith who is with us still.

. . .

The liturgical year is the process of slow, sure immersion in the life of Christ that, in the end, claims us, too, as heralds of that life ourselves.

The continuing proclamation of the Scriptures, the centrality of the Gospels as the foundation of every liturgy, and the ongoing reflection on those readings in homilies year after year do two things: one of them communal, the other personal. First, the liturgical year reminds us as the church what kind of a community we are meant to be. . . .

Second, the liturgical year implants within each of us individually the reprise of those moments that are the substance of the faith. It calls us to face the distance between the ideals we see in the life of Christ and the pale ghost of them we find in our own. It calls us to private and personal reflection on the place of Jesus in the daily exercise of our existence.

1. According to Chittister, what is the purpose of the liturgical year?

2. How does the liturgical year seek to accomplish this purpose?

3. What do you think Chittister means by "the place of Jesus in the daily exercise of our existence"?

The excerpts on this handout are from *The Liturgical Year,* by Joan Chittister (Nashville, TN: Thomas Nelson, 2009), pages 11, 6, 10–11, 13, respectively. Copyright © 2009 by Joan Chittister. Used with permission of Thomas Nelson, Inc., Nashville, TN.

Gospel Reflection Questions

Use this space to take brief, informal notes on your group's five Gospel readings.

1. Looking at these readings *as a whole,* what qualities or characteristics of Jesus emerge most strongly?

2. Which of these qualities or characteristics is most difficult for a young person to live out in today's world? Why? How might prayerful reflection on these readings, in the context of the liturgy, make it easier to live out each quality or characteristic?

3. What do we learn from examining these readings together that might be lost if we looked at them only individually?

4. How do these readings, as a whole, present to us "the standard of what it means to live a Christian life both as the church and as individuals" (Chittister, *The Liturgical Year,* p. 11)?

© 2012 by Saint Mary's Press
Living in Christ Series

Document #: TX002205

Unit 1 Test

Part 1: Fill-in-the-Blank

Place the following events or time periods in the history of ancient Israel in the order in which they occurred by filling in a "1" before the first event or time period that occurred, a "2" before the second, and so forth, up to 15.

_____The Greek period

_____The wilderness years

_____Settlement in Canaan: The era of the judges

_____The return from Exile: Restoration and rebuilding

_____The era of the patriarchs and matriarchs

_____The Exodus from Egypt

_____The united nation of Israel: King David

_____The Israelites enslaved in Egypt

_____The split of the kingdom: The divided monarchy

_____The formation of the Sinai Covenant

_____The rise of the monarchy: King Saul

_____The Babylonian Exile

_____The last king of the united nation: King Solomon

_____The era of the prophets

_____The Roman period

Document #: TX002206

Part 2: Multiple Choice

Write your answers in the blank spaces at the left.

1. _____ Vatican Council II's *Divine Revelation* is often known by its Latin name, which is _____.

    A. *Sacrosanctum Concilium*
    B. *Monasterium Domenici*
    C. *Dei Verbum*
    D. *Opus Dei*

2. _____ Divine Revelation is transmitted through _____.

    A. Scripture
    B. Tradition
    C. the wisdom of well-intentioned people
    D. both A and B but not C

3. _____ The general term for the teachings of the Church is _____.

    A. dogma
    B. doctrine
    C. Magisterium
    D. *verbum*

4. _____ The Church's official teaching office or authority is known as the _____.

    A. dogma
    B. doctrine
    C. Magisterium
    D. *verbum*

5. _____ In the *Lectionary*, the Old Testament and Gospel readings were assigned to particular Sundays based on the principle of _____.

    A. *aggiornamento*
    B. psalmody
    C. harmonious composition
    D. semicontinuous reading

Document #: TX002206

6. _____ In the *Lectionary*, the New Testament readings (usually from the Epistles) were assigned to particular Sundays based on the principle of _____.

   A. *aggiornamento*
   B. psalmody
   C. harmonious composition
   D. semicontinuous reading

7. _____ The part of the liturgy in which the presider helps us to understand the Scripture readings and apply them to our lives is called the _____.

   A. Liturgy of the Word
   B. homily
   C. Prayers of the Faithful
   D. breviary

8. _____ The Liturgy of the Hours may be prayed by _____.

   A. those living in monastic, cloistered settings
   B. the ordained
   C. the baptized
   D. all of the above

9. _____ The heart of the Liturgy of the Hours is _____.

   A. the New Testament
   B. the Eucharist
   C. psalmody
   D. the penitential rite

10. _____ In describing the New Testament, we can say that _____.

    A. it is intimately connected with the Old Testament
    B. it continues the story of God's loving relationship with humanity
    C. it must be viewed and understood in the broader context of the entire Bible
    D. all of the above

Part 3: Essay

Respond to the following with at least one substantial paragraph.

1. Describe the relationship between the Old and New Testaments. Include how the two are connected or interrelated, their commonalities, and key differences between them.

2. What is the *Lectionary*? Explain how the *Lectionary* can help us to grow in faith by discussing *both* of the following:

   - the relationship among the readings proclaimed at any one Sunday liturgy

   - the relationship among the Gospel readings proclaimed on consecutive Sundays

3. What is the Liturgy of the Hours? Explain how it is structured, how it uses Scripture, and how it enables us to grow in unity with the Church throughout the world.

4. Identify and explain the five levels of authority in Magisterial teachings, giving an example of each.

Unit 1 Test Answer Key

Part 1: Fill-in-the-Blank

14, The Greek period

4, The wilderness years

6, Settlement in Canaan: The era of the judges

13, The return from Exile: Restoration and rebuilding

1, The era of the patriarchs and matriarchs

3, The Exodus from Egypt

8, The united nation of Israel: King David

2, The Israelites enslaved in Egypt

10, The split of the kingdom: The divided monarchy

5, The formation of the Sinai Covenant

7, The rise of the monarchy: King Saul

12, The Babylonian Exile

9, The last king of the united nation: King Solomon

11, The era of the prophets

15, The Roman period

Part 2: Multiple Choice

1. C	**5.** C	**9.** C
2. D	**6.** D	**10.** D
3. B	**7.** B	
4. C	**8.** D	

Part 3: Essay

1. The Old and New Testaments are interrelated parts of the Bible that are best understood as a whole. According to Vatican Council II's *Dogmatic Constitution on Divine Revelation* (*Dei Verbum*), the New Testament is "hidden in the Old" and the Old Testament is "made manifest in the New" (16). In other words, the Old Testament *begins* the story of God's loving relationship with humanity, and the New Testament *continues* that story. Both testaments share common themes, such as God's great love for us, God's desire to reveal the divine self to us, and God's concern for the poor and forgotten. The two testaments differ in their focus. The Old Testament focuses on the history of ancient Israel, from the time of the patriarchs until the Greco-Roman period. The New Testament focuses on the life of Jesus and the spread of the Gospel message in the early years of the Church.

© 2012 by Saint Mary's Press
Living in Christ Series

Document #: TX002207

2. The *Lectionary* is not the Bible. It is a collection of readings from the Bible that are assigned to be proclaimed at Mass on weekdays and Sundays. On any given Sunday, four Scripture readings are proclaimed: an Old Testament reading, a Psalm (which is usually sung), a New Testament reading (usually from the Epistles), and a Gospel reading. The Old Testament reading and the Gospel have been assigned to particular Sundays based on the principle of harmonious composition, meaning that these two readings are similar in content, theme, or both. Attentiveness to the commonalities between these readings deepens our understanding of the message God intends to communicate to us through Scripture. Moreover, by attending Sunday liturgy faithfully, we hear a significant portion of the Gospels over time. These Gospel readings are intended to affect us profoundly, as we hear and internalize their message week after week and year after year. They are intended to help us grow closer to Jesus and to become more like him.

3. The Liturgy of the Hours is the prayer of the Church. Although it is most often associated with monks and nuns who live in cloistered settings and structure their whole life around prayer, the Liturgy of the Hours can be prayed by anyone. It is a powerful means of cultivating the discipline of daily, Scripture-based prayer. Whether we pray it individually or communally, this prayer enables us to grow in unity with the Church throughout the world, as we join with all those who offer this prayer each day, from morning to evening.

The Liturgy of the Hours consists almost entirely of Scripture. After an opening invocation, the heart of the Liturgy of the Hours is psalmody: one, two, or three psalms, each of which begins and ends with an antiphon. After a Scripture reading and brief response, the Liturgy concludes with a Gospel canticle, prayers of intercession, and the Lord's Prayer.

4. The Magisterium is the official living teaching authority of the Church. Not all statements issued by the Magisterium are equally authoritative; rather, there are five levels of authority in these teachings or proclamations. Dogmatic statements, such as the Proclamation of the Dogma of the Immaculate Conception, are most authoritative. These are proclaimed by the Pope *ex cathedra,* "from the chair." Next are conciliar statements, which are issued collectively by the entire Magisterium (that is, by all the bishops, including the Pope). Examples include the sixteen documents of Vatican Council II, such as *Divine Revelation.* Papal encyclicals are issued by a Pope in response to a particular situation or need. For example, Pope Leo XIII issued *Rerum Novarum* in 1891 as a response to the growing industrialization of the workplace. Popes may also issue apostolic constitutions, statements, and letters, such as the document that proclaimed the Great Jubilee of the Year 2000. Finally, national bishops' conferences may issue pastoral letters, such as that released by the U.S. bishops in 1986, *Economic Justice for All.* (*Note:* Examples of documents offered for each level of authority may vary.)

The quotation on this handout from *Dogmatic Constitution on Divine Revelation* (*Dei Verbum*, 1965), number 16, is in *Vatican Council II: Volume 1: The Conciliar and Postconciliar Documents*, New Revised Edition, Austin Flannery, general editor (Northport, NY: Costello Publishing, 1996). Copyright © 1975, 1986, 1992, 1996 by Reverend Austin Flannery.

Unit 2 A Catholic Approach to Scripture: Exegetical and Interpretive Methods

Overview

This unit will introduce the students to exegetical and interpretive methods that will allow them to understand more clearly the Catholic approach to Scripture.

Key Understandings and Questions

Upon completing this unit, the students will have a deeper understanding of the following key concepts:

- Various exegetical methods enable us to read and interpret Scripture contextually.
- Literary criticism enables us to analyze a scriptural text by examining its genre, plot, characters, and symbolism.
- Sociohistorical criticism enables us to understand the culture and world in which a scriptural text was written.
- Ideological criticism enables us to understand how our own worldview shapes our interpretation of Scripture.

Upon completing the unit, the students will have answered the following questions:

- What is the purpose of exegesis?
- How does sociohistorical criticism inform our interpretation of Scripture?
- How does literary criticism inform our interpretation of Scripture?
- How does ideological criticism inform our interpretation of Scripture?

How Will You Know the Students Understand?

The following resources will help you to assess the students' understanding of the key concepts covered in this unit:

- handout "Final Performance Task Options for Unit 2" (Document #: TX002217)
- handout "Rubric for Final Performance Tasks for Unit 2" (Document #: TX002218)
- handout "Unit 2 Test" (Document #: TX002227)

Student Book Articles

This unit draws on articles from *The New Testament: The Good News of Jesus Christ* student book and incorporates them into the unit instruction. Whenever the teaching steps for the unit require the students to refer to or read an article from the student book, the following symbol appears in the margin: ▮▮. The articles covered in the unit are from "Section 1: The Word of God," and are as follows:

- "Context: Literary Form" (article 4)
- "Context: Historical and Cultural Situation" (article 5)
- "Context: Scriptural Development" (article 6)
- "Sacred Scripture: A Living Word for Today" (article 7)

The Suggested Path to Understanding

This unit in the teacher guide provides you with one learning path to take with the students, to enable them to begin their study of exegetical and interpretive methods that will allow them to understand more clearly the Catholic approach to Scripture of the New Testament. It is not necessary to use all the learning experiences, but if you substitute other material from this course or your own material for some of the material offered here, check to see that you have covered all relevant facets of understanding and that you have not missed knowledge or skills required in later units.

 Step 1: Preassess what the students already know about exegetical and interpretive methods used in the Catholic approach to Scripture by inviting them to interact with a document from U.S. history.

 Step 2: Follow this assessment by presenting to the students the handouts "Final Performance Task Options for Unit 2" (Document #: TX002217) and "Rubric for Final Performance Tasks for Unit 2" (Document #: TX002218).

 Step 3: Introduce the students to the difference between a contextual and a fundamentalist reading of Scripture by watching a video clip and examining biblical references.

 Step 4: Introduce the students to an exegetical method: literary criticism.

 **Step 5:** Engage the students in interpreting Scripture using literary criticism.

 Step 6: Introduce the students to an exegetical method: sociohistorical criticism.

 **Step 7**: Engage the students in interpreting Scripture using socio-historical criticism.

 Step 8: Introduce the students to an exegetical method: ideological criticism.

Step 9: Engage the students in interpreting Scripture using ideological criticism.

Step 10: Make sure the students are all on track with their final performance tasks, if you have assigned them.

Step 11: Provide the students with a tool to use for reflecting on what they learned in the unit and how they learned.

Background for Teaching This Unit

Visit *smp.org/LivinginChrist* for additional information about these and other theological concepts taught in this unit:

- "A Brief History of Catholic Biblical Interpretation" (Document #: TX002208)
- "How Should We Interpret Scripture?" (Document #: TX002209)
- "Understanding Genres and Literary Forms" (Document #: TX001026)
- "Bible 101: A Basic Introduction to the Word of God" (Document #: TX001000)

The Web site also includes information on these and other teaching methods used in the unit:

- "How to Teach Biblical Research" (Document #: TX002210)
- "Introducing Biblical Criticism" (Document #: TX002211)

Scripture Passages

Scripture is an important part of the Living in Christ series and is frequently used in the learning experiences for each unit. The Scripture passages featured in this unit are as follows:

- Mark 7:24–30 (the Syrophoenician woman)
- Matthew 4:1–11 (the temptation of Jesus)
- Matthew 8:5–13 (healing of the centurion's servant)
- Luke 1:46–55 (Mary's *Magnificat*)
- Luke 8:4–8 (Parable of the Sower)
- Luke 10:25–37 (the Good Samaritan)
- John 8:1–11 (woman caught in adultery)

Vocabulary

The student book and the teacher guide include the following key terms for this unit. To provide the students with a list of these terms and their definitions, download and print the handout "Vocabulary for Unit 2" (Document #: TX002219), one for each student.

. . . .

apocalyptic literature	literary criticism
biblical exegesis	literary forms (genres)
exegete	moral truth
ideological criticism	sociohistorical criticism
literary convention	

Learning Experiences

Explain   **Step 1**

Preassess what the students already know about exegetical and interpretive methods used in the Catholic approach to Scripture by inviting them to interact with a document from U.S. history.

1. **Prepare** by downloading and printing the handout "The Gettysburg Address" (Document #: TX002216), one for each student. In addition, download and print as many copies of the handout "Preassessment Pair Activity" (Document #: TX002215) as are needed so that each student has either one exegetical methodology or one definition. Cut these handouts along the dotted lines to create strips of paper with either a methodology or a definition. (If you have an odd number of students, you may assign a single strip to a pair of students.) Gather three large sheets of newsprint or poster board and markers.

2. **Tell** the students that in this unit they will learn about the Catholic approach to Scripture and will be introduced to three major exegetical methods that will help them to interpret Scripture: literary criticism, sociohistorical criticism, and ideological criticism.

3. **Give** each student a strip of paper that has one of either the exegetical methodologies or the definitions. Explain that each student has either a methodology or a definition. Direct the students to find a partner who has their matching methodology or definition. In other words, each pair should have a methodology and a definition. Allow 2 to 3 minutes for the students to form pairs. After the allotted time, check to see that the students are correctly paired according to the methodology and its definition:

   - **Literary criticism:** A methodology that enables us to analyze a scriptural text by examining its genre, plot, characters, and symbolism.

   - **Sociohistorical criticism:** A methodology that enables us to analyze a scriptural text by examining the culture and world in which a scriptural text was written.

   - **Ideological criticism:** A methodology that enables us to understand a scriptural text by examining how our own worldview shapes our interpretation of Scripture.

4. **Distribute** to each student a copy of the handout "The Gettysburg Address" (Document #: TX002216). Direct the students to read it silently. After they have read the document, ask them to discuss the following questions with their partners and note their responses:

   • What is this document about? What is it communicating? What does it mean?

   • What information would help you to better understand the text?

   Allow approximately 5 minutes for this discussion.

5. **Ask** the pairs to share their responses with the class. Point out examples of questions they have raised that are literary, sociohistorical, or ideological in nature.

6. **Direct** the students to form three groups, based on the methodology and definition they were given (that is, those with literary criticism and its definition form one group; those with sociohistorical criticism and its definition form a second group; those with ideological criticism and its definition form the third group). Distribute poster board or newsprint and markers to each group. Direct each group to respond to the question that is relevant to its methodology:

   • Literary criticism: What kinds of questions would we ask of this text to understand it as a piece of literature?

   • Sociohistorical criticism: What kinds of questions would we ask of this text to understand the social and historical context in which it was written?

   • Ideological criticism: What kinds of questions would we ask of the text to understand how someone's worldview would shape both the writing and the understanding of the text?

   Tell the groups to write these questions on their paper. Allow approximately 10 minutes for this brainstorming.

7. **Draw** the class back together to share responses. Invite the students to consider the following:

   • How can these three different methodologies help us to understand the text?

   • Why might it be useful to interpret a text using different methodologies?

   • How or why do you think these methods will be helpful for our study of the New Testament?

> **Teacher Note**
>
> As students work in their groups, note the areas where they seem to have difficulty, as well as areas in which they already have a strong background.

8. **Conclude** this preassessment learning experience by reminding the students that in this unit they will learn about the Catholic approach to the interpretation of Scripture. Tell them that they not only will learn more about each of these methodologies but also will have an opportunity to use each one to interpret Scripture.

Understand

Step 2

Follow this assessment by presenting to the students the handouts "Final Performance Task Options for Unit 2" (Document #: TX002217) and "Rubric for Final Performance Tasks for Unit 2" (Document #: TX002218).

This unit provides you with two ways to assess that the students have a deep understanding of the most important concepts in the unit: writing a research paper on the Catholic approach to Scripture or illustrating the three exegetical methods studied in class through a group presentation. Refer to "Using Final Performance Tasks to Assess Understanding" (Document #: TX001011) and "Using Rubrics to Assess Work" (Document #: TX001012) at *smp.org/ LivinginChrist* for background information.

> **Teacher Note**
>
> Remind the students to choose their final performance task in accordance with any course requirements you may have established.

> **Teacher Note**
>
> You will want to assign due dates for the performance tasks.
>
> If you have done these performance tasks, or very similar ones, with students before, place examples of this work in the classroom. During this introduction explain how each is a good example of what you are looking for, for different reasons. This allows the students to concretely understand what you are looking for and to understand that there is not only one way to succeed.

1. **Prepare** by downloading and printing the handouts "Final Performance Task Options for Unit 2" (Document #: TX002217) and "Rubric for Final Performance Tasks for Unit 2" (Document #: TX002218), one copy of each for each student.

2. **Distribute** the handouts. Give the students a choice as to which performance task to work on and add more options if you so choose.

3. **Review** the directions, expectations, and rubric in class, allowing the students to ask questions. You may want to say something to this effect:

   ➤ If you wish to work alone, you may choose option 1 only. If you wish to work with one or two other people, you may choose option 2.

   ➤ Near the end of the unit, you will have one full class period to work on the final performance task. However, keep in mind that you should be working on, or at least thinking about, your chosen task throughout the unit, not just at the end.

4. **Explain** the types of tools and knowledge the students will gain throughout the unit so that they can successfully complete the final performance task.

5. **Answer** questions to clarify the end point toward which the unit is headed. Remind the students as the unit progresses that each learning experience builds the knowledge and skills they will need in order to show you that they understand the exegetical and interpretive tools used in the Catholic approach to understanding Scripture.

Understand

Step 3

Introduce the students to the difference between a contextual and a fundamentalist reading of Scripture by watching a video clip and examining biblical references.

1. **Prepare** by obtaining and previewing episode 3, "The Midterms," from season 2 of the TV series *The West Wing.* You may obtain the DVD or download the digital episode from an online source. Specifically, locate the video clip from 33:30 to 36:24 of the episode, in which President Josiah Bartlet challenges a talk radio host about a fundamentalist interpretation of the Bible. Arrange for the use of the equipment needed to play the scene in your classroom. Download and print the handout "Contextual Reading of Scripture" (Document #: TX002220), one for each student.

> **Teacher Note**
>
> Because the scene from *The West Wing* ends with a disparaging comment that includes profanity (starting at 36:26), you may want to preview this to ensure you know when to stop the clip.

2. **Begin** by inviting the students to brainstorm a list of social issues or current events in which the Bible is referenced to either support or refute a particular stance. Examples might include evolution, marriage, abortion, and war. List these items on the board for reference.

3. **Tell** the students that they will see a short video clip (about 2 minutes long) from the TV series *The West Wing,* which aired from 1999 to 2006. In this scene, Martin Sheen, who plays President Josiah Bartlet, has an exchange with a popular talk radio host, Dr. Jacobs. Be aware that President Bartlet is addressing a political rival in a confrontational way. Explain that the purpose of this video clip is not to explore the specific issues presented but rather to understand the difference between a fundamentalist reading of Scripture and the contextual interpretation of Scripture. Show the video clip.

4. **Distribute** the handout "Contextual Reading of Scripture" (Document #: TX002220). Organize the students into small groups of three or four. Give the following explanation and directions:

   ➤ In the video clip, President Bartlet refers to several Scripture quotations. You may have heard of some of these quotations before, while others may be new to you.

   ➤ In your small group, read each of the Scripture citations listed on the handout.

   ➤ After reading the citations with your group, brainstorm a list of questions you would want to ask of the text to help you understand it. For example, you might want to ask, Was this directive or command meant for a particular group of people? Your questions can be as specific or as broad as you like.

Allow 10 to 15 minutes for groups to work on this handout. Circulate around the room to answer student questions and to ensure that groups are on task.

5. **Draw** the class back together, and invite the students to share the questions they would want to ask of the texts. List these questions on the board. As various groups share their questions, direct the students to place a check mark next to the same or similar questions on their papers so that the class can avoid repetition. Advise the students that if the same or similar question has already been listed, they should simply skip that question when sharing their responses with the large group.

6. **Draw** the students' attention to the section "The Senses of Scripture," in article 7 of the student book. Explain that the *literal sense* does not mean "words alone" but "words in context," taking into consideration time and culture, literary genres, and modes of narration current at the time. (See also *CCC*, 110 and 116. Note that the *literal sense* is not defined in the *CCC* as "words alone" as popularly understood, but as "words interpreted by context.") Emphasize that if Scripture is interpreted with the words alone, without context, this is in itself an interpretation most often called a *fundamentalist* reading or interpretation.

   Offer this or a similar example: Imagine that you answered a question like, "What are you doing this afternoon?" with "I'm just going to chill." These words, to many English-speaking Americans, might mean, "I'm planning to be cold." However, someone who knows the time and culture in which these words were spoken and the literary genre of teen slang would understand the *literal sense* of the words as: "I'm going to relax this afternoon." (You may want to ask for other examples.)

7. **Invite** the students to consider the difference between reading and interpreting a text through the words alone (a fundamentalist reading) and contextually (to discover the *literal sense* as defined in *CCC*, 116, and in article 7 of the student book). Direct the students' attention to the following points:

   ➤ A *fundamentalist* reading of Scripture is just one form of interpretation, though many who prefer this way of reading Scripture may not understand that to be the case. Focusing on particular passages and choosing to understand them in a fundamentalist way, while ignoring other passages (as in the case of Dr. Jacobs in the video clip) is in itself an act of interpretation.

   ➤ In contrast, the Catholic approach to Scripture is clearly stated in the *Catechism*: "In order to discover *the sacred authors' intention*, **the reader must take into account the conditions of their time and culture, the literary genres in use at that time, and the modes of feeling, speaking, and narrating then current.** 'For the fact is that truth is differently presented and expressed in the various types of historical writing, in prophetical and poetical texts, and in other forms of literary expression'[1]" (*CCC,* 110; emphasis added). These ways of reading and interpreting Scripture are *contextual methods*.

> ➤ The goal of contextualist exegesis is to discover the authors' intention, that is, the *literal sense*, of Scripture as discussed in the student book section of article 7, "The Senses of Scripture," and in *CCC*, 116.

8. **Conclude** this learning experience by telling the students they will have an opportunity to learn about and practice three different contextual methods of interpreting Scripture throughout this course: literary criticism, sociohistorical criticism, and ideological criticism.

Article 4

Explain   ## Step 4

Introduce the students to an exegetical method: literary criticism.

1. **Prepare** by downloading the PowerPoint "Exegesis and Literary Analysis" (Document #: TX002213). Download and print the handout "Literary Analysis of Luke 10:25–37" (Document #: TX002221), one for each student.

2. **Assign** the students to read article 4, "Context: Literary Form," in the student book as preparation for this learning experience. Ask the students to bring their Bibles to class.

3. **Present** the PowerPoint "Exegesis and Literary Criticism" (Document #: TX002213). Direct the students to take notes. Supplement the material on the slides with your own explanations, taking care to include the "notes" listed for each slide.

4. **Remind** the students, at the conclusion of the PowerPoint presentation, that literary criticism is one of three methodologies they will learn and practice. For each of the three methodologies explored in this unit, students will use the same Gospel text, Luke 10:25–37. This will help them to understand that different methodologies yield different insights when applied to the same text.

5. **Organize** the students into pairs. Distribute the handout "Literary Analysis of Luke 10:25–37" (Document #: TX002221), one copy for each student. Explain that the students will have an opportunity to work with their partners to engage in literary criticism using the Gospel text Luke 10:25–37. Review the directions on the handout. Allow approximately 15 minutes for the students to work on this passage. Circulate around the room to respond to questions and ensure that the students are on task.

6. **Gather** the students after the allotted time to share what they have discovered about this passage through their literary analysis of the text. You may want to continue the discussion by bringing attention to and asking about the following:

Teacher Note

If you have classroom sets of biblical references such as *Saint Mary's Press® Essential Bible Dictionary* and *Saint Mary's Press® Essential Guide to Biblical Life and Times,* make these available at this time. If not, direct the students to write down their questions, and appoint students to look up definitions and terms as they are brought forward during discussion.

➤ This passage is broken up into several parts: The lawyer's question (v. 25); Jesus' counterquestion (v. 26); the lawyer's response (v. 27); Jesus' challenge to the lawyer (v. 28); a follow-up question from the lawyer (v. 29); Jesus' story of the Good Samaritan, which includes a counterquestion (vv. 30–36); the lawyer's answer (v. 37a); and Jesus' mandate (v. 37b).

➤ The characters include a priest, a Levite, and a Samaritan. More details about these social roles will be explored in later units in this course.

➤ Why do you think this story is called the "Good Samaritan"? What does this title presuppose about Samaritans?

➤ What do you notice about the way the lawyer answers Jesus' question in verse 37a? *(Answer: He does not say "the Samaritan" but rather says "the one who treated him with mercy.")*

➤ What does this text tell us about what it means to be a neighbor and about who we look to as our neighbors?

7. **Conclude** this learning experience by reminding the students that literary criticism is one methodology that they will learn and use to understand a Scripture text. Throughout this unit, they will have opportunities to learn about other methodologies and then use them to deepen their understanding of the meaning of a text. The next learning experience will focus on practicing this same methodology but with a different scriptural text.

Step 5

Engage the students in interpreting Scripture using literary criticism.

1. **Prepare** by downloading and printing the handout "Exegetical Methodology: Literary Criticism" (Document #: TX002222), one for each student. Ask the students to bring their Bibles to class. You may want to make available additional resources, such as *Saint Mary's Press® Essential Bible Dictionary*, *Saint Mary's Press® Essential Guide to Biblical Life and Times*, and the *New Jerome Biblical Commentary*.

2. **Explain** to the students that they will have a further opportunity to practice literary analysis of a Scripture text. Organize the students into groups of four.

3. **Distribute** the handout "Exegetical Methodology: Literary Criticism" (Document #: TX002222). Direct the students to write the names of their group members on their paper (section A on the handout). Explain that they will return to these same groupings for subsequent learning experiences. Then explain to the students that their group will choose one of the Scripture passages listed (section B on the handout) and begin a literary analysis of the text (section C on the handout).

   Remind the students that each member of the group should take notes on the group's responses to the questions in section C of the handout. They may use any available resources, such as a Bible dictionary or biblical commentary. Allow 15 to 20 minutes for the students to work on their chosen text. Circulate around the room to answer questions and ensure that groups are on task.

4. **Direct** the students' attention to section D of the handout. Explain that each group will prepare a skit of a "movie trailer" based on the group's literary analysis of the text. The trailer should be succinct and convey the essential information about and significance of the text. Allow 10 to 15 minutes for groups to prepare their trailers. Circulate around the room to answer any questions and to ensure that groups are on task.

> **Teacher Note**
>
> If you would like to ensure that each group studies a different Scripture passage, you may want to assign passages to each group or simply have groups choose a text one by one, not allowing duplication.

5. **Draw** the class back together, and ask the small groups to perform their movie trailers. As time permits, elicit further questions and comments about the texts.

6. **Conclude** this learning experience by reminding the students that literary criticism is just one methodology that helps us to understand and interpret the meaning of a Scripture text. In the next learning experiences, they will learn about sociohistorical criticism and ideological criticism.

Articles
5, 6

Explain

Step 6

Introduce the students to an exegetical method: sociohistorical criticism.

1. **Prepare** by downloading the PowerPoint "Exegesis and Sociohistorical Criticism" (Document #: TX002214). Download and print the handout "Sociohistorical Analysis of Luke 10:25–37" (Document #: TX002223), one for each student.

2. **Assign** the students to read article 5, "Context: Historical and Cultural Situation," and article 6, "Context: Scriptural Development," in their student books as preparation for this learning experience. Ask the students to bring their Bibles to class.

3. **Present** the PowerPoint "Exegesis and Sociohistorical Criticism" (Document #: TX002214). Direct the students to take notes. Supplement the material on the slides with your own explanations, taking care to include the "notes" listed for each slide.

4. **Distribute** the handout "Sociohistorical Analysis of Luke 10:25–37" (Document #: TX002223), one copy for each student. Explain that the students will have an opportunity to work first individually and then together as a class to engage in sociohistorical criticism using the Gospel text Luke 10:25–37. Review the directions on the handout. Allow 15 to 20 minutes for the students to work individually on this passage. Circulate around the room to respond to questions and ensure that the students are on task.

Teacher Note

If you have classroom sets of biblical references such as *Saint Mary's Press® Essential Bible Dictionary* and *Saint Mary's Press® Essential Guide to Biblical Life and Times*, make these available at this time. If not, direct the students to write down their questions, and appoint students to look up definitions and terms as they are brought forward during discussion.

5. **Gather** the large group after the allotted time to share what the students have discovered, as well as any questions they may have about this passage through their sociohistorical analysis of the text. You may want to emphasize the following points:

   ➤ A scholar of the law was someone who was an expert in the Mosaic Law and in interpreting tradition. This person was probably a member of the group known as scribes, a group that was affiliated with the Pharisees.

   ➤ In the time of Jesus, a priest was someone who offered sacrifices in the Temple on behalf of the people of God.

   ➤ A Levite was someone from the tribe of Levi. The Levites were given the responsibility of overseeing the tabernacle and the Temple. The tribe of Levi was the priestly class.

   ➤ A Samaritan was a person from the territory of Samaria, located between Judea and Galilee. The Jews and Samaritans were deeply divided over religious and ethnic differences. For this reason, in the time of Jesus, the Jews despised Samaritans and treated them with disdain.

   ➤ The assumption of the robbers and of the priest and Levite is that the victim of this robbery is dead or nearly dead.

   ➤ The fact that the victim is dead or nearly dead raises questions for both the priest and Levite regarding adherence to Jewish purity laws.

      Touching a dead body made a person impure for seven days; the person had to bathe ritually, with water mixed with the ashes of a red heifer, to become clean again. If an impure person touched another object, it too became unclean, and could transmit uncleanness to anyone who touched it (see Nm 19:11–22). Priests followed especially strict purity laws: they were allowed to come near the bodies of close relatives only, and the high priest was forbidden to come into contact with any corpse at all, even his father or mother (see Lv 21:1–12). (Albl, *Saint Mary's Press® Essential Guide to Biblical Life and Times*, pp. 42–43)

➤ This passage raises several important questions about observing the law:

- Can someone who is not Jewish, and therefore not observant of Jewish law (such as a Samaritan), inherit eternal life?

- Can someone who is Jewish and supposedly observant of the purity laws but who does not observe the greatest law (see v. 27) inherit eternal life?

- What is more important: being a member of God's Chosen People or acting with mercy toward those most in need?

6. **Invite** the class to return to the final question on the handout "Sociohistorical Analysis of Luke 10:25–37" (Document #: TX002223). Direct the students to turn to a partner and discuss how they might answer that question now that they have more information about the history and context of the passage. Allow 2 to 3 minutes for this discussion in pairs. After the allotted time, invite the students to share with the large group what they discussed in pairs.

7. **Conclude** this learning experience by reminding the students that sociohistorical criticism is the second of three methodologies that they will learn and use to understand a Scripture text. The next learning experience will focus on practicing this same methodology but with a different scriptural text.

| Apply | Interpret |

Step 7

Engage the students in interpreting Scripture using sociohistorical criticism.

1. **Prepare** by downloading and printing the handout "Exegetical Methodology: Sociohistorical Criticism" (Document #: TX002224), one for each student. Ask the students to bring their Bibles to class. You may want to make available additional resources, such as *Saint Mary's Press® Essential Bible Dictionary*, *Saint Mary's*

Teacher Note

If you would like to ensure that each group studies a different Scripture passage, you may want to assign passages to each group or simply have groups choose a text one by one, not allowing duplication.

Remind the students that each member of the group should take notes on the group's responses to the questions in section C of the handout. They may use any available resources, such as a Bible dictionary or biblical commentary. Allow 15 to 20 minutes for the students to work on their chosen text. Circulate around the room to answer questions and ensure that the groups are on task.

Press® Essential Guide to Biblical Life and Times, and the *New Jerome Biblical Commentary.*

2. **Explain** to the students that just as they had an opportunity to practice literary analysis of a Scripture text, they will now engage in sociohistorical criticism of a passage. Organize the students into the same groups of four from step 5.

3. **Distribute** the handout "Exegetical Methodology: Sociohistorical Criticism" (Document #: TX002224). Direct the students to write the names of their group members on their paper (section A on the handout). Then explain to the students that their groups will choose a *different* Scripture passage from the one they analyzed in step 5 (section B on the handout), and begin a sociohistorical analysis of the text (section C on the handout).

4. **Direct** the students' attention to section D of the handout. Explain that each group will prepare a newscast based on the group's analysis of the text. The newscast should be succinct and convey the essential information about and significance of the text. Allow 10 to 15 minutes for groups to prepare their newscasts. Circulate around the room to answer any questions and to ensure that the groups are on task.

> **Teacher Note**
>
> If the newscasts are elaborate, you may want to have the students present these in the following class meeting.

5. **Draw** the class back together, and ask the small groups to perform their newscasts. As time permits, elicit further questions and comments about the texts.

6. **Conclude** this learning experience by reminding the students that sociohistorical criticism is the second of three methodologies they will learn in order to understand and interpret the meaning of a Scripture text. In the next learning experiences, they will learn about ideological criticism.

Article 7

 Explain

Step 8

Introduce the students to an exegetical method: ideological criticism.

1. **Prepare** by downloading the PowerPoint "Exegesis and Ideological Criticism" (Document #: TX002212). Download and print the handout "Ideological Analysis of Luke 10:25–37" (Document #: TX002225), one for each student.

2. **Assign** the students to read article 7, "Sacred Scripture: A Living Word for Today," in the student book as preparation for this learning experience. Ask the students to bring their Bibles to class.

3. **Present** the PowerPoint "Exegesis and Ideological Criticism" (Document #: TX002212). Direct the students to take notes. Supplement the material

on the slides with your own explanations, taking care to include the "notes" listed for each slide.

4. **Organize** the students into groups of five. Distribute the handout "Ideological Analysis of Luke 10:25–37" (Document #: TX002225), one copy for each student. Explain that the students will have an opportunity to work in their groups to engage in ideological criticism using the Gospel text Luke 10:25–37. Review the directions on the handout. Allow 15 to 20 minutes for the students to work on this passage. Circulate around the room to respond to questions and ensure that the students are on task.

5. **Gather** the students after the allotted time to share what they have discovered, as well as any questions they may have about this passage through their ideological analysis of the text. Ask them to consider the following:

   ➤ When we study this text through the lens of ideological criticism, what can it teach us about prejudice and discrimination?

   ➤ If we were to translate this passage to our day and age, whom do we consider to be Samaritans? Whom do we judge and label? Whom do we discriminate against?

6. **Conclude** this learning experience by reminding the students that ideological criticism is the third of three methodologies they will learn and use to understand a Scripture text. The next learning experience will focus on practicing this same methodology but with a different scriptural text.

> **Teacher Note**
>
> If you have classroom sets of biblical references such as *Saint Mary's Press® Essential Bible Dictionary* and *Saint Mary's Press® Essential Guide to Biblical Life and Times*, make these available at this time. If not, direct the students to write down their questions, and appoint students to look up definitions and terms as they are brought forward during discussion.

Step 9

Engage the students in interpreting Scripture using ideological criticism.

1. **Prepare** by gathering art supplies, including markers, crayons, and a large poster board or sheet of newsprint for each small group. Download and print the handout "Exegetical Methodology: Ideological Criticism" (Document #: TX002226), one for each student. Ask the students to bring their Bibles to class. You may want to make available additional resources, such as *Saint Mary's Press® Essential Bible Dictionary*, *Saint Mary's Press® Essential Guide to Biblical Life and Times*, and the *New Jerome Biblical Commentary*.

2. **Explain** to the students that just as they had an opportunity to practice both literary and sociohistorical analyses of a Scripture text, they will now

engage in ideological criticism of a passage. Organize the students into the same groups of four from steps 5 and 7.

3. **Distribute** the handout "Exegetical Methodology: Ideological Criticism" (Document #: TX002226). Direct the students to write the names of their group members on their paper (section A on the handout). Then explain to the students that their groups will choose a third Scripture passage to analyze, making sure it is *different from* the ones they analyzed in steps 5 and 7 (section B on the handout), and begin an ideological analysis of the text (section C on the handout).

4. **Direct** the students' attention to section D of the handout. Explain that each group will prepare a billboard based on the group's analysis of the text. The billboard should convey the essential information about and significance of the text. Distribute the art supplies you gathered, and allow 10 to 15 minutes for groups to prepare their billboards. Circulate around the room to answer any questions and to ensure that the groups are on task.

5. **Invite** the small groups to post their billboards around the room. Have each small group explain its billboard. As time permits, elicit further questions and comments about the texts.

6. **Conclude** this learning experience by reminding the students that they have now learned three exegetical methodologies for interpreting scriptural texts: literary, sociohistorical, and ideological criticism methodologies. Through the remainder of this course, they will be asked to engage in interpretation of scriptural texts using these methods.

> **Teacher Note**
>
> If you would like to ensure that each group studies a different Scripture passage, you may want to assign passages to each group or simply have groups choose a text one by one, not allowing duplication.
>
> Remind the students that each member of the group should take notes on the group's responses to the questions in section C of the handout. They may use any available resources, such as a Bible dictionary or biblical commentary. Allow 15 to 20 minutes for the students to work on their chosen text. Circulate around the room to answer questions and ensure that the groups are on task.

Step 10

Make sure the students are all on track with their final performance tasks, if you have assigned them.

If possible, devote 50 to 60 minutes for the students to ask questions about the tasks and to work individually or in their small groups.

1. **Remind** the students to bring to class any work they have already prepared so that they can work on it during the class period. If necessary, reserve the library or media center so the students can do any book or online research. Download and print extra copies of the handouts "Final Performance Task Options for Unit 2" (Document #: TX002217) and "Rubric for

Final Performance Tasks for Unit 2" (Document #: TX002218). Review the final performance task options, answer questions, and ask the students to choose one if they have not already done so.

2. **Provide** some class time for the students to work on their performance tasks. This then allows you to work with the students who need additional guidance with the project.

Step 11

Provide the students with a tool to use for reflecting on what they learned in the unit and how they learned.

This learning experience will provide the students with an excellent opportunity to reflect on the Catholic approach to Scripture using exegetical and interpretive methods, as well as to consider how their understanding of these methods has developed throughout the unit.

1. **Prepare** for this learning experience by downloading and printing the hand-out "Learning about Learning" (Document #: TX001159; see Appendix), one for each student. Ask the students to bring in the homilies they wrote in unit 1, which they will use in this reflective step.

2. **Distribute** the handouts and give the students about 15 minutes to answer the questions quietly.

3. **Direct** the students to review their homilies from unit 1 and to reflect in writing on the following questions:

   • Now that you have learned what information can be gained about a Scripture text using different exegetical methods, what information would you have wanted to know about your assigned Scripture texts before you wrote your homily for unit 1?

   • Which of the three exegetical methods has been most helpful to you in understanding these passages? Why?

4. **Invite** the students to share any reflections they have about the content they learned as well as their insights into the way they learned.

5. **Direct** the students to keep this handout in a separate section of their folder or binder so that they can refer back to it at the conclusion of the course.

Preassessment Pair Activity

✂ _____

literary criticism

✂ _____

a methodology that enables us to analyze a scriptural text by examining its genre, plot, characters, and

symbolism

✂ _____

sociohistorical criticism

✂ _____

a methodology that enables us to analyze a scriptural text by examining the culture and world in which a

scriptural text was written

✂ _____

ideological criticism

✂ _____

Document #: TX002215

✂ _____

a methodology that enables us to understand a scriptural text by examining how our own worldview

shapes our interpretation of Scripture

✂ _____

The Gettysburg Address
by Abraham Lincoln

Four score and seven years ago our fathers brought forth, upon this continent, a new nation, conceived in Liberty, and dedicated to the proposition that all men are created equal.

Now we are engaged in a great civil war, testing whether that nation, or any nation so conceived, and so dedicated, can long endure. We are met here on a great battlefield of that war. We have come to dedicate a portion of it as a final resting place for those who here gave their lives that that nation might live. It is altogether fitting and proper that we should do this.

But in a larger sense we cannot dedicate—we cannot consecrate—we cannot hallow this ground. The brave men, living and dead, who struggled, here, have consecrated it far above our poor power to add or detract. The world will little note, nor long remember, what we say here, but can never forget what they did here.

It is for us, the living, rather to be dedicated here to the unfinished work which they have, thus far, so nobly carried on. It is rather for us to be here dedicated to the great task remaining before us—that from these honored dead we take increased devotion to that cause for which they here gave the last full measure of devotion—that we here highly resolve that these dead shall not have died in vain; that this nation shall have a new birth of freedom; and that this government of the people, by the people, for the people, shall not perish from the earth.

Document #: TX002216

Final Performance Task Options for Unit 2

Important Information for Both Options

The following are the main ideas that you are to understand from this unit. They should appear in this final performance task so that your teacher can assess whether you learned the most essential content.

- Various exegetical methods enable us to read and interpret Scripture contextually.

- Literary criticism enables us to analyze a scriptural text by examining its genre, plot, characters, and symbolism.

- Sociohistorical criticism enables us to understand the culture and world in which a scriptural text was written.

- Ideological criticism enables us to understand how our own worldview shapes our interpretation of Scripture.

In addition to demonstrating understanding of these four main concepts of the unit, your final performance task must contain or demonstrate the following:

- In-depth, substantial content appropriate for an upper-level high school religious studies course

- Responsible and accurate use of Scripture

- Substantive content that creatively and accurately engages with and interprets the material of this unit

- Proper grammar, spelling, and diction

- A neat and well-organized presentation

Option 1: A Research Paper on the Catholic Approach to Scripture

The director of religious education of the local parish has invited you to write a research paper on the Catholic approach to Scripture that can be used as a study tool for candidates of the Rite of Christian Initiation of Adults (RCIA) program. Your paper should include a basic summary of the development of Catholic biblical exegesis. In addition, the paper should conclude with a personal reflection that focuses on what you have learned about exegetical and interpretive methods and how these methods may have shifted your understanding of or approach to Scripture. The research paper should use at least three credible sources (approved by your teacher) that have not been examined in class and should be four to five pages in length.

Document #: TX002217

Option 2: A Group Presentation Using Three Exegetical Tools

Your local parish has invited you and your classmates to do a presentation for an adult Bible study group on the exegetical and interpretive tools used to understand Scripture. Your presentation should include a thorough explanation of what exegesis is, as well as the three exegetical methods studied in this unit: literary criticism, sociohistorical criticism, and ideological criticism. You will choose one Gospel text. Although your group will focus on interpreting just that text, your presentation should demonstrate all three exegetical methods. Consult at least three credible sources (approved by your teacher) other than your textbook. Be sure to discuss your choice of Gospel text with your teacher before beginning work on it. Give your presentation to the class on the day designated by your teacher and prepare a written version to turn in to your teacher.

The presentation must include a visual component (such as a PowerPoint presentation, video, or handouts). The presentation should also include the following:

- an introduction that situates the passage you have chosen within the larger context of the particular Gospel in which it appears

- an overview of the major topics or questions regarding the selected passage that your presentation will explore

- an explanation of each of the three methodologies you will use to interpret the passage you have chosen—that is, literary, sociohistorical, and ideological

- an analysis of the passage from the perspective of each methodology

- a conclusion in which you apply your interpretations of the passage to some aspect of the world today, for example, a concern that many young people face, a problem your school is encountering, or a pressing matter of national or international justice

- a bibliography citing the sources you used in developing your presentation

Rubric for Final Performance Tasks for Unit 2

Criteria	4	3	2	1
Assignment includes all items requested in the instructions.	Assignment includes all items requested, and they are completed above expectations.	Assignment includes all items requested.	Assignment includes over half of the items requested.	Assignment includes less than half of the items requested.
Assignment shows understanding of the following concept: *Various exegetical methods enable us to read and interpret Scripture contextually.*	Assignment shows unusually insightful understanding of this concept.	Assignment shows good understanding of this concept.	Assignment shows adequate understanding of this concept.	Assignment shows little understanding of this concept.
Assignment shows understanding of the following concept: *Literary criticism enables us to analyze a scriptural text by examining its genre, plot, characters, and symbolism.*	Assignment shows unusually insightful understanding of this concept.	Assignment shows good understanding of this concept.	Assignment shows adequate understanding of this concept.	Assignment shows little understanding of this concept.
Assignment shows understanding of the following concept: *Sociohistorical criticism enables us to understand the culture and world in which a scriptural text was written.*	Assignment shows unusually insightful understanding of this concept.	Assignment shows good understanding of this concept.	Assignment shows adequate understanding of this concept.	Assignment shows little understanding of this concept.
Assignment shows understanding of the following concept: *Ideological criticism enables us to understand how our own worldview shapes our interpretation of Scripture.*	Assignment shows unusually insightful understanding of this concept.	Assignment shows good understanding of this concept.	Assignment shows adequate understanding of this concept.	Assignment shows little understanding of this concept.
Assignment uses proper grammar, spelling, and diction.	Assignment has no grammar or spelling errors.	Assignment has one grammar or spelling error.	Assignment has two grammar or spelling errors.	Assignment has more than two grammar or spelling errors.
Assignment uses its assigned or chosen media effectively.	Assignment uses its assigned or chosen media in a way that greatly enhances it.	Assignment uses its assigned or chosen media effectively.	Assignment uses its assigned or chosen media somewhat effectively.	Assignment uses its assigned or chosen media ineffectively.
Assignment is neatly done.	Assignment not only is neat but is exceptionally creative.	Assignment is neatly done.	Assignment is neat for the most part.	Assignment is not neat.

Document #: TX002218

Vocabulary for Unit 2

apocalyptic literature: A literary form that uses highly dramatic and symbolic language to offer hope to a people in crisis.

biblical exegesis: The critical interpretation and explanation of a biblical text.

exegete: A biblical scholar attempting to interpret the meaning of biblical texts.

ideological criticism: A methodology that enables us to analyze a scriptural text by examining how our own worldview shapes our interpretation of Scripture.

literary convention: A defining feature of a particular literary form. An example would be beginning a letter with the greeting "Dear."

literary criticism: A methodology that enables us to analyze a scriptural text by examining its genre, plot, characters, and symbolism.

literary forms (genres): Different kinds of writing determined by their literary technique, content, tone, and purpose (how the author wants the reader to be affected).

moral truth: A truth dealing with the goodness or evil of human acts, attitudes, and values.

sociohistorical criticism: A methodology that enables us to analyze a scriptural text by examining the culture and world in which a scriptural text was written.

Contextual Reading of Scripture

With the members of your group, read the following Scripture quotes. As you read each one, generate a list of questions that you might want to ask of the text to make further sense of it and understand why it was written. Your questions may be general in nature or specific to the text. Be prepared to share your questions with the class.

1. Exodus 21:7

2. Exodus 35:1–3

3. Leviticus 11:4–8

4. Leviticus 11:10–12

5. Leviticus 18:22

6. Leviticus 19:19

7. Leviticus 20:9–10

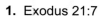 Document #: TX002220

Literary Analysis of Luke 10:25–37

Read Luke 10:25–37 silently. Discuss your responses to the following questions with your partner. Each of you should record your responses on your own handout. Be prepared to share your responses with the class.

1. What is the form or literary genre of the text?

2. How would you summarize the text? Is there a plot? What is the plot?

3. What do you notice about the placement or repetition of words?

4. What particular words are used? What do they mean?

5. What images or symbols are used? How are they used? What is their significance?

6. What characters appear in the text, if any? What do you know about them?

7. How do the characters interact and relate to one another in the text?

8. Using the insights gained from literary criticism, what is the primary message being communicated in this text? What meaning does this text have for us today?

Document #: TX002221

Exegetical Methodology: Literary Criticism

A. Write the names of your group members here.

1. _____

2. _____

3. _____

4. _____

B. Circle the Scripture passage your group has chosen for a literary analysis.

- Mark 7:24–30 (the Syrophoenician woman)

- Matthew 4:1–11 (the temptation of Jesus)

- Matthew 8:5–13 (healing of the centurion's servant)

- Luke 1:46–55 (Mary's *Magnificat*)

- Luke 8:4–8 (Parable of the Sower)

- John 8:1–11 (woman caught in adultery)

C. Using the methodology of literary criticism, analyze your chosen text. Each member of the group should record notes on your group's responses to the questions below, as well as additional comments. You will have 15 to 20 minutes to work on these questions.

1. What is the form or literary genre of the text?

2. How would you summarize the text? Is there a plot? What is the plot?

Document #: TX002222

3. What do you notice about the placement or repetition of words?

4. What particular words are used? What do they mean?

5. What images or symbols are used? How are they used? What is their significance?

6. What characters appear in the text if any? What do you know about them?

7. How do the characters interact and relate to one another in the text?

8. Using the insights gained from literary criticism, what do you think is the primary message being communicated in this text? What meaning does this text have for us today?

D. Based on your group's responses to these questions, create a movie trailer that conveys what you have learned about this text through literary analysis. Be prepared to perform your movie trailer for the class.

Document #: TX002222

Sociohistorical Analysis of Luke 10:25–37

Read Luke 10:25–37 silently. Write your responses to the following questions. It is fine to have more questions than answers.

1. Imagine you are looking out a window into the world of this scriptural text. Some of the areas you need to look at include

    - customs

    - traditions

    - religious practices

    - geography

    - culture

    - society and social norms

    - family life

2. What questions does this text raise about the areas listed above? Write down your questions or describe what you might know next to those items.

3. What social, historical, and cultural cues are found in the text that will help us to better understand the intent of the author and the meaning of the text?

4. What other background information might help us to better understand the text?

5. Using the insights gained from sociohistorical criticism, what do you think is the primary message being communicated in this text? What meaning does this text have for us today?

© 2012 by Saint Mary's Press
Living in Christ Series

Exegetical Methodology: Sociohistorical Criticism

A. Write the names of your group members here (this should be same group you worked with in doing literary criticism).

   1. _____

   2. _____

   3. _____

   4. _____

B. Circle the Scripture passage your group has chosen for a sociohistorical analysis. *Do not* choose a passage you already worked on using the literary criticism methodology.

   - Mark 7:24–30 (the Syrophoenician woman)

   - Matthew 4:1–11 (the temptation of Jesus)

   - Matthew 8:5–13 (healing of the centurion's servant)

   - Luke 1:46–55 (Mary's *Magnificat*)

   - Luke 8:4–8 (Parable of the Sower)

   - John 8:1–11 (woman caught in adultery)

C. Using the methodology of sociohistorical criticism, analyze your chosen text. Each member of the group should record notes on your group's responses to the questions below, as well as additional comments. You will have 15 to 20 minutes to work on these questions.

   1. Imagine you are looking out a window into the world of this scriptural text. Some of the areas you need to look at include the following:

   - Customs

   - Traditions

   - Religious practices

   - Geography

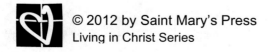
Document #: TX002224

- Culture

- Society and social norms

- Family life

2. What questions does this text raise about the areas listed above? Next to those items, write down your questions or describe what you might know.

3. What social, historical, and cultural cues are found in the text that will help us to better understand the intent of the author and the meaning of the text?

4. What other background information might help us to better understand the text?

5. Using the insights gained from sociohistorical criticism, what do you think is the primary message being communicated in this text? What meaning does this text have for us today?

D. Based on your group's responses to these questions, create a newscast that conveys what you have learned about this text through sociohistorical criticism. Be prepared to perform your newscast for the class.

© 2012 by Saint Mary's Press
Living in Christ Series

Document #: TX002224

Ideological Analysis of Luke 10:25–37

Read Luke 10:25–37 in your small group. Discuss your responses to the following questions with your group. Each of you should record your responses on your own handout. Be prepared to share your responses with the class.

1. What group of people might be viewed as superior in the text? What group of people might be viewed as inferior in the text?

2. How can this text be read and interpreted in a way that can help us liberate people who are dominated, oppressed, or marginalized?

3. In the text, does any particular group of people or a character demonstrate faith, intelligence, or perseverance? Which one or ones?

4. What do you notice about the way in which Jesus speaks about or interacts with this particular person or group of people?

5. In what way might this text be used by a particular group in society to dominate or oppress another group?

6. In what way might this text be used by a particular group in society to support their opinions or perceptions of a specific issue?

Document #: TX002225

Exegetical Methodology: Ideological Criticism

A. Write the names of your group members here (this should be the same group you worked with in doing literary and sociohistorical criticism).

1. _____

2. _____

3. _____

4. _____

B. Circle the Scripture passage that your group has chosen for an ideological analysis. *Do not* choose a passage that you already worked on for the previous two learning experiences.

- Mark 7:24–30 (the Syrophoenician woman)

- Matthew 4:1–11 (the temptation of Jesus)

- Matthew 8:5–13 (healing of the centurion's servant)

- Luke 1:46–55 (Mary's *Magnificat*)

- Luke 8:4–8 (Parable of the Sower)

- John 8:1–11 (woman caught in adultery)

C. Using the methodology of ideological criticism, analyze your chosen text. Each member of the group should record notes on your group's responses to the questions below, as well as additional comments. You will have 15 to 20 minutes to work on these questions.

1. What group of people might be viewed as superior in the text? What group of people might be viewed as inferior in the text?

2. How can this text be read and interpreted in a way that can help us liberate people who are dominated, oppressed, or marginalized?

3. In the text, does any particular group of people or a character demonstrate faith, intelligence, or perseverance? Which one or ones?

Document #: TX002226

4. What do you notice about the way in which Jesus speaks about or interacts with this particular person or group of people?

5. In what way might this text be used by a particular group in society to dominate or oppress another group?

6. In what way might this text be used by a particular group in society to support their opinions or perceptions of a specific issue?

D. Based on your group's responses to these questions, create a billboard that conveys what you have learned about this text through ideological criticism. Be prepared to both display and explain your billboard to the class.

Unit 2 Test

Part 1: Matching

Match each term in column 1 with a description in column 2. Write the letter that corresponds to your choice in the space provided.

Column 1

1. _____contextualist approach

2. _____biblical exegesis

3. _____exegete

4. _____moral truth

5. _____literary forms (genres)

6. _____literary convention

7. _____literary criticism

8. _____sociohistorical criticism

9. _____ideological criticism

10. _____scholar of the law

11. _____priest

12. _____Levite

13. _____Samaritan

Column 2

A. In the time of Jesus, someone who offered sacrifices in the Temple on behalf of the people of God.

B. Different kinds of writing determined by their literary technique, content, tone, and purpose (how the author wants the reader to be affected).

C. A defining feature of a particular literary form. An example would be beginning a letter with the greeting "Dear."

D. A methodology that enables us to analyze a scriptural text by examining the culture and world in which a scriptural text was written.

E. Someone who was an expert in the Mosaic Law and in interpretation of tradition. This person was probably a member of the group known as scribes—a group that was affiliated with the Pharisees.

F. The critical interpretation and explanation of a biblical text.

G. A methodology that enables us to analyze a scriptural text by examining its genre, plot, characters, and symbolism.

H. A truth dealing with the goodness or evil of human acts, attitudes, and values.

I. A group given the responsibility of oversight of the tabernacle and the Temple. They were a priestly class.

J. A biblical scholar attempting to interpret the meaning of biblical texts.

K. A person from the territory located between Judea and Galilee. This group and the Jews were deeply divided over religious and ethnic differences. For this reason, in the time of Jesus, they were despised by the Jews and treated with disdain.

L. The approach to biblical interpretation that pays attention to context in an effort to understand the literal and therefore also the spiritual senses of Scripture. It can be summarized as the approach through which our understanding of the literal sense of Scripture is informed by scientific and historical knowledge.

M. A methodology that enables us to analyze a scriptural text by examining how our own worldview shapes our interpretation of Scripture.

Part 2: Multiple Choice

For each question, choose the methodology to which the question pertains. Write your answer in the blank spaces at the left.

1. _____ What are the social, historical, and cultural cues that will help us to better understand the intent of the author and the meaning of the text?

   A. literary criticism
   B. sociohistorical criticism
   C. ideological criticism

2. _____ What is the form or genre of the text?

   A. literary criticism
   B. sociohistorical criticism
   C. ideological criticism

3. _____ What images or symbols are used? How are they used? What is their significance?

   A. literary criticism
   B. sociohistorical criticism
   C. ideological criticism

4. _____ How can this text be read and interpreted in a way that can help us to liberate people who are dominated, oppressed, or marginalized?

   A. literary criticism
   B. sociohistorical criticism
   C. ideological criticism

5. _____ What can this text tell us about customs, traditions, and religious practices?

   A. literary criticism
   B. sociohistorical criticism
   C. ideological criticism

6. _____ What can this text tell us about society and social norms at the time it was written?

   A. literary criticism
   B. sociohistorical criticism
   C. ideological criticism

Document #: TX002227

7. _____ How would we summarize the text? Is there a plot? What is the plot?

      A. literary criticism
      B. sociohistorical criticism
      C. ideological criticism

8. _____ What do we notice about the placement or repetition of words?

      A. literary criticism
      B. sociohistorical criticism
      C. ideological criticism

9. _____ In what way might this text be used by a particular group in society to support their opinions or perceptions of a specific issue?

      A. literary criticism
      B. sociohistorical criticism
      C. ideological criticism

10. _____ Who are the main characters in the text? What are they like as people? How do they interact with one another?

      A. literary criticism
      B. sociohistorical criticism
      C. ideological criticism

Part 3: Essay

Answer the following questions in an essay of at least three substantial paragraphs.

1. Explain the Catholic approach to the interpretation of Scripture. In particular, summarize all three exegetical methodologies studied in this unit and what role each plays in helping us to understand Scripture. Then make concrete references to one or more Scripture stories to support a more in-depth explanation of at least two of the three methodologies.

2. Read the following passage: John 4:4–29. Choose two of the three exegetical methodologies you have learned in the course of this unit to interpret this scriptural text. Write one paragraph for each of the methodologies, plus a third concluding paragraph in which you offer a relevant interpretation of the passage. Feel free to pose questions you may not be able to answer without the necessary research tools.

    John 4:4–29

    He had to pass through Samaria. So he came to a town of Samaria called Sychar, near the plot of land that Jacob had given to his son Joseph. Jacob's well was there. Jesus, tired from his journey, sat down there at the well. It was about noon.

A woman of Samaria came to draw water. Jesus said to her, "Give me a drink." His disciples had gone into the town to buy food. The Samaritan woman said to him, "How can you, a Jew, ask me, a Samaritan woman, for a drink?" (For Jews use nothing in common with Samaritans.) Jesus answered and said to her, "If you knew the gift of God and who is saying to you, 'Give me a drink,' you would have asked him and he would have given you living water." [The woman] said to him, "Sir, you do not even have a bucket and the cistern is deep; where then can you get this living water? Are you greater than our father Jacob, who gave us this cistern and drank from it himself with his children and his flocks?" Jesus answered and said to her, "Everyone who drinks this water will be thirsty again; but whoever drinks the water I shall give will never thirst; the water I shall give will become in him a spring of water welling up to eternal life." The woman said to him, "Sir, give me this water, so that I may not be thirsty or have to keep coming here to draw water."

Jesus said to her, "Go call your husband and come back." The woman answered and said to him, "I do not have a husband." Jesus answered her, "You are right in saying, 'I do not have a husband.' For you have had five husbands, and the one you have now is not your husband. What you have said is true." The woman said to him, "Sir, I can see that you are a prophet. Our ancestors worshiped on this mountain; but you people say that the place to worship is in Jerusalem." Jesus said to her, "Believe me, woman, the hour is coming when you will worship the Father neither on this mountain nor in Jerusalem. You people worship what you do not understand; we worship what we understand, because salvation is from the Jews. But the hour is coming, and is now here, when true worshipers will worship the Father in Spirit and truth; and indeed the Father seeks such people to worship him. God is Spirit, and those who worship him must worship in Spirit and truth." The woman said to him, "I know that the Messiah is coming, the one called the Anointed; when he comes, he will tell us everything." Jesus said to her, "I am he, the one who is speaking with you."

At that moment his disciples returned, and were amazed that he was talking with a woman, but still no one said, "What are you looking for?" or "Why are you talking with her?" The woman left her water jar and went into the town and said to the people, "Come see a man who told me everything I have done. Could he possibly be the Messiah?"

Unit 2 Test Answer Key

Part 1: Matching

1. L

2. F

3. J

4. H

5. B

6. C

7. G

8. D

9. M

10. E

11. A

12. I

13. K

Part 2: Multiple Choice

1. B

2. A

3. A

4. C

5. B

6. B

7. A

8. A

9. C

10. A

Part 3: Essay

1. The Catholic approach to Scripture underscores the necessity of interpreting Scripture in a way that helps us to discover the author's intentions. We must understand the literary genre of the text, the time and culture in which it was written, and the way of speaking that was prevalent at that time. In other words, we have to understand the context.

Three methodologies can help us explore the context and understand the author's intent. They are literary criticism, sociohistorical criticism, and ideological criticism. Literary criticism is a methodology that enables us to analyze a scriptural text by examining its genre, plot, characters, and symbolism. Sociohistorical criticism is a methodology that enables us to analyze a scriptural text by examining the culture and world in which a scriptural text was written. Ideological criticism is a methodology that enables us to analyze a scriptural text by examining how our own worldview shapes our interpretation of Scripture.

(Two concrete examples from Scripture will vary. Examples could include the following.)
The story of the Good Samaritan: Through sociohistorical analysis we realize that Samaritans were despised in the time of Jesus. In this Gospel text, we see that the priest and Levite walked by the nearly dead victim because they were afraid of defiling themselves. These men of God were too focused on one aspect of the law (not defiling themselves by touching someone who was nearly dead) rather than living the spirit of the law (to love one's neighbor as oneself). The Samaritan, on the other hand, surprises us by truly living out the spirit of the law, thus showing us that it is possible to not be Jewish but still be observant of the law (to love one's neighbor) and, thus, inherit eternal life.

Through literary analysis we see how the text is constructed: When the lawyer asks a question, Jesus responds with a question. When the lawyer assertively answers Jesus' question, Jesus responds with a further challenge. The lawyer then follows up with another question in the hope of making Jesus falter, only to have Jesus give the example of the Good Samaritan, which includes a counterquestion. In

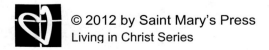

his response to Jesus, we finally see that the lawyer struggles with how to answer, refusing to admit that the Samaritan was a good neighbor; rather, he indicates that the good neighbor was the one who "showed mercy." This exchange concludes with Jesus' mandate for the lawyer (and all of us) to follow the example of the Good Samaritan.

2. Engaging in sociohistorical criticism to analyze the passage, we see that the passage begins with Jesus, a Jew, crossing through the land of Samaria, the enemy of the Jews. When he sees a Samaritan woman at Jacob's well, he asks her for a drink of water. Normally, a Jewish man would not engage in conversation with a Samaritan woman, let alone ask to drink from the same vessel she handled. Both the woman and vessel would be considered impure. Jesus continues to engage in a conversation with the Samaritan woman. What is most profound about this is that it is a *theological* conversation about worship, truth, and the Messiah.

Through literary criticism, we see that the Samaritan woman poses the issue right from the beginning: "How can you, a Jew, ask me, a Samaritan woman, for a drink?" The question is posed in such a way as to point out the dichotomy: you = Jew; me = Samaritan. The exchange, then, between Jesus and the Samaritan woman moves back and forth from the literal to the metaphorical. She is literally talking about water, while Jesus refers to "living water" or the water of life. Is it possible that this literal versus metaphorical conversation continues when they talk about her husbands? Is it possible that the five husbands refers to something else—perhaps groups of people with whom the Samaritans have formed alliances? Through the conversation, she refers to him as "sir," demonstrating a level of respect. Could it be that "sir" is translated as "lord"? The Samaritan woman then takes this theological conversation to another level by making a faith statement about the Messiah: "I know that the Messiah is coming, the one called the Anointed; when he comes, he will tell us everything." Jesus' response is interesting: "I am he." Could the translation actually be "I AM"—in reference to Moses' encounter with God at the burning bush? At the end of this passage, the woman leaves her water jar to tell the others what she has learned and experienced. Her question to them is, Could he possibly be the Messiah?

In his time, Jesus crosses boundaries to engage with people of other cultures, religions, and genders. Out of theological necessity, he reaches out to the Samaritan woman and is not worried about social or religious constraints, customs, or stereotypes. He focuses on fostering her faith and helping her to know that she too can have eternal life. In the end, it is the Samaritan woman who becomes a missionary, sharing her encounter with Jesus with her community.

Unit 3   The Development of the Gospels and the Writing of Mark

Overview

Now that the students possess a basic understanding of a Catholic approach to Scripture, including a firm foundation in exegetical methods, this unit offers them a general overview of the development of the four Gospels before focusing their study on Mark, the first Gospel written.

Key Understandings and Questions

Upon completing this unit, the students will have a deeper understanding of the following key concepts:

- The canon of the New Testament was formed over a period of nearly two centuries in a process that began with the life and teaching of Jesus and proceeded through oral tradition to written tradition and finally the inclusion of inspired texts.
- Mark, Matthew, and Luke are called synoptic Gospels because they share much in common; John differs in form and content.
- Mark portrays Jesus as a suffering Messiah who experiences all the joys and sorrows of human life.
- In the Gospel of Mark, Jesus proclaims the Reign of God in parables and miracles.

Upon completing the unit, the students will have answered the following questions:

- Through what process was the canon of the New Testament formed?
- Why are Mark, Matthew, and Luke called synoptic Gospels?
- What is Mark's Christology?
- In the Gospel of Mark, how does Jesus proclaim the Reign of God?

How Will You Know the Students Understand?

The following resources will help you to assess the students' understanding of the key concepts covered in this unit:

- handout "Final Performance Task Options for Unit 3" (Document #: TX002241)
- handout "Rubric for Final Performance Tasks for Unit 3" (Document #: TX002242)
- handout "Unit 3 Test" (Document #: TX002248)

Student Book Articles

This unit draws on articles from *The New Testament: The Good News of Jesus Christ* student book and incorporates them into the unit instruction. Whenever the teaching steps for the unit require the students to refer to or read an article from the student book, the following symbol appears in the margin: (▇). The articles covered in the unit are from "Section 1: The Word of God" and "Section 2: The Synoptic Gospels and the Acts of the Apostles," and are as follows:

- "Covenants Old and New" (article 2)
- "The Formation of the Gospels" (article 11)
- "An Overview of the Synoptic Gospels" (article 12)
- "The Miracles in Mark's Gospel" (article 13)
- "The Parables in Mark's Gospel" (article 14)
- "Mark's Passion Narrative" (article 15)
- "The Suffering Messiah" (article 16)

The Suggested Path to Understanding

This unit in the teacher guide provides you with one learning path to take with the students, to enable them to begin their study of the Gospels in general and Mark's Gospel in particular. It is not necessary to use all the learning experiences, but if you substitute other material from this course or your own material for some of the material offered here, check to see that you have covered all relevant facets of understanding and that you have not missed knowledge or skills required in later units.

 Step 1: Preassess what the students already know about the Gospels in general and Mark's Gospel in particular by having them complete a timeline learning experience.

 Step 2: Follow this assessment by presenting to the students the handouts "Final Performance Task Options for Unit 3" (Document #: TX002241) and "Rubric for Final Performance Tasks for Unit 3" (Document #: TX002242).

 **Step 3:** Introduce Sustained Silent Reading (SSR), a practice in which students will engage throughout the remainder of the course.

 Step 4: Explain the process through which the New Testament developed.

 **Step 5:** Guide the students in a critical examination of selections from the Infancy Gospel of Thomas, a noncanonical text.

Step 6: Introduce a chart of the four Gospels, which students will begin to work on in this unit and will complete in subsequent units.

 Step 7: Facilitate the students' creation of a section of a "Synoptic Parallels" resource.

 Step 8: Use Martin Luther King Jr.'s "I Have a Dream" speech and passages from the Gospel of Mark to lead students in exploring the concept of the Reign of God.

 Step 9: Present information to the students regarding four key aspects of Mark's Christology, and then guide the students in creating a documentary film or a series of skits to present and explore this information.

 Step 10: Make sure the students are all on track with their final performance tasks, if you have assigned them.

 Step 11: Provide the students with a tool to use for reflecting on what they learned in the unit and how they learned.

Background for Teaching This Unit

Visit *smp.org/LivinginChrist* for additional information about these and other theological concepts taught in this unit:

- "Formation of the Canon" (Document #: TX002233)
- "New Testament Christologies" (Document #: TX002234)
- "Non-canonical Gospels" (Document #: TX002235)
- "Oral Tradition" (Document #: TX002236)
- "Canons and Their Development" (Document #: TX001001)
- "Gospel Comparison Chart" (Document #: TX001175)

The Web site also includes information on these and other teaching methods used in the unit:

- "Using the Jigsaw Process" (Document #: TX001020)
- "Sustained Silent Reading" (Document #: TX002237)

Scripture Passages

Scripture is an important part of the Living in Christ series and is frequently used in the learning experiences for each unit. The Scripture passages featured in this unit are as follows:

- Mark, chapters 1–3
- Matthew, chapters 3, 4, and 8
- Luke, chapters 3–5
- Mark 4:26–29 (Parable of the Seed Growing of Itself, or Secretly)
- Mark 4:30–32 (Parable of the Mustard Seed)
- Mark 10:13–16 (blessing of the children)
- Mark 10:23–27 (the wealthy and the Kingdom of God)
- Mark 12:28–34 (the Greatest Commandment)

Vocabulary

The student book and the teacher guide include the following key terms for this unit. To provide the students with a list of these terms and their definitions, download and print the handout "Vocabulary for Unit 3" (Document #: TX002243), one for each student.

allegory	parable
apocrypha	parousia
canonical	Q Source
centurion	Reign of God
didache	Sanhedrin
kerygma	scribes
Messiah	Son of Man
oral tradition	synoptic Gospels

Learning Experiences

Step 1

Preassess what the students already know about the Gospels in general and Mark's Gospel in particular by having them complete a timeline learning experience.

1. **Prepare** by downloading and printing the handout "New Testament Timeline" (Document #: TX002240), one for each student plus three extras. Copy the three extras on three different colors of paper. Cut the colored copies apart into strips.

2. **Tell** the students that because they now have a firm foundation in a Catholic approach to Scripture, including various exegetical methods, they are ready in this new unit to begin an intensive study of the New Testament, beginning with the Gospels. To give them an overview of the process through which the New Testament developed, they will complete a timeline of major events that occurred during this process. Explain that the timeline will not have dates on it yet, because it is more important for the students at this point to familiarize themselves with the order of events rather than specific dates.

3. **Give** each student one strip of paper from the colored copies of the timeline you have cut apart. If you have fewer than thirty-six students, give some students two strips, but make sure they are the same color. Explain that each student has one or two items from the timeline of events in the development of the New Testament. The strips the students have received make up three complete timelines, which are color-coded. Ask the students to first find their color-coded group members and then, within those groups, to place themselves in the order in which they believe these events to have occurred.

4. **Give** the students 10 to 15 minutes to complete this task. Circulate among the groups but do not offer them assistance right away, because you are trying to ascertain the extent and depth of their prior knowledge.

5. **Instruct** the groups to let you know when they have finished so you can check their work. At that point, you may wish to offer hints as feedback, such as "Items 1 through 5 are correct, but not the remaining ones," or "You have only two out of order; see if you can figure out which ones." Once all groups have completed the timeline with a reasonable degree of accuracy, reconvene the class in the large group.

6. **Distribute** a new, whole copy of the handout "New Testament Timeline" (Document #: TX002240), one for each student. Direct the students to look this over briefly, and then engage them in a brief conversation using these or similar questions:

   - What events did your group find easy to place on the timeline?
   - What events were more difficult to place?
   - What new information did you learn simply from this preassessment learning experience?
   - What questions do you have as we begin this new unit?

7. **Answer** simple factual questions at this time, but defer lengthy discussions to future class sessions. Affirm the students' prior knowledge about the development of the New Testament, as well as their intellectual curiosity in posing questions. You may also wish to clarify that because Mark was the first Gospel written, this introductory unit on the Gospels will include close study of Mark.

8. **Direct** the students to keep the handout "New Testament Timeline" (Document #: TX002240) in their binders so they can refer to it throughout the unit. In a later learning experience, they will fill in the approximate years in which these events occurred.

Step 2

Follow this assessment by presenting to the students the handouts "Final Performance Task Options for Unit 3" (Document #: TX002241) and "Rubric for Final Performance Tasks for Unit 3" (Document #: TX002242).

This unit provides you with three ways to assess that the students have a deep understanding of the most important concepts in the unit: writing an exegetical paper, creating an artistic portrait of Jesus with a written explanation, or developing a museum display with an accompanying audio guide. Refer to "Using Final Performance Tasks to Assess Understanding" (Document #: TX001011) and "Using Rubrics to Assess Work" (Document #: TX001012) at *smp.org/ LivinginChrist* for background information.

> **Teacher Note**
>
> See the appendix for resources describing a semester-long project option in which students can create a portfolio of exegetical papers written as their final performance task for at least four units. You can give students the option to create this portfolio, including a reflective meta-analysis, in place of part or all of their final exam.

Teacher Note

Remind the students to choose their final performance task in accordance with any course requirements you may have established. In addition, if you are offering the semester-long portfolio project to your students (perhaps as part or all of their final exam), explain that the students who wish to begin assembling a portfolio must choose option 1.

Teacher Note

You will want to assign due dates for the performance tasks.

If you have done these performance tasks, or very similar ones, with students before, place examples of this work in the classroom. During this introduction explain how each is a good example of what you are looking for, for different reasons. This allows the students to concretely understand what you are looking for and to understand that there is not only one way to succeed.

1. **Prepare** by downloading and printing the handouts "Final Performance Task Options for Unit 3" (Document #: TX002241) and "Rubric for Final Performance Tasks for Unit 3" (Document #: TX002242), one of each for each student.

2. **Distribute** the handouts. Give the students a choice as to which performance task to work on and add more options if you so choose.

3. **Review** the directions, expectations, and rubric in class, allowing the students to ask questions. You may want to say something to this effect:

   ➤ If you wish to work alone, you may choose any of the three options. If you wish to work with a partner or as part of a group of three, you may choose option 3 only.

   ➤ Near the end of the unit, you will have one full class period to work on the final performance task. However, keep in mind that you should be working on, or at least thinking about, your chosen task throughout the unit, not just at the end.

4. **Explain** the types of tools and knowledge the students will gain throughout the unit so that they can successfully complete the final performance task.

5. **Answer** questions to clarify the end point toward which the unit is headed. Remind the students as the unit progresses that each learning experience builds the knowledge and skills they will need in order to show you that they understand the development of the Gospels, especially the first Gospel, Mark.

Perceive   Interpret

Step 3

Introduce Sustained Silent Reading (SSR), a practice in which students will engage throughout the remainder of the course.

1. **Prepare** by downloading and printing the handout "Sustained Silent Reading Log Instructions" (Document #: TX002244), one for each student. Read or review the method article "Sustained Silent Reading" (Document #: TX002237), available at *smp.org/LivinginChrist.*

2. **Tell** the students that although they will read about the New Testament in their student books, it is far more important for them to read the New Testament itself throughout this course. Although various learning experiences during the course will focus on particular New Testament passages, the bulk of the students' reading will occur during the first 15 minutes of class, using a practice called Sustained Silent Reading (SSR).

3. **Distribute** the handout "Sustained Silent Reading Log Instructions" (Document #: TX002244) and read it aloud with the students. Explain that starting today, most class sessions will follow prayer with an SSR period of about 15 minutes, during which the students will read a designated book of the New Testament at their own pace and then write a brief entry in their reading log. This will provide them with the opportunity to immerse themselves in a particular book of the New Testament as they read it through from beginning to end. Acknowledge that reading Scripture in this way— reading straight through one book, rather than examining selected passages—may be a new experience for many students.

4. **Share** with the students your expectations regarding the SSR log (for example, keeping it in a separate section of their binder or notebook), including your procedure for collecting and assessing this work. Answer any other questions, and then have the students begin reading the Gospel of Mark for this first SSR session. Allow about 15 minutes for this reading.

5. **Remind** the students to write their first SSR log entry when the 15 minutes are almost up if they have not already done so. Advise them to be sure to record the chapters and verses they read, both for their future reference and as a reminder of where to begin reading next time.

6. **Provide** the students with a brief stretch break after SSR before continuing with the day's lesson.

> **Teacher Note**
>
> As you continue the SSR sessions in this unit, have the students continue reading the Gospel of Mark. Those who finish Mark can continue on to Matthew, which will be the first Gospel studied during the next unit.

Article
11

Step 4

Explain the process through which the New Testament developed.

1. **Prepare** by downloading the PowerPoint "The Development of the New Testament" (Document #: TX002238). Make four signs to place in the four corners of your classroom. The signs should read as follows:
   - Travel around the world to share the Good News of Jesus Christ.
   - Go home and write down everything you can remember about Jesus.
   - Go to the desert for time and space to think and reflect.
   - Serve those in need, such as the poor, the sick, orphans, and widows.

2. **Assign** the students to read article 11, "The Formation of the Gospels," in the student book as preparation for this learning experience.

Teacher Note

This learning experience can easily be divided in half, depending on the length of your class sessions.

Teacher Note

Article 11 in the student book ("The Formation of the Gospels"), which the students have read as homework, outlines a three-stage process of the development of the Gospels and the New Testament canon. Note that this unit, including the PowerPoint "The Development of the New Testament" (Document #: TX002238), clarifies a fourth stage: the Church's discernment of texts for inclusion in the canon. You may wish to explain to the students that this fourth stage was an important step in the long process by which the early Christians struggled to figure out who they were and what they believed.

---

3. **Begin** by referring back to the preassessment learning experience and the handout "New Testament Timeline" (Document #: TX002240). Tell the students that the timeline covers a period of approximately 200 years: the length of time it took for the New Testament to take shape. Today's learning experience will explore this process of New Testament development in depth. Direct the students to take notes during the PowerPoint presentation and to write an approximate date, or range of dates, next to each item on their copies of the handout "New Testament Timeline" (Document #: TX002240).

4. **Present** the PowerPoint "The Development of the New Testament" (Document #: TX002238). Be sure to share with the students the information in the "notes" section of each slide. In the notes are further instructions for student learning experiences and sharing to take place during the presentation.

5. **Provide** the students with an opportunity to look back at the material from the PowerPoint presentation and to focus on what was new to them. Direct them to list three pieces of information they learned from this presentation and discussion that they did not know before. Instruct the students to share these items with a partner seated near them. After the partners finish discussing their lists, invite volunteers to share one of their items with the whole class. Affirm the students' growing understanding of the New Testament and their intellectual curiosity.

Explain	Perceive

Step 5

Guide the students in a critical examination of selections from the Infancy Gospel of Thomas, a noncanonical text.

Article
2

Teacher Note

Further prepare for this learning experience by referring to the handout "Using the Jigsaw Process" (Document #: TX001020) as background information for this learning experience.

1. **Prepare** by downloading and printing excerpts from the Infancy Gospel of Thomas (chapters 2, 4, 9, and 14). Links to online versions of the text are available at *smp.org/LivinginChrist.* Make sure you are using the First Greek Form of the Infancy Gospel of Thomas. Make enough copies so that each student will have one excerpt.

2. **Assign** the students to review article 2, "Covenants Old and New," in the student book as preparation for this learning experience.

3. **Begin** by reviewing with the students the four stages in the development of the New Testament that the class covered in the previous learning experience. Remind them that at the fourth stage, the leaders of the early Church faced the task of discerning which of the many texts circulating about Jesus were inspired by the Holy Spirit and therefore should be included in the New Testament canon. Review the criteria that the early Church leaders used to determine which writings were inspired and which were not. The identification of inspired writings—those to be included in the New Testament canon—had to be based on the following four criteria:

   - *apostolic:* based on the preaching and teaching of the Apostles and their closest companions and disciples

   - *community acceptance:* accepted by the Christian communities of the Mediterranean world as being valid and consistent with their beliefs and practices

   - *liturgical:* used in early Christian liturgical celebrations, especially the Eucharist

   - *consistent:* consistent with, not contradicting, other Christian and Hebrew writings that had already been accepted as inspired

   Tell the students that in today's learning experience, they will examine excerpts from one of the Gospels that was not included in the canon: the Infancy Gospel of Thomas.

4. **Organize** the students into four groups. Give each group one of the excerpts from the Infancy Gospel of Thomas. Instruct the groups to read their assigned excerpt aloud and then to discuss the following question:

   • Why was this text not included in the canon? In other words, why did early Church leaders determine that this text was *not* inspired by the Holy Spirit?

   Direct the students to write their group's responses on the back of the excerpt or in their notebooks.

5. **Use** the jigsaw process to reorganize the students into new groups of four people each, so each new group has one representative from each of the original groups. Students should share their findings from their original group with these new groups. Direct the students to take note of similarities among the excerpts they read—especially in the excerpts' depiction of Jesus—which will help them to understand better why these texts were categorized as noncanonical.

6. **Draw** the class back together, and invite the students to share their findings in the large group. In the course of this conversation, be sure to mention the following points:

   ➤ The Christology of these excerpts is not consistent with what the early Church had come to believe about Jesus—for example, in chapter 4, he uses his power to harm rather than to heal.

   ➤ Some of these excerpts (for example, chapter 2) portray Jesus as a magician, which the early Church firmly denied. Unlike a magician, whose power does not depend on people's faith, Jesus' miracles work in cooperation with a person's faith and desire to be healed or saved.

   ➤ In these texts Jesus seems less concerned with service to others and more concerned with protecting his own reputation. Moreover, Jesus does not use his words and deeds to proclaim the Reign of God; rather, he uses them to show off or even to wreak havoc.

   ➤ Because some scholars believe that the Infancy Gospel of Thomas was written in the late second century—by AD 185—it does not meet the criterion of apostolicity. All of the Apostles, and even the second generation of disciples, would have been dead by then.

   ➤ For all of the above reasons, these texts were not proclaimed in the liturgical prayer of the early Christian communities.

   ➤ Because these texts do not satisfy the four criteria for inclusion in the canon, the Infancy Gospel of Thomas was rejected as not inspired by the Holy Spirit.

7. **Conclude** by reminding the students of the following points:

   ➤ The process of discerning which early Christian writings were inspired and which were not took about 100 years (AD 100 to 200, approximately).

➤ It was not a hasty process. Early Church leaders worked carefully and prayerfully to preserve only inspired writings in the canon.

➤ Many of those writings that were not included are still available to us, and they may be interesting reading for historical purposes. However, these noncanonical writings cannot help us to grow in faith, or in relationship with the living Christ, in the way that the inspired writings of the New Testament can.

Article 12

Explain

Step 6

Introduce a chart of the four Gospels, which students will begin to work on in this unit and will complete in subsequent units.

1. **Prepare** by downloading and printing the handout "Chart of the Gospels" (Document #: TX002245), one for each student.

2. **Assign** the students to read article 12, "An Overview of the Synoptic Gospels," in the student book as preparation for this learning experience.

3. **Begin** by telling the students that one of the key understandings of this course is the idea that each of the four Gospels is unique. It is important to develop an appreciation for and understanding of this uniqueness so that we do not blur the distinctions among the Gospels. Also it is essential to be able to compare and contrast the four Gospels on significant points. Filling out a chart will help the students to accomplish these objectives.

4. **Distribute** the handout "Chart of the Gospels" (Document #: TX002245). Explain that the students will be expected to complete the "Mark" column of the chart during this unit, the "Matthew" and "Luke" columns during unit 4, and the "John" column during unit 5.

5. **Emphasize** that the students are not simply to copy this information from the student book. Rather, they are expected to begin with the student book and to supplement with other information they learn in class and through research on their own. Help them to understand that in creating a personalized chart for themselves, they are building a valuable reference that they may use throughout this course.

> **Teacher Note**
>
> You can provide class time for the students to work on the "Mark" column now, or you may wish to assign this as homework.

6. **Organize** the students into pairs on the day designated as the due date for the "Mark" column. Instruct the students to compare their work with that of their partners, checking for agreement on the more objective items (such as date and authorship) and noting similarities or differences in their responses to the more subjective items (such as the

personal reaction). Circulate among the pairs, offering feedback and correcting misinformation as needed.

7. **Remind** the students to keep the chart in their binders so they can refer to it throughout this unit and continue completing it in subsequent units.

Article 12

Step 7

Facilitate the students' creation of a section of a "Synoptic Parallels" resource.

1. **Prepare** by downloading and printing the handout "Synoptic Parallels Questions" (Document #: TX002246), one for each student. Familiarize yourself with the teacher answer key that accompanies this handout, "Synoptic Parallels Questions Teacher Answer Key" (Document #: TX002247). Distribute one piece of newsprint to every three students in your class and have markers available. Ask the students to bring their Bibles for this class session. Examine a copy of a Gospel parallels book if you are not familiar with this resource or explore an online version. Links to various Gospel parallels resources are available at *smp.org/LivinginChrist.*

2. **Begin** by reviewing some background information about the synoptic Gospels from article 12, "An Overview of the Synoptic Gospels," in the student book.

   ➤ The word *synoptic,* which means "seen together," is used to describe the Gospels of Mark, Matthew, and Luke, because they are so similar to one another and contain common points of view.

   ➤ A close examination of these Gospels reveals that Matthew and Luke incorporated almost all of Mark into their respective Gospels.

   ➤ In addition, Biblical scholars have surmised that Matthew and Luke had access to a second common source, known as the *Quelle,* or Q source. *Quelle* is a German word that means "source." This theoretical source is hypothesized to have contained all material that is found in Matthew and Luke but not in Mark.

   ➤ Finally, Matthew and Luke each appear to have used at least one other source to which no other Evangelist had access, which explains the content that is unique to Matthew's Gospel or to Luke's Gospel.

3. **Tell** the students that although common sources (e.g., Mark and Q) explain why the synoptic Gospels are so similar, the uniqueness of each is also important. The synoptic Gospels differ in their organization, use, and presentation of material, and each has elements not found in the other two synoptics. Explain that in this learning experience, the students will create part of a "Synoptic Parallels" resource to help them understand the ways in which the synoptic Gospels are similar to and different from one another.

4. **Organize** the class into three to six groups, assigning one or two groups to each synoptic Gospel. Groups should have no more than six people. Distribute the handout "Synoptic Parallels Questions" (Document #: TX002246), and direct the students to circle on the handout the Gospel that has been assigned to their group. Explain that the students are to search for the answers to the handout questions *only* in their assigned Gospel and *only* in the designated chapters of that Gospel. Reassure them that they will not be able to answer every question. Allow at least 10 minutes for the groups to work.

Teacher Note

If the students inquire about John's Gospel, you may simply wish to mention that John differs significantly from the synoptics in both form and content. John's Gospel will be studied in depth in a future unit.

5. **Use** the jigsaw method to reorganize the students into new groups of three to six students, with each group composed of one or two Mark students, one or two Matthew students, and one or two Luke students. In these new groups, the students should share their responses to the questions on the handout, with fellow group members filling in the answers to the questions they could not answer in their original groups. Circulate among the groups, pointing out circumstances in which the answer to a question may vary depending on the Gospel being consulted: for example, Luke's unique identification of John the Baptist as Zechariah's son (question 1), or the more detailed account of Jesus' temptation offered by Matthew and Luke (question 3).

6. **Facilitate** a brief conversation, using these or similar questions, before proceeding to the next part of this group learning experience:

   • Why could you not answer all of the questions in your original groups? *(Answer: Not every synoptic Gospel contains the same information.)*

   • What are some examples of questions that had slightly different answers, depending on which Gospel you were reading? *(Answer: Questions 1, 3, and 7 are good examples of this.)*

7. **Explain** that the students will now use the information they have discovered to create part of a "Synoptic Parallels" resource. Such resources, which are available in books or online, present the synoptic Gospels side by side in columns to facilitate comparison and contrast. Illustrate on the board as you provide the following further directions:

   ➤ Each group will create one "Synoptic Parallels" poster. Your poster must have three columns, one for each synoptic Gospel, which present the chapters that you read to complete the handout.

   ➤ If two or three Gospels contain the same story, list those stories side by side in the respective columns. This helps us to spot similarities, as well as slight variations, easily.

   ➤ If a Gospel does not contain a story, leave the area in that Gospel's column blank. This helps us to spot information that one or more Evangelists did not include at all or included in a different section.

➤ On the posters, designate passages using chapter and verses, as well as brief descriptions (such as "the healing of Peter's mother-in-law").

➤ You must account for all three chapters read for each Gospel. The poster must not omit any verses.

8. **Distribute** newsprint and markers to each group. Allow at least 15 minutes for the groups to work.

9. **Post** the students' work in the classroom as the groups finish. Draw the students' attention to the usefulness of the "Synoptic Parallels" posters as a visual aid. They make it easier to notice similarities, such as the prominence of John the Baptist in all three synoptics, and differences, such as Luke's unique presentation of Jesus' preaching in the synagogue at Nazareth.

10. **Conclude** by telling the students that their posters represent only a small part of an actual "Synoptic Parallels" resource because they worked with only three chapters from each Gospel. There are books and online resources that present the entire text of the synoptic Gospels (and sometimes of John, as well) in parallel columns, providing an invaluable research tool. If possible, show the students one or more examples of these printed or online resources.

Step 8

Understand

Use Martin Luther King Jr.'s "I Have a Dream" speech and passages from the Gospel of Mark to lead students in exploring the concept of the Reign of God.

1. **Prepare** by downloading and printing the text of the Rev. Dr. Martin Luther King Jr.'s "I Have a Dream" speech, one for each student. Links to online versions of the speech are available at *smp.org/LivinginChrist.*

2. **Begin** by introducing the concept of the Reign of God, using these or similar words:

➤ The Reign of God is also known as the Kingdom of God or Kingdom of Heaven. For our purposes, we will consider all of these terms to be synonymous.

➤ The Reign of God is the defining focus of Jesus' ministry in the synoptic Gospels. It is a vision of how the world will be when God reigns completely. When we pray, in the Lord's Prayer, "your kingdom come, your will be done on earth as it is in Heaven," we are praying for the coming of God's Reign.

Teacher Note

Consider finding audio or video of the speech to present to your students. A link to a video of the speech is provided at *smp.org/LivinginChrist.*

➤ The Reign of God is both "now and not yet." In more theological terms, it is both "realized and unrealized."

➤ On the one hand, Jesus begins his ministry by proclaiming "the kingdom of God is at hand" (Mark 1:15). This means that Jesus, in his earthly life, ushered in the Reign of God: in this sense, the Reign of God is "now" and "realized." It has already begun, and we have access to the blessings and salvation it promises.

➤ On the other hand, we know that the Reign of God is not yet fully here, not fully realized. It takes only a glance at a newspaper or online news site to see that not everyone has embraced the Gospel message of peace, healing, reconciliation, unity, and forgiveness. In this sense, we humans have not yet allowed God to reign fully in our hearts or in our world.

➤ Although the Reign of God is sometimes called the Kingdom of Heaven, it is not only about our life with God in Heaven. It is about our life on earth, as well. When the Reign of God comes fully, the vision of the Lord's Prayer will be realized: God's will, or desire for the world, will be lived out both on earth and in Heaven.

3. **Tell** the students that eventually they will investigate Jesus' proclamation of the Reign of God in all three synoptic Gospels. However, they will begin their exploration of this important concept by studying a famous speech by the Rev. Dr. Martin Luther King Jr.—his "I Have a Dream" speech, given on August 28, 1963, during the March on Washington. Both the structure and content of this speech can help us to better understand the Reign of God, especially how it is both "now" and "not yet."

4. **Distribute** copies of the speech. Have the students take turns reading the speech aloud. (Or play either the audio MP3 file or the video of the speech, if you are using that option, and then have the students follow along silently while listening to or watching the speech.) Invite the students to consider the following questions as they listen, jotting down brief notes:

   • What is Dr. King's vision of how the world should be?

   • How is this vision similar to the Reign of God? How is it different?

   • At the time King gave this speech (August 28, 1963), what aspects of his vision had already been attained? What did he identify as goals still to be achieved?

   Note that the speech, in its entirety, is approximately 16 minutes in length.

5. **Direct** the students to meet with a partner to discuss their responses to the above questions at the conclusion of the speech. Encourage them to share not vague, overall impressions but rather specific observations rooted in the text of the speech. Allow about 10 minutes for this conversation.

6. **Draw** the class back together to share their responses in the large group. You may wish to mention these points if the students do not:

   ➤ King envisions a country and world in which all people are truly free, especially African Americans, whose rights and freedoms in this country were historically restricted and compromised.

   ➤ He wants the United States to live up to the promise enshrined in the Declaration of Independence—that all people are created equal, with certain "unalienable rights."

   ➤ He wishes to make this vision a reality in a way that embodies and promotes dignity, nonviolence, and justice. In other words, he will not resort to violence to attain peace.

   ➤ Many aspects of King's vision are similar to the Reign of God, including his emphasis on the equality of all "God's children," his concern for justice for the oppressed and marginalized, and his commitment never to resort to violence or to "drink from the cup of bitterness and hatred." In fact, he quotes from and alludes to Scripture throughout the speech.

   ➤ However, King's speech is tied to a particular historical and political situation: that of the U.S. civil rights movement. In this speech he tries to galvanize greater support for this movement. In contrast, the Reign of God is not primarily a political reality, and it can be fully attained only with God's grace. Humans do not create the Reign of God; rather, God does—with our help and cooperation.

   ➤ At the time of his speech, King's vision was, in many ways, already realized, because African Americans had secured the right to vote and to attend integrated schools. Also, the March on Washington itself was a major accomplishment and milestone in this movement. However, King points to numerous examples in which his vision is "not yet," such as ongoing police brutality toward African Americans, continued segregation, and lack of economic opportunity.

7. **Continue** with this learning experience by telling the students to keep these points from King's speech in mind as they now explore the Reign of God as presented in the Gospel of Mark. King's ideas and approach, which are so firmly rooted in Scripture, can shed light on this important biblical concept.

8. **Organize** the students into five groups. Assign each group one of the following passages from Mark's Gospel, each of which depicts Jesus' teaching about the Reign of God.

   • Mark 4:26–29: Parable of the Seed Growing of Itself, or Secretly

   • Mark 4:30–32: Parable of the Mustard Seed

   • Mark 10:13–16: blessing of the children

   • Mark 10:23–27: the wealthy and the Kingdom of God

   • Mark 12:28–34: the Greatest Commandment

9. **Direct** the students to work in their small groups to read their assigned passage and write responses to the following questions:
   - What does this passage tell us about the Reign of God?
   - How does this passage portray the Reign of God as "now and not yet"?

   Circulate among the groups to offer assistance as needed. You may also wish to provide Bible dictionaries to aid the students in their analysis.

10. **Explain** to the students that each group will now create a "human sculpture" that applies their passage's presentation of the Reign of God to the world today. Provide these instructions for creating a human sculpture:
    - Each group must decide on the scene it will depict.
    - One member of each group will work as the group's sculptor.
    - The sculptor will "sculpt" the other members of the group into the desired scene, by directing them to sit or stand, moving their arms and legs, and even directing them to smile, frown, or look angry or surprised.

    Give the groups no more than 10 minutes to prepare their human sculptures. Ensure that they depict not the passage itself but rather a scene that applies the passage's understanding of the Reign of God to the contemporary world.

11. **Invite** each group to share its work with the class by reading its passage aloud and then presenting the human sculpture. Solicit comments, feedback, and questions from the class, and offer your own observations as well.

12. **Conclude** this learning experience by returning to King's "I Have a Dream" speech. Explain that much as King used scriptural imagery evocative of the Reign of God to attempt to rectify an injustice prevalent in his time period, so too are we invited to proclaim the Reign of God in our own time. You may wish to refer to examples from the human sculptures as you encourage the students to find ways in their daily lives to cooperate with God's grace in bringing the Reign of God to greater fulfillment.

Articles
13, 14,
15, 16

Step 9

Present information to the students regarding four key aspects of Mark's Christology, and then guide the students in creating a documentary film or a series of skits to present and explore this information.

1. **Prepare** by downloading the PowerPoint "Mark's Christology" (Document #: TX002239) and arranging for the use of an LCD projector in your classroom.

2. **Assign** the students to read article 13, "The Miracles in Mark's Gospel"; article 14, "The Parables in Mark's Gospel"; article 15, "Mark's Passion Narrative"; and article 16, "The Suffering Messiah"; in the student book as preparation for this learning experience.

3. **Begin** by telling the students that over the course of the next two or three class sessions, they will work in groups to produce a documentary film or a series of skits to present and explore Mark's Christology. Assure the students that a PowerPoint presentation will help them to understand the most essential information from the student book articles that they will need to complete this task successfully. This information falls into four categories: Jesus' miracles, Jesus' parables, Jesus the human being, and the suffering Jesus.

4. **Organize** the students into pairs. These pairs will engage in a brief conversation at several points during the PowerPoint presentation. The students may need to refer to their student books during the presentation. Direct them to take notes.

5. **Present** the PowerPoint "Mark's Christology" (Document #: TX002239), being sure to share the information found in the "notes" for each slide.

6. **Respond** to any comments or questions the students have at the conclusion of the presentation. If little time remains, continue with this learning experience during the next class session. Otherwise, give the students a brief stretch break before proceeding.

7. **Invite** the students to use the information you have just presented, as well as additional information from their student books, to work in groups to produce a documentary (in the form of a film or a series of skits, whichever option you have chosen) titled "Mark's Christology."

Teacher Note

Decide which format you would like your students to use for this step: making a documentary film or developing skits. It is best for all groups to follow one consistent format. You may simply decide based on your knowledge of your students' skills and gifts and on your own comfort level with technology. Or you may wish to allow some student input into this decision. If you decide to have the students make a documentary film, be sure they have access to the equipment necessary to accomplish this. Arrange for the use of a computer and an LCD projector to play the groups' documentary segments on the due date.

8. **Divide** the class into four groups, and assign each group one of the four main topics from the PowerPoint presentation: the miracles of Jesus, the parables of Jesus, the human Jesus, and the suffering Jesus.

9. **Explain** that each group is to use information from the student book and its notes from the PowerPoint presentation to produce a 3- to 5-minute segment of the documentary that will focus on the group's particular topic. Each group must incorporate into its segment at least two different passages from Mark's Gospel. You may wish to ensure that the groups do not overlap in the passages they select.

10. **Allow** the students a significant amount of class time to work: ideally at least one full class period, and more if they need time for recording. Encourage them to present the material creatively. For example, they might interview someone who witnessed one of Jesus' miracles; show an archival video clip of Jesus telling a parable; invite a childhood friend of Jesus into the studio to offer a personal testimony; or stage a debate among people present during Jesus' Passion and death.

11. **Ask** each group to present its segment on the day the segments are due. Offer comments and invite conversation and questions as appropriate.

12. **Conclude** by helping the students to realize that this learning experience has immersed them in the unique elements of Mark's Christology. They have now mastered a significant amount of the information they need for the successful completion of their final performance task.

> **Teacher Note**
>
> If you have a large class, you may wish to designate a fifth group of students responsible for producing a creative introduction and conclusion to the documentary.

> **Teacher Note**
>
> If your students have produced particularly high-quality work, be alert for opportunities for them to use that work in other venues. For example, they could screen their film for a Confirmation class or an adult education class in the parish or present their skits to a ninth-grade class that is beginning to study the Gospels.

Step 10

Make sure the students are all on track with their final performance tasks, if you have assigned them.

If possible, devote 50 to 60 minutes for the students to ask questions about the tasks and to work individually or in their small groups.

1. **Remind** the students to bring to class any work they have already prepared so that they can work on it during the class period. If necessary, reserve the library or media center so the students can do any book or online research. Download and print extra copies of the handouts "Final Performance Task Options for Unit 3" (Document #: TX002241) and "Rubric for Final Performance Tasks for Unit 3" (Document #: TX002242). Review the final performance task options, answer questions, and ask the students to choose one if they have not already done so.

2. **Provide** some class time for the students to work on their performance tasks. This then allows you to work with the students who need additional guidance with the project.

Step 11

Provide the students with a tool to use for reflecting on what they learned in the unit and how they learned.

This learning experience will provide the students with an excellent opportunity to reflect on how their understanding of the development of the Gospels, including Mark, the first Gospel written, has developed throughout the unit.

1. **Prepare** for this learning experience by downloading and printing the handout "Learning about Learning" (Document #: TX001159; see Appendix), one for each student. Ask the students to bring in the handout "New Testament Timeline" (Document #: TX002240), which they worked on at the beginning of this unit.

2. **Distribute** the handout and give them about 15 minutes to answer the questions quietly. For the question "How did your understanding of the unit's subject matter change throughout the unit?" refer the students back to the handout "New Testament Timeline" (Document #: TX002240). Invite them to consider these questions:

   • Which two or three events did you learn the most about in the course of this unit? What did you learn about those events? What learning experience or experiences helped that learning to occur?

   • What event do you still want to learn more about? What do you want to learn?

3. **Invite** the students to share any reflections they have about the content they learned as well as their insights into the way they learned.

4. **Direct** the students to keep this handout in a separate section of their folder or binder so that they can refer back to it at the conclusion of the course.

New Testament Timeline

✂_____

Jesus' birth

✂_____

Jesus' public ministry of proclaiming the Reign of God in word and deed

✂_____

Jesus' Passion and death

✂_____

Jesus' Resurrection

✂_____

missionary campaign: Jesus' disciples travel around the world preaching about him

✂_____

the writing of Paul's letters

✂_____

the writing of Mark's Gospel

✂_____

the writing of Matthew's Gospel

✂_____

the writing of Luke's Gospel

✂_____

the writing of John's Gospel

✂_____

the writing of noncanonical texts

✂_____

the formation of the New Testament canon

✂_____

Document #: TX002240

Final Performance Task Options for Unit 3

Important Information for All Three Options

The following are the main ideas that you are to understand from this unit. They should appear in this final performance task so that your teacher can assess whether you learned the most essential content.

- The canon of the New Testament was formed over a period of nearly two centuries in a process that began with the life and teaching of Jesus and proceeded through oral tradition to written tradition and finally the inclusion of inspired texts.

- Mark, Matthew, and Luke are called synoptic Gospels because they share much in common; John differs in form and content.

- Mark portrays Jesus as a suffering Messiah who experiences all the joys and sorrows of human life.

- In the Gospel of Mark, Jesus proclaims the Reign of God in parables and miracles.

In addition to demonstrating understanding of these four main concepts of the unit, your final performance task must also contain or demonstrate the following:

- In-depth, substantial content appropriate for an upper-level high-school religious studies course

- Responsible and accurate use of Scripture

- Substantive content that creatively and accurately engages with and interprets the material of this unit

- Proper grammar, spelling, and diction

- A neat and well-organized presentation

Option 1: An Exegetical Paper

Choose one passage from the Gospel of Mark, approximately five to fifteen verses in length. Ask your teacher to approve the passage that you select. Then, research and write a four- to five-page exegetical paper in which you interpret that passage. Use one of the exegetical methods you studied in unit 2, and consult at least three sources of information other than your textbook. Your paper should follow this structure:

- An introduction that situates Mark's Gospel in general, and the passage you have chosen in particular, within the larger context of the development of the Gospels

- An overview of the major topics or questions regarding the selected passage that your paper will explore

Document #: TX002241

- A explanation of the methodology you will use to interpret the passage—that is, literary, sociohistorical, or ideological

- At least three substantive body paragraphs in which you analyze the passage using the methodology you have chosen and present your interpretation

- A conclusion in which you apply your interpretation of the passage to some aspect of the world today: for example, a concern that many young people face, a problem that your school is encountering, or a pressing matter of national or international justice

- A bibliography

Option 2: An Artistic Portrait of Jesus with a Written Explanation

Create a portrait of Jesus that effectively captures Mark's Christology. Your portrait must be your own original creation, using any artistic media. It may be any size. Write a one-page (minimum) explanation to accompany your portrait. This written piece should situate Mark's Gospel within the larger context of the development of the Gospels and explain how your portrait reflects Mark's Christology.

Option 3: A Museum Display with an Accompanying Audio Guide

Imagine that the small museum attached to your diocese's cathedral is preparing a special exhibit on the Bible. You are entering a contest to create one section of this exhibit: a display that explores the development of the Gospels, including Mark, the first Gospel written. This display may include images, timelines, artistic pieces, and charts, all with accompanying labels and explanations.

To enter the contest, you must create either a small-scale physical model of the display or a digital version of the display. In either case, you must also submit an accompanying audio guide that offers listeners an in-depth explanation of each part of the display. Be sure to check with your teacher regarding the required format for your audio guide—that is, whether it should be an MP3, wav, Windows Media Player, or other format.

© 2012 by Saint Mary's Press
Living in Christ Series

Rubric for Final Performance Tasks for Unit 3

Criteria	4	3	2	1
Assignment includes all items requested in the instructions.	Assignment includes all items requested, and they are completed above expectations.	Assignment includes all items requested.	Assignment includes over half of the items requested.	Assignment includes less than half of the items requested.
Assignment shows understanding of the following concept: *The canon of the New Testament was formed over a period of nearly two centuries in a process that began with the life and teaching of Jesus and proceeded through oral tradition to written tradition and finally the inclusion of inspired texts.*	Assignment shows unusually insightful understanding of this concept.	Assignment shows good understanding of this concept.	Assignment shows adequate understanding of this concept.	Assignment shows little understanding of this concept.
Assignment shows understanding of the following concept: *Mark, Matthew, and Luke are called synoptic Gospels because they share much in common; John differs in form and content.*	Assignment shows unusually insightful understanding of this concept.	Assignment shows good understanding of this concept.	Assignment shows adequate understanding of this concept.	Assignment shows little understanding of this concept.
Assignment shows understanding of the following concept: *Mark portrays Jesus as a suffering Messiah who experiences all the joys and sorrows of human life.*	Assignment shows unusually insightful understanding of this concept.	Assignment shows good understanding of this concept.	Assignment shows adequate understanding of this concept.	Assignment shows little understanding of this concept.
Assignment shows understanding of the following concept: *In the Gospel of Mark, Jesus proclaims the Reign of God in parables and miracles.*	Assignment shows unusually insightful understanding of this concept.	Assignment shows good understanding of this concept.	Assignment shows adequate understanding of this concept.	Assignment shows little understanding of this concept.
Assignment uses proper grammar, spelling, and diction.	Assignment has no grammar or spelling errors.	Assignment has one grammar or spelling error.	Assignment has two grammar or spelling errors.	Assignment has more than two grammar or spelling errors.

Assignment uses its assigned or chosen media effectively.	Assignment uses its assigned or chosen media in a way that greatly enhances it.	Assignment uses its assigned or chosen media effectively.	Assignment uses its assigned or chosen media somewhat effectively.	Assignment uses its assigned or chosen media ineffectively.
Assignment is neatly done.	Assignment not only is neat but is exceptionally creative.	Assignment is neatly done.	Assignment is neat for the most part.	Assignment is not neat.

Vocabulary for Unit 3

allegory: A literary form in which something is said to be like something else, in an attempt to communicate a hidden or symbolic meaning.

apocrypha: Writings about Jesus or the Christian message not accepted as part of the canon of Scripture.

canonical: When referring to Scripture, *canonical* means included in the canon—that is, part of the collection of books the Church recognizes as the inspired Word of God.

centurion: The commander of a unit of approximately one hundred Roman soldiers.

didache: A Greek word meaning "teaching," referring to the preaching and instruction offered to all who have already accepted Jesus.

kerygma: A Greek word meaning "proclamation" or "preaching," referring to the announcement of the Gospel or the Good News of divine salvation offered to all through Jesus Christ. *Kerygma* has two senses. It is both an event of proclamation and a message proclaimed.

Messiah: Hebrew word for "anointed one." The equivalent Greek term is *Christos*. Jesus is the Christ and the Messiah because he is the Anointed One.

oral tradition: The handing on of the message of God's saving plan through words and deeds.

parable: A story intended to call a particular audience to self-knowledge and conversion through an implicit comparison of the audience to someone or something in the story; the use of parables as invitations to choose the Kingdom of God was a central feature of Jesus' teaching ministry.

parousia: The second coming of Christ at the end of time, fully realizing God's plan and the glorification of humanity.

Q Source: A hypothetical written collection of the teachings of Jesus shared among the early followers of Christianity surmised by Scripture scholars to be a source for both Matthew and Luke.

Reign of God: The defining focus of Jesus' ministry in the synoptic Gospels—a vision of how the world will be when God reigns completely. Also known as the Kingdom of God or the Kingdom of Heaven.

Sanhedrin: An assembly of Jewish religious leaders—chief priests, scribes, and elders —who functioned as the supreme council and tribunal during the time of Jesus.

scribes: People associated with the Pharisees or Sadducees who were skilled copyists, professional letter writers, and interpreters and teachers of the Law.

Son of Man: A messianic title from the Book of Daniel, used to describe a figure who receives authority over other nations from God; the only messianic title in the Gospels used by Jesus to describe himself.

synoptic Gospels: From the Greek for "seeing the whole together," the name given to the Gospels of Matthew, Mark, and Luke because they are similar in style and content.

Document #: TX002243

Sustained Silent Reading Log Instructions

At the end of each Sustained Silent Reading (SSR) period, make an entry in your SSR Log. In each dated entry, record what you read (biblical book, chapters, and verses), and write two or three sentences that reflect on or pose questions about what you read. The following questions are designed to prompt your thinking and writing; try to vary the question or questions you answer each time you make an entry in your log. You may use drawings to supplement, but not replace, your writing. See the example provided.

- What surprised you about this reading?

- How does this reading connect with your life?

- What do you like about what you read?

- What do you dislike or find disturbing?

- What aspects (for example, characters or events) of the reading can you visualize easily? What do they look like? Which are harder to visualize? Why?

- With what character in this reading can you most identify? Why?

- How does this reading help you to better understand the world in which the New Testament was written?

- What person, or what group of people, could most benefit from the message of this reading? Why?

- What questions do you have about this reading?

Sample Entry

September 24, 2011

Mark 2:23—4:41

I love how Jesus shows deep compassion for so many people: for the man with the withered hand, for the great crowd of sick people who seem to follow him everywhere, and for his own disciples. But there are times when Jesus seems a little harsh, which puzzles me—for example, why does he always insist that people keep his identity and his power a secret? My favorite story in this section is when Jesus calms the storm: sometimes I feel like my life is one storm after another, and so I feel really comforted by the image of Jesus calming those storms and helping me not to be afraid.

Document #: TX002244

Chart of the Gospels

	Mark	Matthew	Luke	John
When was the Gospel written?				
Is it synoptic? (circle one)	Y N	Y N	Y N	Y N
What is known about the author?				
Who was the intended audience?				
What is the Christology?				
How does Jesus proclaim the Reign of God?				
List three of its particular emphases or themes.				

Document #: TX002245

List two unique aspects of the Passion narrative.				
List two unique aspects of the Resurrection narrative.				
What is one other interesting fact about this Gospel or one way in which it is unique?				
What is your personal reaction to this Gospel? For example, is it appealing to you? Difficult? Why?				

Synoptic Parallels Questions

Circle the Gospel on which your group is focusing:

Mark, chapters 1–3   Matthew, chapters 3–4 and 8   Luke, chapters 3–5

Please wait for directions from your teacher before beginning work.

1.   Who appears in the desert proclaiming a baptism of repentance for the forgiveness of sins?

2.   What happens to Jesus in the Jordan River?

3.   What happens to Jesus in the desert?

4.   Describe Jesus' healing of the paralytic. For example, what does Jesus say? Why are some people in the surrounding crowd not pleased with Jesus' action? What else is interesting or unusual about this story?

5.   Who does Jesus identify as his true family members—his brother, sister, and mother?

6.   Why does Jesus go to live in Capernaum, in the region of Zebulun and Naphtali?

7.   Who are the first four disciples Jesus calls to follow him? What are the circumstances or events surrounding this call?

© 2012 by Saint Mary's Press
Living in Christ Series

Document #: TX002246

8. Who approaches Jesus and asks to be cured? How does Jesus respond?

9. Who approaches Jesus and asks for someone else to be healed? For whom does he ask for healing? How does Jesus respond?

10. What family member of Peter's does Jesus heal?

11. What does Jesus do in the synagogue at Nazareth? How do people respond to him initially? How do they respond after he continues teaching them?

12. What explanation does Jesus offer for why his disciples do not fast?

13. How does Jesus heal the Gadarene demoniacs? Where does he send the demons?

14. What does Jesus do before he leaves Capernaum?

15. What is the name of the tax collector whom Jesus calls to follow him? What, and whom, does the tax collector host at his home shortly thereafter? Who objects to this event, and why? How does Jesus respond to that objection?

Synoptic Parallels Questions Teacher Answer Key

Note: These answers apply only to the chapters that the students read and work with in this learning experience—Mark, chapters 1–3, Matthew, chapters 3–4 and 8, and Luke, chapters 3–5. If a given story appears in another chapter of any of the Gospels, that information is not reflected here. The Gospels to which the questions apply are included in these answers.

1. Who appears in the desert proclaiming a baptism of repentance for the forgiveness of sins?

Mark, Matthew, and Luke: John the Baptist—identified by Luke as John, son of Zechariah.

2. What happens to Jesus in the Jordan River?

Mark, Matthew, and Luke: He is baptized.

3. What happens to Jesus in the desert?

Mark, Matthew, and Luke: He is tempted. Matthew and Luke offer much more detail in identifying the three temptations and Jesus' response to each.

4. Describe Jesus' healing of the paralytic. For example, what does Jesus say? Why are some people in the surrounding crowd not pleased with Jesus' action? What else is interesting or unusual about this story?

Mark and Luke: Because a large crowd has gathered around Jesus, people carrying a paralyzed man on a mat cannot reach Jesus. As a result they dismantle part of the roof and lower the man through it. Jesus first proclaims that the man's sins are forgiven. Then the scribes (Luke also mentions the Pharisees) state that Jesus is blaspheming, for only God can forgive sins. Finally, Jesus directs the man to stand, pick up his mat, and go home, which he does. The story ends with the crowd proclaiming their amazement and glorifying God.

5. Who does Jesus identify as his true family members—his brother, sister, and mother?

Mark: Whoever listens to his teachings and does the will of God.

6. Why does Jesus go to live in Capernaum, in the region of Zebulun and Naphtali?

Matthew: So that what had been spoken through the prophet Isaiah (see Isaiah 8:23—9:1) might be fulfilled. Note that Mark and Luke also write of Jesus' returning to Galilee, but only Matthew quotes the prophet Isaiah as the reason for this.

7. Who are the first four disciples Jesus calls to follow him? What are the circumstances or events surrounding this call?

Mark and Matthew: Jesus calls two sets of brothers who are fishermen—Simon Peter and Andrew, and James and John. He simply calls them, and they leave their nets and boats to follow him.

Luke: Andrew is not mentioned. Moreover, Luke incorporates a miracle into this call story, in which Jesus directs Simon to let down his nets for a catch, and they catch so many fish that the nets begin to break. Upon witnessing this miracle, Simon proclaims that he is a sinful man, and all three men leave everything to follow Jesus.

8. Who approaches Jesus and asks to be cured? How does Jesus respond?

Mark, Matthew and Luke: A leper. Jesus responds by curing him immediately and directing him to show himself to the priest, offering the gift that Moses had prescribed.

9. Who approaches Jesus and asks for someone else to be healed? For whom does he ask for healing? How does Jesus respond?

Matthew: A centurion approaches Jesus and asks him to heal his servant, who is paralyzed. When Jesus agrees to come to the man's home to cure the servant, the centurion objects, stating that he is not worthy for Jesus to enter under his roof: Jesus' words alone should be enough for healing. After praising the centurion's faith, Jesus proclaims that what the man has believed will, in fact, happen: at that very hour the servant is healed.

10. What family member of Peter's does Jesus heal?

Mark and Luke: Peter's mother-in-law.

11. What does Jesus do in the synagogue at Nazareth? How do people respond to him initially? How do they respond after he continues teaching them?

Luke: He reads from the scroll of the prophet Isaiah and proclaims that the passage has been fulfilled in their hearing. At first, they respond positively to him and are amazed by his teaching. However, after he cites examples from the Old Testament and explains that prophets are not welcome in their hometowns, the people drive him out of town and attempt to throw him off a cliff.

12. What explanation does Jesus offer for why his disciples do not fast?

Mark, Matthew, and Luke: Jesus says that wedding guests do not fast while the bridegroom is with them; rather, they fast when the bridegroom is taken away from them. The implication is that Jesus is identifying himself as the bridegroom.

13. How does Jesus heal the Gadarene demoniacs? Where does he send the demons?

Matthew: Jesus heals the Gadarene demoniacs by sending the demons who are tormenting them into a herd of swine. The swine then rush down the cliff into the sea and drown.

Document #: TX002247

14. What does Jesus do before he leaves Capernaum?

Mark and Luke: He goes away in the early morning to a deserted place, away from the crowds. Mark indicates that Jesus prayed there.

15. What is the name of the tax collector whom Jesus calls to follow him? What, and whom, does the tax collector host at his home shortly thereafter? Who objects to this event, and why? How does Jesus respond to that objection?

Mark and Luke: Jesus calls Levi (identified by Mark as the son of Alphaeus) to follow him. Levi then hosts a dinner at his home, with tax collectors and sinners among those in attendance. When the scribes and Pharisees object to Jesus' eating and drinking with these people, Jesus proclaims that those who are sick, not those who are well, need a physician. He has come to call not the righteous, but sinners.

Unit 3 Test

Part 1: Multiple Choice

Write your answers in the blank spaces at the left.

1. _____ Which of the following is *not* a synoptic Gospel?

   A. Mark
   B. Luke
   C. Matthew
   D. John

2. _____ Which of the following is a noncanonical Gospel?

   A. John
   B. Mark
   C. Thomas
   D. Paul

3. _____ Which of the following books of the New Testament was written first?

   A. Mark's Gospel
   B. Paul's First Letter to the Thessalonians
   C. John's Gospel
   D. Genesis

4. _____ Writings recognized by the early Church as canonical had to be _____.

   A. apostolic—connected with the life and teachings of the Apostles.
   B. accepted by the community—that is, by a wide variety of Christian communities
   C. simple—easy to understand
   D. both A and B but not C

5. _____ The two common sources that Matthew and Luke used to write their Gospels were _____.

   A. Mark and John
   B. Mark and Q
   C. Mark and Paul
   D. Paul and the Torah

Document #: TX002248

6. _____ The Reign of God _____.

    A. is completely realized here and now
    B. will begin at some point in the future
    C. is something we can experience only after we die
    D. is both "now" and "not yet"

7. _____ The word from the Greek for "seeing the whole together" is _____.

    A. *dynameis*
    B. synoptic
    C. *Christos*
    D. *diakonia*

8. _____ The original hearers and readers of Mark's Gospel were facing the possibility of _____.

    A. not having enough money to meet their basic needs
    B. having to learn a new language
    C. persecution and martyrdom
    D. none of the above

9. _____ Which of the following Gospels was written first?

    A. Matthew
    B. Mark
    C. Luke
    D. John

10. _____ The "oral tradition" stage of the development of the Gospels is also known as the _____.

    A. missionary campaign stage
    B. desert fathers stage
    C. apostolic stage
    D. all of the above

Document #: TX002248

Part 2: Matching

Match each description in column 2 with a term from column 1. Write the letter that corresponds to your choice in the space provided. (*Note:* There are two extra descriptions in column 2.)

Column 1

1. _____*kerygma*

2. _____*didache*

3. _____apocrypha

4. _____*Quelle*

5. _____synoptic Gospels

6. _____scribes

7. _____messiah

8. _____parousia

9. _____Sanhedrin

10. _____Son of Man

Column 2

A. A Greek word meaning "proclamation" or "preaching," referring to the announcement of the Gospel or the Good News of divine salvation offered to all through Jesus Christ

B. Mark, Luke, and Matthew

C. A Greek word meaning "teaching," referring to the preaching and instruction offered to all who have already accepted Jesus

D. Writings about Jesus or the Christian message not accepted as part of the canon of Scripture

E. Luke, Paul, and John

F. A hypothetical written collection of the teachings of Jesus shared among the early followers of Christianity

G. A list of special, sacred, or authoritative writings

H. People associated with the Pharisees or Sadducees who were skilled copyists, professional letter writers, and interpreters and teachers of the Law

I. Hebrew word for "anointed one"

J. An assembly of Jewish religious leaders—chief priests, scribes, and elders—who functioned as the supreme council and tribunal during the time of Jesus

K. A messianic title from the Book of Daniel

L. A Greek word that means "arrival"; refers to the second coming of Jesus

Part 3: Essay

Answer each of the following questions in an essay of at least three substantial paragraphs.

1. Describe the process by which the canon of the New Testament developed, using as much detail as you are able. Include relevant dates.

2. Describe Mark's Christology. Support your points with references to at least two specific stories or passages from the Gospel of Mark.

3. What is the Reign of God? In Mark's Gospel, how does Jesus proclaim the Reign of God? Support your response with references to at least two specific stories or passages from the Gospel of Mark.

Unit 3 Test Answer Key

Part 1: Multiple Choice

1.	D	**5.**	B	**9.**	B
2.	C	**6.**	D	**10.**	A
3.	B	**7.**	B		
4.	D	**8.**	C		

Part 2: Matching

1.	A	**5.**	B	**9.**	J
2.	C	**6.**	H	**10.**	K
3.	D	**7.**	I		
4.	F	**8.**	L		

Part 3: Essay

Student responses will vary. The following points are possible responses for each question.

1. The canon of the New Testament developed over a period of nearly two centuries. It began with the lifetime of the earthly Jesus, approximately 4 BC to AD 30. After Jesus' death and Resurrection, the early disciples traveled around the Mediterranean world on a missionary campaign, sharing their belief in Jesus. During these travels, they developed an oral tradition as they shared stories and recollections about Jesus' life by word of mouth. One of the key leaders of this movement was Saint Paul. In the course of his travels and preaching, he wrote letters to developing Christian communities in many cities. These letters, or Epistles, became the earliest writings of the New Testament.

Around AD 65 to 70, the early Christians made a significant shift from oral tradition to written tradition. A number of factors drove this shift. First, those people who had known Jesus during his earthly life were beginning to die. The early Christians wanted to record information about Jesus' life and ministry before all the people who had known the earthly Jesus passed away. Second, the early Christians thought that Jesus would be returning soon, perhaps within their lifetimes. When this parousia did not occur, they felt the need to preserve information about Jesus' life for future generations. Third, beginning in AD 66, the Jews revolted against the Roman occupation. The Romans destroyed Jerusalem, including the Temple, in the year 70, with the last rebels surviving at the fortress Masada until 73. These catastrophic events caused the early Christians to be concerned for the long-term stability and survival of Christianity. This motivated them to create a more permanent record of Jesus' life. All of these factors resulted in the writing of many documents about Jesus, most notably the Gospels: beginning with Mark, followed by Matthew and Luke, and ending with John.

All of the New Testament writings were composed by AD 100. However, the process of forming the canon—determining which of the first-century writings about Jesus were inspired by the Holy Spirit—took another 100 years. Writings selected to be in the canon had to be apostolic, accepted by the community, liturgical, and consistent with writings that had already been accepted as inspired. Those writings that were not included in the New Testament are called noncanonical, extracanonical, or apocryphal writings.

2. More than the other Gospels, Mark emphasizes the humanity of Jesus, presenting him as someone who embraces all the joys and sorrows of human life. Mark portrays Jesus as experiencing the full range of human emotions, such as compassion for those in need of healing, love for children brought to him to be blessed, indignation toward those who try to keep the children away from him, frustration with the disciples' lack of understanding, and anger with those buying and selling in the Temple area. Jesus also experiences the physical realities of human life, like fatigue, thirst, and hunger. The latter even prompts him to curse a fruitless fig tree in exasperation.

In his suffering and death, in particular, the full humanity of Jesus is revealed, in all its frailty and vulnerability. Jesus is abandoned by his friends; expresses fear, distress, and sorrow; cries out to God for help; and ultimately suffers the agonizing death of a convicted criminal, condemned to die by crucifixion.

Although all of the Gospels contain a Passion narrative—an account of Jesus' suffering and death—Mark emphasizes Jesus' suffering as the focal point toward which his entire life and ministry are directed. We see this emphasis in, for example, Jesus' three predictions of his coming Passion. This sharp focus on Jesus' suffering can partially be explained by the historical circumstances in which this Gospel was written and the audience to whom it was directed. The first readers and hearers of this Gospel were facing the possibility of persecution, or even martyrdom, for their faith in Jesus. Mark intended to strengthen the resolve of these people by giving them a powerful example of a suffering Messiah.

3. The Reign of God, also known as the Kingdom of God or the Kingdom of Heaven, is the defining focus of Jesus' ministry in the synoptic Gospels. It is a vision of how the world will be when God reigns completely. In Mark's Gospel, Jesus proclaims the Reign of God in miracles and parables.

In the miracles—in Greek *dynameis,* or "act of power"—Jesus demonstrates his own power, allows people to experience God's power through him, and establishes his identity as the Messiah and the Son of God. The saving power that Jesus extends demonstrates that the Reign of God is here and now: it has already begun. For example, when Jesus heals a paralyzed man, he first proclaims that the man's sins are forgiven, and then he instructs the man to stand, pick up his mat, and go home. Jesus shows that his power—a power that encompasses both the physical and spiritual realms—is available to heal and save us now.

In the parables, Jesus uses images drawn from everyday life to craft stories that call his listeners to self-knowledge and conversion. For example, in telling the Parable of the Sower, Jesus draws on the common experience of his listeners, many of whom were experienced farmers. He uses this story to exhort his audience to be "good soil," in which the Reign of God may flourish and reach its full realization.

Unit 4   The Gospels of Matthew and Luke

Overview

Now that the students understand the development of the Gospels, and in particular the Gospel of Mark, this unit focuses on the Gospels of Matthew and Luke. The students will study each Gospel's Christology, as well as how Jesus proclaims the Reign of God in each of these Gospels.

Key Understandings and Questions

Upon completing this unit, the students will have a deeper understanding of the following key concepts:

- Matthew portrays Jesus as the New Moses, the fulfillment of the ancient promises made to the people of Israel.
- In the Gospel of Matthew, Jesus proclaims the Reign of God in powerful teachings to disciples of every generation.
- Luke portrays Jesus as a universal Savior, extending God's love and mercy to all people.
- In the Gospel of Luke, Jesus proclaims the Reign of God in acts of compassion on behalf of the poor and marginalized.

Upon completing the unit, the students will have answered the following questions:

- What is Matthew's Christology?
- In the Gospel of Matthew, how does Jesus proclaim the Reign of God?
- What is Luke's Christology?
- In the Gospel of Luke, how does Jesus proclaim the Reign of God?

How Will You Know the Students Understand?

The following resources will help you to assess the students' understanding of the key concepts covered in this unit:

- handout "Final Performance Task Options for Unit 4" (Document #: TX002255)
- handout "Rubric for Final Performance Tasks for Unit 4" (Document #: TX002256)
- handout "Unit 4 Test" (Document #: TX002265)

Student Book Articles

This unit draws on articles from *The New Testament: The Good News of Jesus Christ* student book and incorporates them into the unit instruction. Whenever the teaching steps for the unit require the students to refer to or read an article from the student book, the following symbol appears in the margin: (■■). The articles covered in the unit are from "Section 2: The Synoptic Gospels and the Acts of the Apostles," and are as follows:

- "Matthew's Infancy Narrative" (article 17)
- "The Kingdom in Matthew's Gospel" (article 18)
- "The Question of Authority" (article 19)
- "The Paschal Mystery according to Matthew" (article 20)
- "Luke's Infancy Narrative" (article 21)
- "The Universal Nature of Covenant Love" (article 22)
- "Luke's Passion Narrative" (article 23)
- "Luke's Post-Resurrection Appearance Narratives" (article 24)

The Suggested Path to Understanding

This unit in the teacher guide provides you with one learning path to take with the students, to enable them to begin their study of the Gospels of Matthew and Luke. It is not necessary to use all the learning experiences, but if you substitute other material from this course or your own material for some of the material offered here, check to see that you have covered all relevant facets of understanding and that you have not missed knowledge or skills required in later units.

 Step 1: Preassess what the students already know about the Gospels of Matthew and Luke by engaging them in a "sorting" exercise.

 Step 2: Follow this assessment by presenting to the students the handouts "Final Performance Task Options for Unit 4" (Document #: TX002255) and "Rubric for Final Performance Tasks for Unit 4" (Document #: TX002256).

 **Step 3:** Continue the practice of Sustained Silent Reading (SSR).

 Step 4: Encourage the students to use their imagination to understand a scriptural character by developing a dramatic monologue.

 **Step 5:** Examine passages in the Gospel of Matthew that portray Jesus as the New Moses and as the fulfillment of the ancient promises made to the people of Israel.

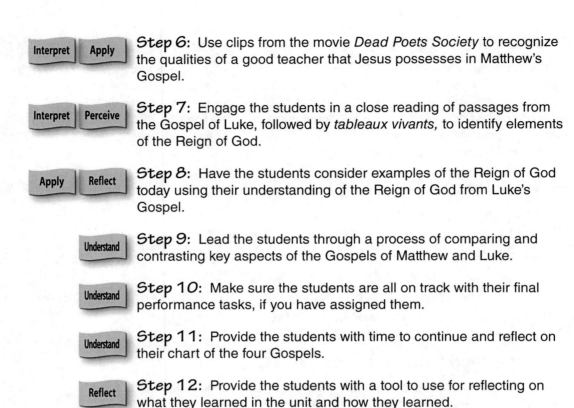

Interpret | Apply — *Step 6*: Use clips from the movie *Dead Poets Society* to recognize the qualities of a good teacher that Jesus possesses in Matthew's Gospel.

Interpret | Perceive — *Step 7*: Engage the students in a close reading of passages from the Gospel of Luke, followed by *tableaux vivants,* to identify elements of the Reign of God.

Apply | Reflect — *Step 8*: Have the students consider examples of the Reign of God today using their understanding of the Reign of God from Luke's Gospel.

Understand — *Step 9*: Lead the students through a process of comparing and contrasting key aspects of the Gospels of Matthew and Luke.

Understand — *Step 10*: Make sure the students are all on track with their final performance tasks, if you have assigned them.

Understand — *Step 11*: Provide the students with time to continue and reflect on their chart of the four Gospels.

Reflect — *Step 12*: Provide the students with a tool to use for reflecting on what they learned in the unit and how they learned.

Background for Teaching This Unit

Visit *smp.org/LivinginChrist* for additional information about these and other theological concepts taught in this unit:

- "Parables" (Document #: TX001056)
- "The New Testament and Other Early Christian Literature" (Document #: TX001058)
- "Gospel Comparison Chart" (Document #: TX001175)
- "Matthew's Sermon on the Mount" (Document #: TX001311)

The Web site also includes information on these and other teaching methods used in the unit:

- "Using the Jigsaw Process" (Document #: TX001020)
- "Sustained Silent Reading" (Document #: TX002237)
- "Bloom's Taxonomy" (Document #: TX002250)

Scripture Passages

Scripture is an important part of the Living in Christ series and is frequently used in the learning experiences for each unit. The Scripture passages featured in this unit are as follows:

- Exodus 20:7 (Second Commandment)
- Exodus 20:13 (Fifth Commandment)
- Exodus 20:14 (Sixth Commandment)
- Exodus 21:12 (law regarding personal injury)
- Leviticus 19:18 (Law of Love)
- Leviticus 24:20 (an eye for an eye)
- Deuteronomy 24:1–5 (marriage laws)
- Matthew 1:1—2:23 (infancy narrative)
- Matthew 5:1–12 (Sermon on the Mount)
- Matthew 5:21–26 (teaching about anger)
- Matthew 5:27–30 (teaching about adultery)
- Matthew 5:31–32 (teaching about divorce)
- Matthew 5:33–37 (teaching about oaths)
- Matthew 5:38–42 (teaching about retaliation)
- Matthew 5:43–48 (love of enemies)
- Matthew 6:5–8 (teaching about prayer)
- Matthew 6:25–34 (dependence on God)
- Matthew 7:1–5 (judging others)
- Matthew 13:18–23 (Parable of the Sower)
- Matthew 13:24–30 (Parable of the Weeds among Wheat)
- Matthew 13:31–33 (Parable of the Mustard Seed)
- Matthew 26:1—28:20 (Passion and Resurrection narrative)
- Luke 1:5—2:52 (infancy narrative)
- Luke 7:11–17 (raising of the widow's son)
- Luke 8:40–56 (Jairus's daughter and the woman with a hemorrhage)
- Luke 16:19–31 (Parable of the Rich Man and Lazarus)
- Luke 17:11–17 (cleansing of the ten lepers)
- Luke 21:1–4 (widow's mite)
- Luke 22:1—24:53 (Passion and Resurrection narrative)

Vocabulary

The student book and the teacher guide include the following key terms for this unit. To provide the students with a list of these terms and their definitions, download and print the handout "Vocabulary for Unit 4" (Document #: TX002257), one for each student.

Amen

Beatitudes

commission

eschatological meal

fiat

infancy narrative

Koine Greek

Passover

Samaritan

Solomon

synonymous parallelism

Learning Experiences

| Explain | ## Step 1 |

Preassess what the students already know about the Gospels of Matthew and Luke by engaging them in a "sorting" exercise.

1. **Prepare** by downloading and printing the handout "Preassessment Activity on the Gospels of Matthew and Luke" (Document #: TX002254). Cut apart the items along the dotted lines, creating twenty-six slips of paper, and retain the answer key for your reference. Gather two pieces of 8½-x-11-inch paper. On one paper write, "Gospel of Matthew," and on the other write, "Gospel of Luke." Tape the signs on opposite walls of the room. Gather one or two rolls of masking tape. (You may wish to have two rolls of masking tape, one for each side of the room, or you can simply pass around the tape when students receive their handout.)

2. **Introduce** the new unit with the following or similar words:
   ➤ We have had the opportunity to explore the formation of the Gospels, and so far we have focused on the Gospel of Mark. In this unit we will continue our study of the synoptic Gospels by learning about the Gospels of Matthew and Luke.

3. **Distribute** the slips of paper cut from the handout "Preassessment Activity on the Gospels of Matthew and Luke" (Document #: TX002254), one slip for each student. If you have fewer than twenty-six students, continue to distribute the slips until all have been handed out. If you have more than twenty-six students, you may allow two students to work on a single slip. Tell the students that they will have 2 minutes to determine with which Gospel the piece of information on their slip belongs. Point out the signs on either side of the classroom and ask the students to tape their slip below the appropriate Gospel heading.

4. **Direct** the students to walk around and look at the slips of information they have posted under each Gospel sign. Ask them to use their student books and Bibles to confirm that they posted their own slips correctly and to determine whether any other slips belong with the other Gospel.

5. **Review** the slips of information under both Gospel signs with the class once the students have finalized their placement. Use the answer key found at the end of the handout to review the placements with the students. Then organize the students into pairs to discuss the following questions:
   • What information did you already know about these two Gospels?
   • What information was difficult to figure out?

- What information is new to you?
- What pieces of information surprised you?
- What questions do you have about these two Gospels?

Allow no more than 5 minutes for the student pairs to discuss their responses.

6. **Invite** volunteers to share their responses with the class. Note their responses to help you tailor the following learning experiences based on the students' prior knowledge. You may choose to list their comments on the board or on a piece of poster board that you can refer to throughout the unit.

7. **Lead** a general discussion with the students about their responses. Invite them to consider the following:
   - Why did the early Church include both of these Gospels in the canon?
   - What significance might these two Gospel accounts have for our faith?

8. **Conclude** this learning experience by telling the students that they will explore both Gospels in greater depth during this unit. You may also choose to leave the information for both Gospels posted on the walls for the duration of the unit. If you choose to administer the test at the end of this unit, be sure to remove the items from the wall before the test.

Step 2

Follow this assessment by presenting to the students the handouts "Final Performance Task Options for Unit 4" (Document #: TX002255) and "Rubric for Final Performance Tasks for Unit 4" (Document #: TX002256).

This unit provides you with three ways to assess that the students have a deep understanding of the most important concepts in the unit: writing an exegetical paper focused on the infancy narratives of Matthew and Luke, using art to compare and contrast the Christology of Matthew and Luke, or creating a lesson plan for a Confirmation class that relates the distinctiveness of these two Gospels. Refer to "Using Final Performance Tasks to Assess Understanding" (Document #: TX001011) and "Using Rubrics to Assess Work" (Document #: TX001012) at *smp.org/LivinginChrist* for background information.

1. **Prepare** by downloading and printing the handouts "Final Performance Task Options for Unit 4" (Document #: TX002255) and "Rubric for Final Performance Tasks for Unit 4" (Document #: TX002256), one of each for each student.

2. **Distribute** the handouts. Give the students a choice as to which performance task to work on and add more options if you so choose.

3. **Review** the directions, expectations, and rubric in class, allowing the students to ask questions. You may want to say something to this effect:

   ➤ If you wish to work alone, you may choose any of the three options. If you wish to work with a partner, you may choose option 2 or 3. To work with a group of three, choose option 3 only.

   ➤ Near the end of the unit, you will have one full class period to work on the final performance task. However, keep in mind that you should be working on, or at least thinking about, your chosen task throughout the unit, not just at the end.

4. **Explain** the types of tools and knowledge the students will gain throughout the unit so that they can successfully complete the final performance task.

5. **Answer** questions to clarify the end point toward which the unit is headed. Remind the students as the unit progresses that each learning experience builds the knowledge and skills they will need in order to show you that they understand the Gospels of Matthew and Luke.

> **Teacher Note**
>
> Remind the students to choose their final performance task in accordance with any course requirements you may have established. In addition, if you are offering the semester-long portfolio project to your students (perhaps as part or all of their final exam), explain that students who wish to assemble a portfolio must choose option 1.

> **Teacher Note**
>
> You will want to assign due dates for the performance tasks.
>
> If you have done these performance tasks, or very similar ones, with students before, place examples of this work in the classroom. During this introduction explain how each is a good example of what you are looking for, for different reasons. This allows the students to concretely understand what you are looking for and to understand that there is not only one way to succeed.

Step 3

Continue the practice of Sustained Silent Reading (SSR).

Teacher Note

Consistently including a 15-minute SSR session in every subsequent class session will enable your students to read both Matthew's and Luke's Gospel in their entirety during this unit and, more broadly, to cultivate the discipline of careful, reflective reading.

1. **Prepare** by downloading and making extra copies, if needed, of the unit 3 handout "Sustained Silent Reading Log Instructions" (Document #: TX002244). Review these instructions with the students, and remind them of your expectations regarding the SSR log (for example, keeping it in a separate section of their binder or notebook), including your procedure for collecting and assessing this work.

2. **Tell** the students to begin reading Matthew's Gospel during today's SSR session. Allow them to read for 15 minutes. Near the end of this time, remind them to make an entry in their SSR log. Explain that after they finish reading the Gospel of Matthew during the SSR sessions, they should begin reading Luke's Gospel.

3. **Provide** the students with a brief stretch break after SSR before continuing with the day's lesson.

Step 4

Encourage the students to use their imagination to understand a scriptural character by developing a dramatic monologue.

Teacher Note

Note which character each student has chosen or been assigned. Once the characters have been selected, prepare a schedule for the students to deliver their monologues that coincides with the learning experiences of the unit and the material being presented. It will be helpful to schedule all monologues to be presented before step 9, which asks the students to review the presentations they have seen. Give the students advance notice of three days or more before they will be required to deliver their monologues.

1. **Prepare** by downloading and printing the handout "Dramatic Monologues" (Document #: TX002258), one for each student.

2. **Explain** to the students that they will have an opportunity to create dramatic monologues based on various characters from the Gospels of Matthew and Luke and that they will use their imagination to "get inside" the mind and heart of a scriptural character in order to better understand Scripture and appreciate biblical characters as human beings.

3. **Distribute** the handout "Dramatic Monologues" (Document #: TX002258), and read it aloud with the students. Explain that the presentations of their dramatic monologues will be interspersed throughout this unit, based on which characters the students choose for this learning experience. Advise the students that each of them must choose or be assigned a different character from Scripture.

4. **Share** your expectations with the students regarding the development of the dramatic monologues and their presentation, including props and costumes. Answer any questions they may have regarding this ongoing learning experience.

Step 5

Examine passages in the Gospel of Matthew that portray Jesus as the New Moses and as the fulfillment of the ancient promises made to the people of Israel.

Article
17

1. **Prepare** by downloading the PowerPoint "Matthew's Christology" (Document #: TX002253) and arranging for the use of an LCD projector as needed. Download and print the handout "Jesus and the Law of Moses" (Document #: TX002259), one for each student.

2. **Assign** the students to read Matthew 1:1—2:23, as well as article 17, "Matthew's Infancy Narrative," in the student book as preparation for this learning experience.

3. **Tell** the students that they will have an opportunity to explore Matthew's Christology in depth by comparing scriptural texts from the Old Testament and Matthew's Gospel. Organize the students into groups of three or four. During and after the PowerPoint presentation, the group members will be asked to engage in conversation with one another about the texts.

4. **Present** the PowerPoint "Matthew's Christology" (Document #: TX002253). Allow the students to refer to their student books during the presentation. Direct them to take notes.

5. **Explain** to the students after the presentation that they will now explore a few examples from Matthew's Gospel in which Jesus refers to the Law of Moses or addresses some specific question or challenge related to Mosaic Law. Direct the students to remain in their small groups. Distribute the handout "Jesus and the Law of Moses" (Document #: TX002259). Assign one set of Scripture passages to each group. If there are more than seven groups, more than one group can work with the same set of passages. Allow approximately 10 minutes for the groups to read their assigned passages and discuss the questions on the handout.

6. **Invite** each small group to share a brief summary of its Scripture passage and to lead a general discussion about its findings.

7. **Conclude** this learning experience by reminding the students that the allusions to Moses continue throughout Matthew's Gospel. In addition, the author of Matthew portrays Jesus as a great teacher—a theme that the next learning experience will explore in greater detail.

Step 6

Use clips from the movie Dead Poets Society to recognize the qualities of a good teacher that Jesus possesses in Matthew's Gospel.

Articles
18, 19

1. **Prepare** by downloading and printing the handout "Jesus, the Teacher" (Document #: TX002260), one for each student. Acquire a copy of the movie *Dead Poets Society* (1989, 128 minutes, rated A-III and PG). Locate and preview the two clips that will be used for this learning experience: "On Poetry" (21:00–23:35) and "Finding a Voice" (42:58–44:30) Arrange for a television and DVD player, or a computer with an LCD projector.

2. **Assign** the students to read article 18, "The Kingdom in Matthew's Gospel," and article 19, "The Question of Authority," in the student book as preparation for this learning experience.

> **Teacher Note**
>
> Further prepare for this learning experience by referring to the handout "Using the Jigsaw Process" (Document #: TX001020) as background information for this learning experience.

3. **Begin** this learning experience by reminding the students that in the Gospel of Matthew, Jesus is portrayed as the New Moses and as the quintessential teacher who proclaims the Reign of God to disciples of every generation. Explain that as a way to delve more deeply into this understanding of Jesus and what it means to be a good teacher, the class will watch two brief video clips from the movie *Dead Poets Society.* Provide context as follows:

➤ The story is set at Welton Academy, a conservative and aristocratic all-boys prep school.

➤ In this traditional environment, John Keating (played by Robin Williams) is an English teacher who uses unconventional teaching methods to inspire his students.

4. **Direct** the students to consider the following questions while watching the two movie clips:

• How would you describe Keating's teaching methods?

• What is Keating trying to teach his students?

- What is unusual about his teaching method or about what he is teaching, especially given the context in which this movie takes place?
- Based on these clips, what characteristics make Keating a good teacher?

   Play the movie clips for the class.

5. **Invite** the students to share their responses to the questions in a brief "pair share." Allow 2 to 3 minutes. Then invite the students to share their insights with the class. You may want to record their responses on the board. Some observations may include the following:

   - Keating uses unusual methods that catch the students' attention (e.g., ripping out pages from a book, standing on his desk).
   - He encourages them to think about and feel poetry for themselves, rather than "rating" it on a graph. He brings poetry alive and makes it relevant to their lives.
   - He inspires them with his passion for poetry.
   - He uses positive affirmation.
   - He encourages students to think for themselves.

6. **Tell** the students that they will now explore the characteristics of a good teacher as exemplified by Jesus in the Gospel of Matthew. Distribute the handout "Jesus, the Teacher" (Document #: TX002260), one for each student. Organize the students into groups of three. Assign to each group one of the passages from the Gospel of Matthew. If you have more than ten groups, you may assign the same passage to more than one group. If you have fewer than ten groups, not all passages need to be assigned. Direct the groups to read their assigned passage and then discuss the questions on the handout. Allow approximately 15 minutes for this part of the learning experience.

7. **Use** the jigsaw method to reorganize the small groups into three large groups. If possible, each large group should have one member from each of the original small groups. Instruct the new groups to have each member share with the group a brief summary of his or her small group's passage and answers to the discussion questions on the handout. Group members should then share their insights about Jesus' teaching.

8. **Draw** the class back together. Invite representatives from each of the large groups to share their observations with the class. Remind the students of the following:

   ➤ At the end of Matthew's Gospel, Jesus directs his disciples in this way: "Go, therefore, and make disciples of all nations, baptizing them in the name of the Father, and of the Son, and of the holy Spirit, teaching them to observe all that I have commanded you. And behold, I am with you always, until the end of the age" (Matthew 28:19–20).

➤ This means we are called to be teachers following the example of Jesus. We may not all train to be professional religion teachers or teach in our parish religious education programs. As Jesus' disciples we are all called to preach the Gospel through our words and actions.

➤ We all have opportunities every day to teach or coach, and not just about Jesus. We can teach a classmate a new formula in math, show a younger sibling how to shoot a basketball, explain to our grandparents how to use a social networking Internet site, or introduce a transfer student to the ways to get around school. When we give patient explanations, model care and concern, and reach out to someone who needs our help, our words and actions follow the example of and reflect our faith in Jesus, the Teacher.

9. **Direct** the students to take a few minutes to write answers to the following reflection questions:

- In what ways are you a teacher?
- How do you proclaim the Reign of God? Give concrete examples of ways you have taught someone else.
- What characteristics of a good teacher do you possess?
- How would you like to grow or change in order to become a better teacher?

Invite the students to share their responses in pairs or with the entire class.

10. **Conclude** this learning experience by reminding the students of the following:

➤ There is a saying attributed to Saint Francis of Assisi: "Preach the Gospel at all times. If necessary, use words."

➤ We preach with our lives. When this seems like a task too difficult or insurmountable, we can be strengthened in the promise of Jesus Christ: "I am with you always, until the end of the age" (Matthew 28:20).

Step 7

Engage the students in a close reading of passages from the Gospel of Luke, followed by tableaux vivants, *to identify elements of the Reign of God.*

Articles
21, 22

1. **Prepare** by downloading the PowerPoint "Luke's Christology and the Reign of God" (Document #: TX002252), and arrange for the use of an LCD projector as needed. Download and print the handouts "The Reign of God in the Gospel of Luke" (Document #: TX002261) and "The Reign of God in the Gospel of Luke and Today" (Document #: TX002262), one of each for each student.

2. **Assign** the students to read article 21, "Luke's Infancy Narrative," and article 22, "The Universal Nature of Covenant Love," in the student book as preparation for this learning experience.

3. **Tell** the students that they will have an opportunity to explore in depth the Christology found in the Gospel of Luke, as well as its understanding of the Reign of God.

4. **Present** the PowerPoint "Luke's Christology and the Reign of God" (Document #: TX002252). Allow the students to refer to their student books during the presentation. Direct them to take notes. Conclude the presentation by reminding the students that in Luke's Gospel, Jesus is especially concerned with those who are poor, marginalized, and forgotten. The author of Luke wants to show that Jews and Gentiles, women, the poor, and outcasts (such as lepers, Samaritans, and tax collectors) all experience Jesus' compassion and forgiveness.

5. **Explain** that the students will now explore aspects of Luke's Christology and the ways in which Jesus proclaims the Reign of God. Organize the students into groups of six. Distribute the handout "The Reign of God in the Gospel of Luke" (Document #: TX002261), one copy for each student. Assign to each group one of the Scripture passages. If you have more than six groups, you may assign the same passage to more than one group. Read the directions together and clarify any questions the students may have. Allow 15 to 20 minutes for the groups to work.

> **Teacher Note**
>
> The handout includes the passage of Luke 8:40–56 twice. You can have one group focus on the role of Jairus's daughter in the passage and have another group focus on the woman with a hemorrhage.

6. **Inform** the students that they will now create *tableaux vivants* based on their Scripture passage. Clarify that *tableaux vivants* are "living pictures" or still-life scenes formed by a group of actors or objects, carefully posed to communicate a story or concept. They are meant to be silent scenes. Explain that each group will create three *tableaux vivants* that portray or communicate how Jesus proclaims the Reign of God. You may want to lead an example for the students before they begin. Allow no more than 10 minutes for groups to create their *tableaux vivants.*

7. **Begin** the presentations of the *tableaux vivants.* To allow each group to set up the scene and then alert the class to look at the scene, use the terms *open curtains* (meaning "open your eyes") and *close curtains* (meaning "close your eyes"). After the presentations, lead a discussion of what the students have learned about the Christology and aspects of the Reign of God found in the Gospel of Luke. Invite the students to compare these insights with what they have already learned about the Christologies and the proclamation of the Reign of God in the Gospels of Mark and Matthew.

8. **Conclude** this learning experience by distributing the handout "The Reign of God in the Gospel of Luke and Today" (Document #: TX002262) as a homework assignment for the next step. Clarify that the students who choose the Luke 8:40–56 passage should focus on either Jairus's daughter or the woman with a hemorrhage, as indicated by italics on the handout.

| Apply | Reflect | **Step 8** |

Have the students consider examples of the Reign of God today using their understanding of the Reign of God from Luke's Gospel.

1. **Ask** the students to gather in their groups from the previous learning experience (step 7). Direct the students to share in their groups what they learned about the particular group of people or issue they researched as homework. Allow approximately 10 minutes for this small-group discussion.

2. **Use** the jigsaw method to reorganize the small groups into six new groups after the allotted time. Have the students present their research findings to their new groups. Other group members should take notes on these presentations. In particular, for each presentation each group member should list two concrete things he or she has learned, as well as one question.

3. **Draw** the class back together to lead a large-group discussion. Invite the students to share what they have learned and the questions they have. Ask them to consider the following questions:

   • How do these Scripture passages and the issues you studied call for our faith-filled response to these contemporary issues?

   • As disciples of Jesus and people of faith, how are we called to respond to these and other issues of social justice in order to proclaim the Reign of God in our own time and place?

4. **Help** the students to formulate some concrete actions they can take (as individuals or as a class) in response to the issues, the people, and the circumstances they have studied. Examples include a letter-writing campaign, an educational campaign for the school community, or a fund-raiser, such as a bake sale with proceeds to be donated to a related charity.

Articles
20, 23,
24

Step 9

Lead the students through a process of comparing and contrasting key aspects of the Gospels of Matthew and Luke.

1. **Prepare** by downloading and printing the handouts "Comparing and Contrasting Infancy Narratives in the Gospels of Matthew and Luke" (Document #: TX002263) and "Comparing and Contrasting the Passion and Resurrection Narratives in the Gospels of Matthew and Luke" (Document #: TX002264), one of each for each student. Gather three large pieces of poster board and markers.

2. **Assign** the students to read article 20, "The Paschal Mystery according to Matthew"; article 23, "Luke's Passion Narrative"; and article 24, "Luke's Post-Resurrection Appearance Narratives"; in the student book as preparation for this learning experience.

3. **Begin** this learning experience by reminding the students that they have learned about some similarities and differences between the Gospels of Matthew and Luke. Explain that now they will do a more focused comparison between the two Gospels, paying special attention to the infancy narratives, the dramatic monologues presented in class, and the Passion and Resurrection narratives.

4. **Organize** the students into groups of three or four. Distribute the handout "Comparing and Contrasting Infancy Narratives in the Gospels of Matthew and Luke" (Document #: TX002263). Review the directions with the class. Allow 10 to 15 minutes for the groups to work on the handout.

5. **Invite** volunteers from each group to share their responses with the class. Instruct the students to listen attentively, both to avoid repeating responses and to ensure that they note any information that their group did not include in their analysis.

6. **Direct** the students to consider the dramatic monologues presented in class. You may want to refer to the handout "Dramatic Monologues" (Document #: TX002258) as a reference or simply list on the board the various characters the students chose from each Gospel. Direct the small groups to spend a few minutes brainstorming what aspects of the characters were unique to each Gospel, as well as what each character had in common in both Gospels.

> ### Teacher Note
> You may want to refer the students to their notes from the PowerPoint presentations on Matthew and Luke as an additional resource.

7. **Ask** for three volunteers and give them the sheets of poster paper and markers. Invite the groups to share their findings with the class. As each group shares, ask the volunteers to note the similarities on the first sheet, the findings unique to the Gospel of Matthew on the second sheet, and the findings unique to the Gospel of Luke on the third sheet.

8. **Distribute** the handout "Comparing and Contrasting the Passion and Resurrection Narratives in the Gospels of Matthew and Luke" (Document #: TX002264). Instruct the students to return to their small groups to compare and contrast the Passion and Resurrection narratives from the Gospels of Matthew and Luke. Allow approximately 15 minutes for the students to work with their group members.

9. **Draw** the class back together, and invite volunteers to share what they learned from comparing and contrasting the structures, characters, and other aspects of the Passion and Resurrection narratives of Matthew's and Luke's Gospels. Finally, invite volunteers from the groups to share what they learned about the Christologies or theological emphases found in Matthew and Luke. Ask the students to consider the following questions:

   ➤ Why is it important that we understand these distinct Christologies in Matthew and Luke?

   ➤ What significance might the Christologies found in these Gospels have for our faith?

   ➤ In what ways do these Gospels speak to your own understanding of and relationship with Jesus?

10. **Conclude** this learning experience by reminding the students that Mark, Matthew, and Luke are synoptic Gospels that have much in common because of the shared source, Q. Explain that the students will have an opportunity to explore the unique Christology of the Gospel of John in the next unit.

Step 10

Make sure the students are all on track with their final performance tasks, if you have assigned them.

If possible, devote 50 to 60 minutes for the students to ask questions about the tasks and to work individually or in their small groups.

1. **Remind** the students to bring to class any work they have already prepared so that they can work on it during the class period. If necessary, reserve the library or media center so the students can do any book or online research. Download and print extra copies of the handouts "Final Performance Task Options for Unit 4" (Document #: TX002255) and "Rubric for Final Performance Tasks for Unit 4" (Document #: TX002256). Review the final performance task options, answer questions, and ask the students to choose one if they have not already done so.

2. **Provide** some class time for the students to work on their performance tasks. This then allows you to work with the students who need additional guidance with the project.

Step 11

Provide the students with time to continue and reflect on their chart of the four Gospels.

1. **Ask** the students to bring their copies of the unit 3 handout "Chart of the Gospels" (Document #: TX002245) for this class session. At this point, the part of the chart that pertains to Mark's Gospel should be complete.

2. **Provide** about 15 minutes for the students to work individually to complete the Matthew and Luke sections of the chart. Emphasize that the students are not to simply copy this information from the student book. Rather, they are expected to begin with the student book and to supplement with other information they learn in class and through research on their own. Help them to understand that in creating a personalized chart for themselves, they are building a valuable reference that they may use throughout this course.

3. **Organize** the students into pairs. Instruct the students to compare their work on the Gospels of Matthew and Luke with that of their partners, checking for agreement on the more objective items (such as date and authorship) and noting similarities or differences in their responses to the more subjective items (such as the personal reaction). Circulate among the pairs, offering feedback and correcting misinformation as needed.

4. **Remind** the students to keep the chart in their binders so that they can refer to it throughout this unit and continue completing it in subsequent units.

Step 12

Provide the students with a tool to use for reflecting on what they learned in the unit and how they learned.

This learning experience will provide the students with an excellent opportunity to reflect on the distinct Christologies and understanding of the Reign of God found in the Gospels of Matthew and Luke, as well as how their understanding of these Gospels has developed throughout the unit.

1. **Prepare** for this learning experience by downloading and printing the handout "Learning about Learning" (Document #: TX001159; see Appendix), one for each student.

2. **Distribute** the handout and give the students about 15 minutes to answer the questions quietly.

3. **Invite** the students to share any reflections they have about the content they learned as well as their insights into the way they learned.

4. **Direct** the students to keep this handout in a separate section of their folder or binder so that they can refer back to it at the conclusion of the course.

Preassessment Learning Experience on the Gospels of Matthew and Luke

✂ _____

Jesus' genealogy is traced back to Adam.

✂ _____

Symbol for this Gospel is a man.

✂ _____

Jesus' genealogy is traced back to Abraham.

✂ _____

The newborn Jesus is placed in a manger, symbolizing that he is the Bread of Life.

✂ _____

Image of Jesus in this Gospel is the New Moses and Teacher of the New Law.

✂ _____

Image of Jesus in this Gospel is merciful, compassionate, and especially concerned for the poor, marginalized, women, and non-Jews.

✂ _____

Written around AD 80.

✂ _____

Written primarily for a community of Jewish Christians, with some Gentiles.

✂ _____

Sources were the Gospel of Mark, Q, and the L-Source.

✂ _____

The angel Gabriel appears to Zechariah to announce the birth of John.

✂ _____

Document #: TX002254

✂──

Author is most likely a Jewish Christian.

✂──

Symbol for this Gospel is an ox.

✂──

Jesus is the fulfillment of the Covenant.

✂──

Written primarily for Gentile (Greek) Christians, represented by "Theophilus."

✂──

Sources were the Gospel of Mark, Q, and the M-Source.

✂──

The Magi follow the star to where Jesus was born.

✂──

Jesus proclaims the New Law from a mountain.

✂──

In the post-Resurrection account of the road to Emmaus, two disciples recognize Jesus in the breaking of the bread.

✂──

The authority of Jesus and the Apostles is directly established in this Gospel.

✂──

Written between AD 80 and 85.

✂──

Being a disciple of Christ is compatible with being a faithful Jew.

✂──

Document #: TX002254

✂ _____

Author is a Gentile Christian.

✂ _____

Themes focus on Mary, concern for the poor, and the meal representing the Reign of God.

✂ _____

The angel Gabriel appears to Mary to announce the birth of Jesus.

✂ _____

An angel announces the birth of Jesus to Joseph.

✂ _____

In this Gospel, there is an emphasis on Jesus praying and on parables about prayer.

✂ _____

Answer Sheet

The Gospel of Matthew	The Gospel of Luke
Symbol for this Gospel is a man.	Symbol for this Gospel is an ox.
Jesus' genealogy is traced back to Abraham.	Jesus' genealogy is traced back to Adam.
Image of Jesus in this Gospel is the New Moses and Teacher of the New Law.	Image of Jesus in this Gospel is merciful, compassionate, and especially concerned for the poor, marginalized, women, and non-Jews.
Written around AD 80.	Written between AD 80 and 85.
Written primarily for a community of Jewish Christians, with some Gentiles.	Written primarily for Gentile (Greek) Christians, represented by "Theophilus."
Author is most likely a Jewish Christian.	Author is a Gentile Christian.
Jesus is the fulfillment of the Covenant.	Themes focus on Mary, concern for the poor, and the meal representing the Reign of God.
Sources were the Gospel of Mark, Q, and the M-Source.	Sources were the Gospel of Mark, Q, and the L-Source.
Being a disciple of Christ is compatible with being a faithful Jew.	The angel Gabriel appears to Zechariah to announce the birth of John.
An angel announces the birth of Jesus to Joseph.	The angel Gabriel appears to Mary to announce the birth of Jesus.
The Magi follow the star to where Jesus was born.	The newborn Jesus is placed in a manger, symbolizing that he is the Bread of Life.
Jesus proclaims the New Law from a mountain.	In this Gospel, there is an emphasis on Jesus praying and on parables about prayer.
The authority of Jesus and the Apostles is directly established in this Gospel.	In the post-Resurrection account of the road to Emmaus, two disciples recognize Jesus in the breaking of the bread.

Final Performance Task Options for Unit 4

Important Information for All Three Options

The following are the main ideas that you are to understand from this unit. They should appear in this final performance task so that your teacher can assess whether you learned the most essential content:

- Matthew portrays Jesus as the New Moses, the fulfillment of the ancient promises made to the people of Israel.

- In the Gospel of Matthew, Jesus proclaims the Reign of God in powerful teachings to disciples of every generation.

- Luke portrays Jesus as a universal Savior, extending God's love and mercy to all people.

- In the Gospel of Luke, Jesus proclaims the Reign of God in acts of compassion on behalf of the poor and marginalized.

In addition to demonstrating understanding of these four main concepts of the unit, your final performance task must also contain or demonstrate the following:

- In-depth, substantial content appropriate for an upper-level high-school religious studies course

- Responsible and accurate use of Scripture

- Substantive content that creatively and accurately engages with and interprets the material of this unit

- Proper grammar, spelling, and diction

- A neat and well-organized presentation

Option 1: An Exegetical Paper

Based on the infancy narratives in the Gospels of Matthew and Luke, write an exegetical paper that demonstrates the distinctiveness of these two Gospels. Use one of the exegetical methods you studied in unit 2, and consult at least three sources of information other than your student book. Your paper should follow this structure:

- An introduction that situates the infancy narratives within the broader contexts of the Gospels of Matthew and Luke

- An overview of the major topics, questions, or problems regarding the infancy narratives that your paper will explore

Document #: TX002255

- A explanation of the methodology you will use to compare and contrast the passages, as well as interpret them—that is, literary, sociohistorical, or ideological—and a brief justification for your choice of that methodology

- At least three substantive body paragraphs in which you compare and contrast the infancy narratives using the methodology you have chosen and present your interpretation of the texts

- A bibliography

Option 2: Comparison and Contrast of the Christology of Matthew and Luke Using Art

Because of your scriptural expertise, as well as your artistic ability, a curator of a local art gallery has asked you to create two images of Jesus that illustrate the distinct Christologies of the Gospel of Matthew and the Gospel of Luke for an exhibit that features art based on those two Gospels. Your presentation for the curator should include the following:

- Two original images of Jesus from the Gospels—one from Matthew and one from Luke. (With your teacher's approval, you may use two art pieces from another source. Be sure to include the artists' names and the sources of the art.)

- A three- to four-page paper that clearly compares and contrasts the two images and explains how they illustrate the distinct natures of the Gospels of Matthew and Luke. Include at least two references from each Gospel (four scriptural references total) that explain the distinct Christology of each Gospel.

Option 3: A Lesson Plan for Your Local Parish Confirmation Class

The director of religious education at your local parish has asked for your help in preparing students for Confirmation. In particular, she would like you to teach a class about the Gospels of Matthew and Luke to help her students understand the Gospels' similarities, as well as what makes them distinct. Your lesson plan should include the following:

- A detailed outline for an hour-long class

- One or more visual components (such as a handout or PowerPoint presentation)

- At least one interactive activity that allows students to engage with the Gospel texts and with one another to understand what is unique about each Gospel and its Christology

Rubric for Final Performance Tasks for Unit 4

Criteria	4	3	2	1
Assignment includes all items requested in the instructions.	Assignment includes all items requested, and they are completed above expectations.	Assignment includes all items requested.	Assignment includes over half of the items requested.	Assignment includes less than half of the items requested.
Assignment shows understanding of the following concept: *Matthew portrays Jesus as the New Moses, the fulfillment of the ancient promises made to the people of Israel.*	Assignment shows unusually insightful understanding of this concept.	Assignment shows good understanding of this concept.	Assignment shows adequate understanding of this concept.	Assignment shows little understanding of this concept.
Assignment shows understanding of the following concept: *In the Gospel of Matthew, Jesus proclaims the Reign of God in powerful teachings to disciples of every generation.*	Assignment shows unusually insightful understanding of this concept.	Assignment shows good understanding of this concept.	Assignment shows adequate understanding of this concept.	Assignment shows little understanding of this concept.
Assignment shows understanding of the following concept: *Luke portrays Jesus as a universal Savior, extending God's love and mercy to all people.*	Assignment shows unusually insightful understanding of this concept.	Assignment shows good understanding of this concept.	Assignment shows adequate understanding of this concept.	Assignment shows little understanding of this concept.
Assignment shows understanding of the following concept: *In the Gospel of Luke, Jesus proclaims the Reign of God in acts of compassion on behalf of the poor and marginalized.*	Assignment shows unusually insightful understanding of this concept.	Assignment shows good understanding of this concept.	Assignment shows adequate understanding of this concept.	Assignment shows little understanding of this concept.
Assignment uses proper grammar, spelling, and diction.	Assignment has no grammar or spelling errors.	Assignment has one grammar or spelling error.	Assignment has two grammar or spelling errors.	Assignment has more than two grammar or spelling errors.
Assignment uses its assigned or chosen media effectively.	Assignment uses its assigned or chosen media in a way that greatly enhances it.	Assignment uses its assigned or chosen media effectively.	Assignment uses its assigned or chosen media somewhat effectively.	Assignment uses its assigned or chosen media ineffectively.
Assignment is neatly done.	Assignment not only is neat but is exceptionally creative.	Assignment is neatly done.	Assignment is neat for the most part.	Assignment is not neat.

Document #: TX002256

Vocabulary for Unit 4

Amen: A Hebrew word that expresses agreement. When used at the beginning of a teaching, as Jesus uses it, the word adds authority to what follows.

Beatitudes: The teachings of Jesus that begin the Sermon on the Mount and that summarize the New Law of Christ. The Beatitudes describe the actions and attitudes by which one can discover genuine happiness, and they teach us the final end to which God calls us: full communion with him in the Kingdom of Heaven.

commission: To commission someone is to send him or her on mission. Jesus commissioned the Apostles to carry out his mission to the world.

eschatological meal: The Eucharist, which anticipates the heavenly banquet that Jesus will share with the faithful when the Kingdom of God is fully realized at the end of time. The word *eschatological* derives from *eschaton*, meaning "the end of time."

fiat: Latin for "let it be done," words Mary spoke to the angel at the Annunciation.

infancy narrative: The accounts of Jesus' birth and early life.

Koine Greek: The dialect of the Greek language most commonly used from around 300 BC to AD 300, and the language in which the New Testament books were originally written.

Passover: The night the Lord passed over the house of the Israelites marked by the blood of the lamb, and spared the firstborn sons from death. It also is the feast that celebrates the deliverance of the Chosen People from bondage in Egypt and the Exodus from Egypt to the Promised Land.

Samaritan: An inhabitant of Samaria. The Samaritans, an interreligious and interracial people (Jewish and Assyrian), rejected the Jerusalem Temple and worshipped instead at Mount Gerizim. The hostility between Jews and Samaritans is often recounted in the New Testament.

Solomon: David's son, a king of Israel renowned for his wisdom.

synonymous parallelism: A device used in Hebrew poetry in which the same idea is expressed in two adjacent lines but in different words, thus expanding and emphasizing the idea in a balanced composition.

Document #: TX002257

Dramatic Monologues

Using our imagination to "get inside" the mind and heart of a scriptural character can help us to better understand the Scriptures and appreciate biblical characters as human beings.

1. Choose one of the biblical characters from the list of characters designated for this activity (see the bottom of the handout).

2. Spend some time "getting acquainted" with this person through the careful and repeated reading of one or more biblical texts featuring that person or that person's friends, family, or associates. You may use a biblical commentary or dictionary to look up additional information about your character and the particular passage or passages in which he or she appears. Using your imagination, try to see events, experiences, and so on, from your character's point of view.

3. Prepare a dramatic monologue of at least 2 minutes in which you talk about *one* particular event, experience, or choice in your character's life from his or her point of view.

- You are going for depth rather than breadth, so do not just speak or write about your character's life generally. Help us to think about what was going through your character's mind and heart at that time and in that particular interaction with Jesus.

- Use your imagination, but do not stray from the biblical text in ways that make no sense.

- You do not need to summarize the story; rather, try to give new, original insights about the character.

- You may use updated or current language to express your character's context, but your character should not be portrayed in a modern situation.

- Imagine that you really are this person—what would you say about your situation?

4. Type your monologue—this will be handed in on the due date.

5. Deliver your monologue to the class on the due date.

- Your monologue should be delivered or performed, not read.

- Be very familiar with your text—almost memorize it.

- Make good and frequent eye contact with the class.

Document #: TX002258

Characters from Matthew's Gospel

Joseph (chapter 1)

King Herod (chapter 2)

John the Baptist (chapter 3)

Simon Peter

Centurion (whose servant was healed) (chapter 8)

Woman with the hemorrhage (chapter 9)

Canaanite woman (chapter 15)

Rich young man (chapter 19)

One of two blind men healed by Jesus (chapter 20)

Woman who anointed Jesus (chapter 26)

Judas (chapters 26 and 27)

Caiaphas (chapter 26)

Pilate (chapter 27)

Mary Magdalene (chapters 27 and 28)

Characters from Luke's Gospel

Zechariah (chapter 1)

Elizabeth (chapter 1)

Mary, Jesus' Mother

The angel Gabriel (chapter 1)

A shepherd (chapter 2)

John the Baptist (chapter 3)

Simon Peter

Gerasene demoniac (chapter 8)

Woman with a hemorrhage (chapter 8)

Jairus (chapter 8)

Martha (chapter 10)

Crippled woman cured on the Sabbath (chapter 13)

The thankful leper (chapter 17)

The rich official (chapter 18)

Zacchaeus (chapter 19)

Cleopas (chapter 24)

Document #: TX002258

Jesus and the Law of Moses

Circle the set of scriptural texts that you and your group members have been assigned to read. As a group, compare the texts and discuss the questions listed below.

    A. Exodus 20:7 and Matthew 5:33–37

    B. Exodus 20:13 and Matthew 5:21–26

    C. Exodus 20:14 and Matthew 5:27–30

    D. Exodus 21:12 and Matthew 5:21–26

    E. Leviticus 19:18 and Matthew 5:43–48

    F. Leviticus 24:20 and Matthew 5:38–42

    G. Deuteronomy 24:1–5 and Matthew 5:31–32

For Discussion

1. Based on your reading of these two scriptural texts, what is significant about how Jesus reinterprets the Mosaic Law?

2. For Matthew's Jewish audience, which was familiar with Mosaic Law, why might this reinterpretation have been troublesome or difficult to accept?

3. For Matthew's Gentile audience, why might this reinterpretation have been appealing?

Jesus, the Teacher

Circle the passage that you and your group members have been assigned to read.

Matthew 5:1–12

Matthew 5:21–26

Matthew 5:38–42

Matthew 5:43–48

Matthew 6:5–8

Matthew 6:25–34

Matthew 7:1–5

Matthew 13:18–23

Matthew 13:24–30

Matthew 13:31–33

As a group, read your assigned passage and then discuss the questions listed below. All the group members should note their responses on a separate sheet of paper so they can share them with the class.

1. How would you describe Jesus' teaching method in this passage?

2. What is Jesus trying to teach the people?

3. What is unusual about his teaching method or about what he is teaching, especially given the context in which he lived and taught?

4. What does this scriptural text teach us about the Reign of God?

5. What else do we know about how and what Jesus teaches in the Gospel of Matthew? Give concrete examples to support your claims.

Document #: TX002260

The Reign of God in the Gospel of Luke

1. Circle the passage that you and your group have been assigned.

Luke 7:11–17 (raising of the widow's son)

Luke 8:40–56 (*Jairus's daughter* and the woman with a hemorrhage)

Luke 8:40–56 (Jairus's daughter and *the woman with a hemorrhage*)

Luke 16:19–31 (Parable of the Rich Man and Lazarus)

Luke 17:11–17 (cleansing of the ten lepers)

Luke 21:1–4 (widow's mite)

2. Read your assigned passage as a group.

3. Take time to do some research on the significance of characters, words, and so forth, in your passage. In other words, do a mini-exegesis of the text.

4. List in this space what you have learned.

5. As a group, discuss the following questions. Be sure each member of your group writes his or her responses in the space provided.

   A. Based on this passage, how would you characterize Jesus and his actions?

   B. What can we glean from this passage about Luke's Christology?

   C. What does this passage tell us about the Reign of God in the Gospel of Luke?

The Reign of God in the Gospel of Luke and Today

In the list below, find the Scripture passage you studied in class with your group. The list equates the Scripture passage with a modern group of people and the issue these people face or circumstances in which they live. Research the group of people and issue that relates to your Scripture passage. *You only need to research the one group.* On a separate piece of paper, respond to the questions below this list, and be prepared to present your findings in class.

- Luke 7:11–17 (raising of the widow's son) = Mothers of the Plaza de Mayo (Argentina)

- Luke 8:40–56 (*Jairus's daughter* and the woman with a hemorrhage) = human trafficking of young girls

- Luke 8:40–56 (Jairus's daughter and *the woman with a hemorrhage*) = social stigmas associated with women who have been raped

- Luke 16:19–31 (Parable of the Rich Man and Lazarus) = poverty in Haiti before and after the earthquake of January 12, 2010

- Luke 17:11–17 (cleansing of the ten lepers) = HIV/AIDS in Africa

- Luke 21:1–4 (widow's mite) = elderly women and poverty

Questions

1. Who are the poor and marginalized in this situation?

2. Describe the situation or circumstances in which they live or the suffering they endure or have endured.

3. What actions are being taken to change their situation?

4. What actions still need to be taken? How might people your age participate in or support these needed actions?

5. In what ways is this issue or situation similar to the Gospel passage you read from Luke?

© 2012 by Saint Mary's Press
Living in Christ Series

Comparing and Contrasting Infancy Narratives in the Gospels of Matthew and Luke

With the members of your group, review the infancy narratives found in Matthew 1:1—2:23 and Luke 1:5—2:52. Refer to your student book and notes from class, as well.

What similarities and differences do you see between the infancy narratives in the Gospels of Matthew and Luke? Use the table below to write your analysis. Include information about Jesus' genealogy, the Annunciation of his birth, and those who first visited Jesus.

Infancy Narratives

	Unique to Matthew	In Both Matthew and Luke	Unique to Luke
Structure			
Characters			
Other			

Document #: TX002263

Comparing and Contrasting the Passion and Resurrection Narratives in the Gospels of Matthew and Luke

With the members of your group, read the Passion and Resurrection narratives found in Matthew 26:1—28:20 and Luke 22:1—24:53. Refer to your student book and notes from class, as well. What similarities and differences do you see between the Passion and Resurrection narratives in the Gospels of Matthew and Luke? Use the table below to write your analysis.

Passion and Resurrection Narratives

	Unique to Matthew	In Both Matthew and Luke	Unique to Luke
Structure			
Characters			
Other			
Christology			

Unit 4 Test

Part 1: Matching

Determine which Gospel the information describes. Write "M" for Matthew and "L" for Luke.

1. _____ Jesus' genealogy is traced back to Adam.

2. _____ Symbol for this Gospel is a man.

3. _____ Jesus' genealogy is traced back to Abraham.

4. _____ The newborn Jesus is placed in a manger, symbolizing that he is the Bread of Life.

5. _____ Image of Jesus in this Gospel is the New Moses and Teacher of the New Law.

6. _____ Image of Jesus in this Gospel is merciful, compassionate, and especially concerned for the poor, marginalized, women, and non-Jews.

7. _____ Written around AD 80.

8. _____ Written primarily for a community of Jewish Christians, with some Gentiles.

9. _____ Sources were the Gospel of Mark, Q, and the L-Source.

10. _____ The angel Gabriel appears to Zechariah to announce the birth of John.

11. _____ Author is most likely a Jewish Christian.

12. _____ Symbol for this Gospel is an ox.

13. _____ Jesus is the fulfillment of the Covenant.

14. _____ Written primarily for Gentile (Greek) Christians, represented by "Theophilus."

15. _____ Sources were the Gospel of Mark, Q, and the M-Source.

16. _____ The Magi follow the star to where Jesus was born.

17. _____ Jesus proclaims the New Law from a mountain.

18. _____ In the post-Resurrection account of the road to Emmaus, two disciples recognize Jesus in the breaking of the bread.

19. _____ The authority of Jesus and the Apostles is directly established in this Gospel.

20. _____ Written between AD 80 and 85.

21. _____ Being a disciple of Christ is compatible with being a faithful Jew.

22. _____ Author is a Gentile Christian.

23. _____ Themes focus on Mary, concern for the poor, and the meal representing the Reign of God.

24. _____ The angel Gabriel appears to Mary to announce the birth of Jesus.

25. _____ An angel announces the birth of Jesus to Joseph.

26. _____ In this Gospel, there is an emphasis on Jesus praying and on parables about prayer.

Part 2: Essay

Answer the following question in three to five substantial paragraphs.

1. Compare and contrast the Christologies of Matthew and Luke. Support your response with relevant details, passages, or stories from each of the Gospels. In your concluding paragraph, explain which Gospel most speaks to you and your faith journey and why.

Document #: TX002265

Unit 4 Test Answer Key

Part 1: Matching

1. L	**10.** L	**19.** M
2. M	**11.** M	**20.** L
3. M	**12.** L	**21.** M
4. L	**13.** M	**22.** L
5. M	**14.** L	**23.** L
6. L	**15.** M	**24.** L
7. M	**16.** M	**25.** M
8. M	**17.** M	**26.** L
9. L	**18.** L	

Part 2: Essay

Student responses will vary. The following points are possible responses.

In the Gospel of Matthew, Jesus is presented as the New Moses who has come to fulfill the covenant as promised to the people of Israel. The Gospel begins with the genealogy of Jesus, followed by the Annunciation of Jesus' birth to Joseph. To escape Herod and his intention to do away with the potential threat of the Messiah, Joseph follows the instructions from his dream and takes Mary and Jesus to Egypt. The reader is reminded of Joseph, son of Jacob, who was sold into slavery and who later saved his family from starvation during a time of famine. In the same way, the Joseph of the New Testament flees with his family to Egypt to save them. In Matthew 2:15, the words of the prophet Hosea are quoted in reference to Jesus: "Out of Egypt I called my son." The return from Egypt, then, fulfills these words of the prophet.

In contrast, the Gospel of Luke begins with the annunciation of John's birth to Zechariah, followed by the Annunciation of Jesus' birth to Mary. Although Mary is silent in Matthew's Gospel and Joseph takes a more prominent role, the opposite is true for Luke's Gospel: Mary takes center stage in salvation history, while Joseph is silent. Both Mary's and Zechariah's canticles help us to see that Jesus will be the Savior of all, especially the poor and oppressed. This theme is played out in the birth of Jesus in a stable's manger, because there was no room at the inn. Rather than being visited by the Magi (as in the Gospel of Matthew), the Holy Family is surrounded by lowly shepherds. Only later in Luke's infancy narrative do we encounter the genealogy of Jesus.

The overall structures of both Gospels differ, as well. Following the infancy narrative in the Gospel of Matthew, five sections are reminiscent of the Jewish law or five books of the Pentateuch. Luke, on the other hand, structures the Gospel around a journey. Both Gospels end with some reminder of how they began. Luke begins with the Bread of Life in the manger who gives sustenance to all, and he concludes with the breaking of bread with the disciples on the road to Emmaus. In Matthew 1:23, the angel quotes the prophet Isaiah and says, "Behold, the virgin shall be with child and bear a son, / and they shall name him Emmanuel." The reader is reminded in Matthew that *Emmanuel* means "God is with us." Matthew concludes the Gospel with Jesus' words, "I am with you always, until the end of the age" (28:20).

Unit 5

The Gospel of John

Overview

Now that the students have completed an in-depth study of the synoptic Gospels, this unit immerses them in the theological emphases and literary features of John's Gospel.

Key Understandings and Questions

Upon completing this unit, the students will have a deeper understanding of the following key concepts:

- The Gospel of John consists of a prologue, the Book of Signs, the Book of Glory, and an epilogue.
- John portrays Jesus as the Divine Son of God.
- The Gospel of John presents the person of Jesus through metaphors and symbolism.
- Careful exegesis of John's Gospel enables us to avoid any damaging anti-Semitic misinterpretations.

Upon completing the unit, the students will have answered the following questions:

- What is the structure of John's Gospel?
- What is John's Christology?
- What literary tools does John use to present Jesus?
- Why must we carefully examine John's portrayal of the Jewish people?

How Will You Know the Students Understand?

The following resources will help you to assess the students' understanding of the key concepts covered in this unit:

- handout "Final Performance Task Options for Unit 5" (Document #: TX002273)
- handout "Rubric for Final Performance Tasks for Unit 5" (Document #: TX002274)
- handout "Unit 5 Test" (Document #: TX002280)

Student Book Articles

This unit draws on articles from *The New Testament: The Good News of Jesus Christ* student book and incorporates them into the unit instruction. Whenever the teaching steps for the unit require the students to refer to or read an article from the student book, the following symbol appears in the margin: (📖). The articles covered in the unit are from "Section 3: The Johannine Writings," and are as follows:

- "Comparison and Contrast: John and the Synoptic Gospels" (article 28)
- "Allegory in the Seven Signs" (article 29)
- "The Paschal Mystery in the Gospel of John" (article 30)
- "John's Post-Resurrection Accounts" (article 31)

The Suggested Path to Understanding

This unit in the teacher guide provides you with one learning path to take with the students, to enable them to begin their study of the Gospel of John. It is not necessary to use all the learning experiences, but if you substitute other material from this course or your own material for some of the material offered here, check to see that you have covered all relevant facets of understanding and that you have not missed knowledge or skills required in later units.

 Step 1: Preassess what the students already know about the Gospel of John by engaging them in a "myths and facts" exercise.

 Step 2: Follow this assessment by presenting to the students the handouts "Final Performance Task Options for Unit 5" (Document #: TX002273) and "Rubric for Final Performance Tasks for Unit 5" (Document #: TX002274).

 **Step 3:** Continue the practice of Sustained Silent Reading (SSR).

 **Step 4:** Use the teaching strategies of critical questioning and the jigsaw process to guide the students in exploring selected passages from John that highlight this Gospel's Christology.

 **Step 5:** Begin a series of learning experiences in which the students explore the structure of John's Gospel, beginning with the prologue.

 **Step 6:** Facilitate the students' examination of the Book of Signs, emphasizing how the signs move those who witness them to greater faith.

 **Step 7:** Guide the students in searching for and analyzing artwork that depicts selected scenes from the Book of Glory.

 **Step 8:** Lead the students in reflecting on and praying with some of the metaphors and symbols John uses to present the person of Jesus.

 Step 9: Facilitate a critical examination of selected passages from John's Gospel that have often been misinterpreted as anti-Semitic.

 Step 10: Make sure the students are all on track with their final performance tasks, if you have assigned them.

 Step 11: Provide the students with time to complete and reflect on their chart of the four Gospels.

 Step 12: Provide the students with a tool to use for reflecting on what they learned in the unit and how they learned.

Background for Teaching This Unit

Visit *smp.org/LivinginChrist* for additional information about these and other theological concepts taught in this unit:

- "Jesus and Judaism" (Document #: TX002267)
- "The Passion According to John" (Document #: TX002268)
- "Gospel Comparison Chart" (Document #: TX001175)

The Web site also includes information on these and other teaching methods used in the unit:

- "Critical Questioning Method of Engaging with Texts" (Document #: TX001316)
- "Using a Mind Map" (Document #: TX001009)
- "Using the Jigsaw Process" (Document #: TX001020)
- "Sustained Silent Reading" (Document #: TX002237)

Scripture Passages

Scripture is an important part of the Living in Christ series and is frequently used in the learning experiences for each unit. The Scripture passages featured in this unit are as follows:

- John 1:35–51 (the call of the first disciples)
- John 2:1–12 (the wedding at Cana)
- John 3:1–15 (visit of Nicodemus)
- John 4:4–42 (Samaritan woman at the well)
- John 6:1–21 (multiplication of the loaves and walking on water)
- Genesis 1:1—2:4 (the first Creation story)

- Proverbs 8:22–36 (preexistent Wisdom, God's partner in creation)
- Wisdom 7:22—8:1 (the spirit and light of Wisdom)
- Exodus 25:8–22 (the tabernacle, God's dwelling place among the Israelites)
- Exodus 40:34–38 (God's glory filling the tabernacle)
- 1 Kings 8:10–13,27–30 (God's glory filling Solomon's Temple)
- John 4:46–54 (healing of the royal official's son)
- John 5:1–18 (healing a sick man at the pool of Bethesda)
- John 9:1–41(healing of the man born blind)
- John 11:1–45 (raising of Lazarus)
- John 13:1–17 (Jesus washing the disciples' feet)
- John 19:25–27 (the Beloved Disciple and the women at the foot of the cross)
- John 19:31–37 (piercing of Jesus' side)
- John 20:11–18 (post-Resurrection appearance to Mary Magdalene at the empty tomb)
- John 20:24–29 (doubting Thomas)
- John 6:35 (I am the bread of life)
- John 8:12 (I am the light of the world)
- John 11:25 (I am the resurrection and the life)
- John 14:26 (I am the way, the truth, and the life)
- John 15:5 (I am the vine, and you are the branches)
- John 5:18–47 (Jesus doing his Father's work)
- John 6:32–59 (The bread of life discourse)
- John 7:11–36 (Jesus teaching in the Temple at the Feast of Tabernacles)
- John 8:31–59 (Jesus and Abraham)
- John 18:28—19:16 (Jesus' trial before Pilate and sentence of crucifixion)

Vocabulary

The student book and the teacher guide include the following key terms for this unit. To provide the students with a list of these terms and their definitions, download and print the handout "Vocabulary for Unit 5" (Document #: TX002275), one for each student.

collect	New Eve
I AM	schism
metaphor	symbol

Learning Experiences

Step 1

Preassess what the students already know about the Gospel of John by engaging them in a "myths and facts" exercise.

1. **Prepare** by downloading and printing the handout "The Gospel of John: Myths and Facts" (Document #: TX002272), one for each student. Download the PowerPoint "The Gospel of John: Myths and Facts" (Document #: TX002270), and arrange for the use of an LCD projector in your classroom.

2. **Introduce** the unit with the following or similar statements:

    ➤ Unlike the prior two units, this entire unit will focus on one Gospel: the Gospel of John.

    ➤ Because John is so different from the synoptic Gospels, it makes sense to devote a whole unit to John.

    ➤ For a variety of reasons, John is often misunderstood from theological, exegetical, and literary perspectives. Therefore, we are beginning this unit with an exercise that will help to determine the extent to which you are able to distinguish myths about John's Gospel from facts.

3. **Distribute** the handout "The Gospel of John: Myths and Facts" (Document #: TX002272), and review the directions with the students. Assure them that this is simply a preassessment to see what they already know, not a test to be graded. Give them about 10 minutes to complete the handout. For your own information, note that items 1, 2, 4, 5, 7, 10, and 13 are myths; items 3, 6, 8, 9, 11, 12, and 14 are facts.

4. **Invite** the students to have a brief conversation with another student seated near them to compare their responses, noting any items on which they disagree. Allow 2 to 3 minutes for the partners to discuss their answers.

5. **Present** the PowerPoint "The Gospel of John: Myths and Facts" (Document #: TX002270), which will reveal the correct answers along with some introductory information about these topics. Direct the students to take brief notes on their handouts, especially regarding items to which they responded incorrectly.

6. **Direct** the students to turn back to their partners to share the following:
   - their "score"—the number of items correctly identified as myths or facts
   - one item that surprised them the most—that is, a myth they thought for sure was a fact or vice versa
   - one question they have about John's Gospel

7. **Draw** the class back together, and invite several volunteers to share the substance of their partner conversation, especially the items that surprised them and their questions. Affirm the students' prior knowledge about John's Gospel, as well as their intellectual curiosity in posing questions. Allow the students to keep the handout so that they can refer back to it near the end of the unit.

Step 2

Follow this assessment by presenting to the students the handouts "Final Performance Task Options for Unit 5" (Document #: TX002273) and "Rubric for Final Performance Tasks for Unit 5" (Document #: TX002274).

This unit provides you with three ways to assess that the students have a deep understanding of the most important concepts in the unit: writing an exegetical paper, creating a triptych that artistically presents the first three sections of John's Gospel, or developing a detailed outline for a 1-hour presentation at a conference on monotheistic religions. Refer to "Using Final Performance Tasks to Assess Understanding" (Document #: TX001011) and "Using Rubrics to Assess Work" (Document #: TX001012) at *smp.org/LivinginChrist* for background information.

1. **Prepare** by downloading and printing the handouts "Final Performance Task Options for Unit 5" (Document #: TX002273) and "Rubric for Final Performance Tasks for Unit 5" (Document #: TX002274), one of each for each student.

2. **Distribute** the handouts. Give the students a choice as to which performance task to work on and add more options if you so choose.

> **Teacher Note**
>
> Remind the students to choose their final performance task in accordance with any course requirements you may have established. In addition, if you are offering the semester-long portfolio project to your students (perhaps as part or all of their final exam), explain that the students who wish to assemble a portfolio must choose option 1.

Teacher Note

You will want to assign due dates for the performance tasks.

If you have done these performance tasks, or very similar ones, with students before, place examples of this work in the classroom. During this introduction explain how each is a good example of what you are looking for, for different reasons. This allows the students to concretely understand what you are looking for and to understand that there is not only one way to succeed.

3. **Review** the directions, expectations, and rubric in class, allowing the students to ask questions. You may want to say something to this effect:

   ➤ If you wish to work alone, you may choose any of the three options. If you wish to work with a partner, you may choose option 2 or 3. If you wish to work as part of a group of three, you may choose option 3 only.

   ➤ Near the end of the unit, you will have one full class period to work on the final performance task. However, keep in mind that you should be working on, or at least thinking about, your chosen task throughout the unit, not just at the end.

4. **Explain** the types of tools and knowledge the students will gain throughout the unit so that they can successfully complete the final performance task.

5. **Answer** questions to clarify the end point toward which the unit is headed. Remind the students as the unit progresses that each learning experience builds the knowledge and skills they will need in order to show you that they understand the Gospel of John.

Step 3

Continue the practice of Sustained Silent Reading (SSR).

Teacher Note

Consistently including a 15-minute SSR session in every subsequent class session will enable your students to read John's Gospel in its entirety during this unit and, more broadly, to cultivate the discipline of careful, reflective reading.

1. **Prepare** by downloading and making extra copies, if needed, of the unit 3 handout "Sustained Silent Reading Log Instructions" (Document #: TX002244). Review these instructions with the students, and remind them of your expectations regarding the SSR log (for example, keeping it in a separate section of their binder or notebook), including your procedure for collecting and assessing this work.

2. **Tell** the students to begin reading John's Gospel during today's SSR session. Allow them to read for 15 minutes. Near the end of this time, remind them to make an entry in their SSR log.

3. **Provide** the students with a brief stretch break after SSR before continuing with the day's lesson.

Explain | **Interpret** | ## Step 4

Use the teaching strategies of critical questioning and the jigsaw process to guide the students in exploring selected passages from John that highlight this Gospel's Christology.

1. **Prepare** by downloading and printing the handout "Exploring John's Christology" (Document #: TX002276), one for each student. Ask the students to bring their Bibles for this class session. You may also wish to have copies of biblical and theological dictionaries available for student use.

2. **Review** with the students the strategy of critical questioning, also known as "level questions." Tell them that this strategy involves asking themselves questions about a reading that tap into three levels of understanding:

   1. what the reading says on a basic, literal (i.e., words alone) level
   2. what the reading says on a deeper level
   3. why the reading matters today

   Consider writing these levels of understanding on the board for the students to use as reference during this learning experience. Point out to the students that these questions progress from basic, content-oriented items to questions that encompass broad philosophical issues. Also advise them that questions on all three levels should never be answerable with a simple yes-or-no response.

   > **Teacher Note**
   >
   > Further prepare for this learning experience by referring to the handouts "Critical Questioning Method of Engaging with Texts" (Document #: TX001316) and "Using the Jigsaw Process" (Document #: TX001020) as background information for this learning experience.

3. **Organize** the students into five groups, and distribute the handout "Exploring John's Christology" (Document #: TX002276). Assign each group one of the five passages from John's Gospel listed on the handout. Ask the students to follow steps 1 through 3 on the handout. Within their groups, the students should read the passage together and then write three questions for each critical questioning level (i.e., nine questions total) on the passage. Allow about 15 minutes for this process. Circulate among the groups to offer assistance as needed.

4. **Reorganize** the students into new groups, comprising one person from each of the original groups, using the jigsaw process. If the number of students in your class is not divisible by five, have each "extra" student join one of the groups. Invite the students to proceed to step 4 on the handout, using their level 1 and level 2 questions to summarize for their new groups the passage they read. Have the other group members take notes on a separate sheet of paper as each person shares.

5. **Have** the groups proceed to step 5 on the handout, examining their level 3 questions, which should probe the deeper, more abstract issues raised by these passages. Ask them to note what similarities and differences they notice among these questions. The students will use these questions as the basis for discussing the last item (step 6) on the handout. Direct the students to work within their groups to construct an answer to the question in step 6 that accounts for what they have learned from all five passages.

6. **Draw** the class back together, and facilitate a large-group discussion focused on the question in step 6 from the handout. Be sure to address the following points if the students do not mention them:

   ➤ In John's Gospel Jesus is frequently portrayed as knowing information to which he would not have had access via merely human means. For example, in John 1:42, he knows Simon's name without being told, and in John 6:15, he knows that the crowd wants to carry him off and make him king.

   ➤ Jesus is presented as being in total control of his life, decisions, and priorities. For example, in John 6:5–6, he has already planned to work a miracle—his question about feeding the people, posed to Philip, was only a test. In John, chapter 1, he calls the first disciples (Andrew, Simon, Philip, and Nathanael) with little effort—a simple invitation to "come and see" or "follow me" is enough for them to respond. He even gives Simon a new name—Cephas, or Peter—at their first meeting.

   ➤ Jesus' powerful "signs"—the word John uses to identify Jesus' miracles—move those who witness these events to believe in him. For example, those who witness the transformation of the water into wine at Cana "began to believe in him" (2:11); those present at the feeding of the crowd proclaim that Jesus is "truly the Prophet, the one who is to come into the world" (6:14).

   ➤ Jesus' ministry is marked by long, often complicated theological conversations with individuals and groups. We observe this in his conversations with Nicodemus in chapter 3 and with the unnamed Samaritan woman in chapter 4.

   ➤ On many occasions, Jesus either directly states or indirectly alludes to his identity as the Divine Son of God. For example, in conversing with Nicodemus, he states that "no one has gone up to heaven except the one who has come down from heaven, the Son of Man" (3:13), that is, himself. In his lengthy exchange with the Samaritan woman, he responds to her belief in a "Messiah . . . the one called the Anointed; . . . he will tell us everything" with the clear assertion that "I am he, the one who is speaking with you" (4:25–26).

7. **Help** the students to understand that these passages, considered together, give us a clear view of John's unique Christology. Although all four canonical Gospels present Jesus as fully human and fully divine, John emphasizes Jesus' divinity in all the ways mentioned above. In theology this Christology is sometimes called a "high" Christology. In contrast, Christology like that of Mark's Gospel, which emphasizes Jesus' humanity, is called a "low" Christology.

8. **Conclude** by reminding the students that the Gospel of John was the last canonical Gospel written, between AD 90 and 100. Prompt them to consider how this may have shaped John's approach in presenting Jesus.

   ➤ Perhaps it took time—years, or even decades—for the early Christian community to grow in understanding the fullness of Jesus' identity and mission.

   ➤ This may explain why Mark, the first Gospel, emphasizes Jesus' humanity, while John, the last Gospel, emphasizes his divinity.

Step 5

Begin a series of learning experiences in which the students explore the structure of John's Gospel, beginning with the prologue.

Article 28

1. **Prepare** by downloading the PowerPoint "The Structure of John's Gospel" (Document #: TX002271) and arranging for the use of an LCD projector in your classroom. Download and print the handout "Old Testament Themes and Images in John's Prologue" (Document #: TX002277), one for each student. Distribute six pieces of newsprint, and have markers and other art supplies available. If your students are not using the *New American Bible, Revised Edition* (NABRE), download and make copies of the footnotes for John 1:1–18 from the NABRE at the Web site of the U.S. Conference of Catholic Bishops (USCCB). Also make available biblical and theological dictionaries.

2. **Assign** the students to read article 28, "Comparison and Contrast: John and the Synoptic Gospels," as well as the introductory material for the Gospel of John found in the student book in preparation for this learning experience.

3. **Begin** by asking the students to recall that John's Gospel has a unique structure, very different from that of the synoptic Gospels. John's Gospel consists of a prologue, a Book of Signs, and a Book of Glory. Explain that the student book also identifies chapter 21 of John's Gospel as an epilogue, which biblical scholars believe was a later addition to the text. Tell the students that today they will receive some basic information about the

structure of the Gospel of John and engage in close study of the prologue. In subsequent learning experiences, they will examine the Book of Signs and the Book of Glory.

4. **Present** the PowerPoint "The Structure of John's Gospel" (Document #: TX002271). Direct the students to take notes. After you conclude the presentation, invite brief comments or questions from the students. Remind them that this has been only an overview; they will explore the prologue, Book of Signs, and Book of Glory in greater depth today and in subsequent class sessions. You may wish to give the students a brief stretch break before proceeding.

5. **Organize** the students into pairs. Direct them to open their Bibles to John's prologue (1:1–18). Distribute a copy of the footnotes to any students who are not using the NABRE. Read the prologue aloud together as a class. Then draw the students' attention to the footnotes:

   ➤ Examining the footnotes that accompany a biblical text can be an important first step in biblical research and exegesis.

   ➤ The footnotes draw our attention to important issues of translation and meaning and also to connections with other passages in both Testaments.

   ➤ The footnotes for John's prologue are extensive and merit our consideration.

6. **Have** the students work with their partners, reading the footnotes carefully and recording in their notebooks three interesting facts they discover about the prologue from the footnotes. Allow about 10 minutes for the students to work.

7. **Draw** the class back together, and invite the students to volunteer what they discovered in the footnotes. Emphasize the extent to which our understanding of a text can deepen when we take the time to study the footnotes carefully.

   If the students did not comment on the references to the Old Testament found in the footnotes, point these out to them. Remind them that the footnotes draw our attention to the ways in which John incorporates theological concepts, themes, and images from the Old Testament into the prologue. Explain that the students will now examine some of the Old Testament passages to which John refers or alludes.

> **Teacher Note**
>
> If little time remains, you may continue this learning experience during the next class session.

8. **Direct** each pair of students to join with one or two other pairs near them (as determined by class size) to form six new groups. Distribute copies of the handout "Old Testament Themes and Images in John's Prologue" (Document #: TX002277). Assign each group one of the Old Testament passages listed on the handout, and provide each group with biblical or theological dictionaries. Review the questions on the handout with the students. Advise them that answering these questions will help them to

work toward creating a group image to post in the classroom, as directed in step 8 on the handout. Hand out the art paper and supplies. Allow 20 to 30 minutes for the groups to work; near the end of the allotted time, remind the groups to start working on their image if they have not started already. Circulate among the groups to offer help as needed, especially with creating the image.

9. **Invite** each group to share and explain its completed image to the class, as time permits. Offer clarifying comments as needed, including the following:

> **Teacher Note**
>
> If time is limited, you may wish to have the groups complete and share their images during the next class session.

> ➤ The prologue evokes a connection with Genesis from the first verse: "In the beginning." This emphasizes Jesus' preexistence with God the Father from all eternity.

> ➤ The prologue's emphasis on Jesus as the Word (in Greek, *logos*) bears a strong resemblance to the way in which Wisdom is portrayed in the Old Testament. Like the Word, Wisdom is also pre-existent, present with God at the beginning of time, during the creation of the world. The Word and Wisdom are both also described with the beautiful, striking imagery of light shining in darkness.

> ➤ The well-known line "the Word became flesh and dwelt among us" (v. 14) is literally translated as *tabernacled* among us." This makes an explicit connection with the tabernacle, or portable shrine, that the Israelites built to worship God during their years in the wilderness.

➤ In the Old Testament, God's glory filled that tabernacle and later filled the Temple built by King Solomon. According to John's prologue, that same glory of God is now visible in a new way: in Jesus, the Word made flesh.
10. **Conclude** by reminding the students that like the infancy narratives in Luke and Matthew, John's prologue functions as an overture to the rest of the Gospel: that is, it introduces many of the Gospel's key theological themes. Encourage the students to keep these themes in mind and to notice them as they resurface in the Book of Signs and the Book of Glory. Finally, affirm the students' close and careful study of the prologue. Note that they probably did not realize how much meaning could be derived from a relatively brief passage.

11. **Post** the images the students created in one section of the classroom, if space permits. As other work is posted regarding the Book of Signs and the Book of Glory, you will be creating a valuable visual reminder of the structure of John's Gospel.

Step 6

Facilitate the students' examination of the Book of Signs, emphasizing how the signs move those who witness them to greater faith.

Articles
29, 30,
31

1. **Prepare** by writing on the board these questions that the students will answer regarding the signs in the Book of Signs:

   - What is the attitude of the people surrounding Jesus at the *beginning* of the story?
   - In what way or ways is this attitude different by the *end* of the story?
   - Who comes to greater faith in Jesus in the course of the story? Who, if anyone, resists or rejects this faith?
   - Does this story symbolize faith through any particular image? If so, how?
   - How does the sign reveal Jesus' glory (that is, his divinity and his heavenly home)?

   Gather paper (legal-sized or larger) and art supplies for the students to create their storyboards.

2. **Assign** the students to read article 29, "Allegory in the Seven Signs"; article 30, "The Paschal Mystery in the Gospel of John"; and article 31, "John's Post-Resurrection Accounts"; in the student book as preparation for this learning experience. Ask them to bring their Bibles for this class session.

Teacher Note

In this learning experience, the multiplication of the loaves and the walking on water are considered together, because they appear back-to-back in John, chapter 6. Because the multiplication of the loaves and the wedding at Cana were both studied in step 4, you also may wish to ensure that the students who worked with those passages in step 4 study a different passage today.

---

3. **Begin** by prompting the students to recall the structure of John's Gospel: the prologue, the Book of Signs, and the Book of Glory, plus the epilogue. Today's class will focus on the Book of Signs.

4. **Organize** the students into six groups. Assign each group one of these signs:

   - turning water into wine at the wedding at Cana (2:1–12)
   - healing of the royal official's son (4:46–54)
   - healing a sick man at the pool of Bethesda (5:1–18)
   - multiplication of the loaves, and walking on water (6:1–21)
   - healing of the man born blind (9:1–41)
   - raising of Lazarus (11:1–45)

5. **Direct** the students to read their assigned passage and to write brief responses to the questions you have written on the board. Allow 10 to 15 minutes for the students to work.

6. **Draw** the class back together, and invite each group to report its findings to the class. Direct the students to note similarities among the groups' findings. In particular, draw their attention to the following commonalities among the signs:

   ➤ In all the signs, belief or faith, or the lack thereof, is a central focus.

   ➤ In the accounts of the signs, an individual (like the man born blind, as in 9:38) or a group of people (like the disciples, as in 2:11) comes to greater faith in Jesus because they have witnessed or participated in a sign.

   ➤ However, not everyone who witnesses a sign comes to greater faith. In fact, sometimes the signs prompt greater hostility toward Jesus or toward those who believe in him, as in 5:18 and 9:34.

   ➤ These varied reactions to the signs help us to understand that the signs are not magic tricks that automatically lead to expressions of awe and faith. Rather, the internal attitude of the person witnessing the sign is key: if someone is open to faith, the sign allows that faith to grow and deepen. If someone persists in unbelief and hostility, even the greatest sign—raising Lazarus from the dead—has no transformative effect.

7. **Have** the students work in the same groups to create a storyboard of the sign on which they have been focusing. Explain that a storyboard is like a comic strip, but with no dialogue or captions—the flow of the story is evident simply from the images. Tell the students that their storyboards must contain at least six images, at least one of which must attempt to capture the moment at which an individual or group comes to greater faith because of the sign. Acknowledge that this intangible reality can be difficult to express in an image, and suggest that the careful use of color, symbol, or abstraction can help. Allow the groups 20 to 25 minutes to create their storyboards.

8. **Display** the storyboards in the classroom, and direct the students to take a "gallery tour" to examine the work of their classmates. In particular, invite them to notice how the various groups depicted the moment at which a person or group came to greater faith because of the sign. Draw the class back together, and invite comments, questions, and reflections.

9. **Post** the storyboards in a second section of your classroom, as you continue to create a visual reference for the three sections of John's Gospel.

10. **Transition** into the homework assignment using these or similar words:

    ➤ The people who witnessed the signs had to have open minds, hearts, and spirits for the signs to move them to greater faith. If they were closed even to the *possibility* of faith, then the signs would have had no effect on them, or even a negative effect.

➤ The events of our own lives are similar. If we are open to faith, both the joys and struggles of our lives can be "signs" for us; that is, they can reveal the presence of God to us and deepen our relationship with the One who called us into being, who loves us unconditionally, and who leads us to the truth.

➤ Think about a past or present event or experience in your life that could be a "sign" for you of God's glory and infinite love. This event or experience may on the surface seem ordinary, but when interpreted through the eyes of faith, it can be profoundly meaningful. Examples include taking a risk to try something new; completing a challenging school assignment; experiencing the birth of a sibling, niece, or nephew; engaging in community service; or coping with the illness or death of a family member.

➤ As homework, write a substantial paragraph in which you describe this event or experience and reflect on how it has moved you to greater faith.

11. **Have** volunteers take a few minutes during the next class session to share their homework reflections (perhaps as part of the prayer to begin class). Conclude these reflections by inviting students to connect both the "signs" of John's Gospel and the "signs" of their ordinary lives with the Sacraments. Just as the signs prompt greater faith in those who are open to it, so too the Sacraments lead us to a more profound relationship with God if we are open to that possibility.

Step 7

Guide the students in searching for and analyzing artwork that depicts selected scenes from the Book of Glory.

1. **Prepare** by reserving the computer lab for this class session or by ensuring that the students will have access to laptops with an Internet connection. Gather five large pieces of newsprint and some markers, and arrange for the use of an LCD projector for student presentations of the artwork they find. Download and make copies of the handout "Analyzing Artistic Depictions of the Book of Glory" (Document #: TX002278), one for each student.

2. **Begin** by prompting the students to recall the structure of John's Gospel: the prologue, the Book of Signs, and the Book of Glory, plus the epilogue. Point out that today's class will focus on the Book of Glory, and in particular those aspects of the Book of Glory that are unique to John's account of Jesus' Passion, death, and Resurrection.

3. **Distribute** the handout "Analyzing Artistic Depictions of the Book of Glory" (Document #: TX002278), and read through the directions together. Then organize the students into five groups, and assign each group one of the passages from the Book of Glory that are listed on the handout. Give the groups a piece of newsprint and some markers to record their responses to the questions posed on the handout. Have the students follow the directions on the handout. Allow the next 30 to 40 minutes for them to search for images, create their PowerPoint presentations, and analyze the images they select. The Web sites listed on the handout should provide ample images from which to choose; supervise the students to ensure that they are not visiting other sites.

4. **Have** each group present its PowerPoint presentation to the class. The groups can use their notes from the newsprint to comment on and analyze each image. Invite reflections, questions, and reactions from the class. In particular, engage the students in a discussion of the extent to which viewing these images has enhanced, focused, or broadened their understanding of the Gospel of John in general and the Book of Glory in particular. If time is short, student presentations of their findings may occur during the next class session.

> **Teacher Note**
>
> Discourage the students from searching for images via Internet search engines, because this approach is likely to be time-consuming and unproductive due to the volume of inappropriate or unhelpful images that such a search may yield.

5. **Post** the students' notes on their images in a third section of the classroom, completing the students' visual reference to the prologue, Book of Signs, and Book of Glory.

6. **Transition** into the homework assignment. Direct the students' attention to the visual reference for the structure of John's Gospel that they have created over the past several class sessions: the images connecting the prologue with various Old Testament passages; the storyboards on the Book of Signs; and the notes on the artistic depictions of the Book of Glory. Invite the students to consider all of this and then to write, as homework, at least one substantial paragraph in which they reflect on the following questions:

   - How is the Gospel of John different from the synoptic Gospels?
   - In particular, how is the Gospel of John unique from a literary perspective, a theological perspective, and a Christological perspective?

   Tell the students to be sure to address all three parts of John's Gospel in their response (excluding the epilogue).

Step 8

Lead the students in reflecting on and praying with some of the metaphors and symbols John uses to present the person of Jesus.

1. **Prepare** by obtaining large sheets of paper, 8½-x-14-inch (legal-sized) or 11-x-17-inch (tabloid-sized), one sheet for each student. Gather markers, crayons, or colored pencils. Ask the students to bring their Bibles to class. For the prayer that concludes this learning experience, you will need a chime to call the students to quiet meditation, or five small candles if a chime is unavailable.

Teacher Note

Further prepare for this learning experience by referring to the handout "Using a Mind Map" (Document #: TX001009) as background information for this learning experience.

---

2. **Begin** by reviewing with the students the following points that appear in the student book articles they have read as homework in previous steps:

   ➤ More than the other Gospels, the Gospel of John uses metaphors, symbolism, and allegory to communicate information about Jesus' identity and mission.

   ➤ One of the unique ways John does this is through the "I AM" statements. These are an allusion to Exodus 3:14, in which God revealed the Divine Name to Moses as "I am who I am." John uses these "I AM" statements (in Greek, *ego eimi*) to affirm Jesus' divinity.

   ➤ Some of the "I AM" statements stand alone; for example, "Amen, amen, I say to you, before Abraham came to be, I AM" (John 8:58). In others, John uses "I AM" to introduce an image, symbol, or metaphor that gives us profound insight into Jesus' identity and mission.

   ➤ Today's learning experience provides the opportunity to reflect on and pray with some of the beautiful, poetic language of John's Gospel, seeking a deeper understanding of the mission that lies at the heart of the person of Jesus and of our own call to share in that mission.

3. **Organize** the students into five groups. Assign each group one of the following verses from John's Gospel:

   • "I am the bread of life; whoever comes to me will never hunger, and whoever believes in me will never thirst" (6:35).

   • "I am the light of the world. Whoever follows me will not walk in darkness, but will have the light of life" (8:12).

   • "I am the resurrection and the life; whoever believes in me, even if he dies, will live" (11:25).

- "I am the way and the truth and the life. No one comes to the Father except through me" (14:6).
- "I am the vine, you are the branches. Whoever remains in me and I in him will bear much fruit, because without me you can do nothing" (15:5).

4. **Explain** that the students will be creating a mind map, using the central image of the Scripture verse they have just been assigned. If needed, remind the students that a mind map is a visual form of brainstorming, in which words, ideas, images, or symbols radiate outward from a central concept—similar to spokes on a wheel, although not necessarily as uniform. Each of these points may have subpoints branching out from it—the "map" illustrates the relationships among the various ideas. Remind the students that as with all brainstorming, there are no wrong "answers"; in fact, allowing the mind to free-associate with an image allows us to generate ideas that we may not have considered in a more restricted or structured exercise.

> **Teacher Note**
>
> The first part of this exercise is completed individually. You may wish for students to remain at their own desks for now, and then direct them to move when they need to collaborate with their group members.

> **Teacher Note**
>
> If your students are familiar with mind maps, you may truncate this sample exercise or skip it entirely.

5. **Illustrate** a mind map by showing a sample exercise on the board with an image not being used for this learning experience, such as "I am the good shepherd" (John 10:14). Invite the students to brainstorm ideas around this image as you record their thoughts on the board in the format of a mind map. For example, they may consider characteristics of a shepherd (patient, hardworking, strong, dedicated, willing to take risks for the sheep); the idea that a shepherd is a model for leadership (a leader who is willing to serve, who gives everything for the good of the group, and who does not seek accolades or recognition); and groups of people today who may need a "good shepherd" (people with addictions, those who are victims of violence, the unemployed, or people suffering from depression or mental illness). Help the students come to a good understanding of the concept of a mind map.

6. **Distribute** the large sheets of paper, one to each student, as well as markers, crayons, or colored pencils. Direct the students to write the central image from their assigned verse—bread, light, resurrection/life, way/truth/life, or vine—in the center of their paper. Then have the students work independently to create a mind map for that image. Allow 10 to 15 minutes for this process. You may wish to play soft, meditative background music to encourage the students to work quietly and reflectively.

7. **Have** the students gather with other students who worked on the same verse they did. Allow about 5 minutes for them to share and compare their mind maps. Invite them to notice how one image, rich in meaning, can generate numerous ideas.

8. **Direct** the students to work in their groups to use the ideas recorded on their mind maps to compose a collect that will be offered aloud at the conclusion of the class session. Explain that a collect is a prayer offered on behalf of a group ("collecting" the group's thoughts and needs) that often follows a specific format, commonly referred to as "YOU—WHO—DO—THROUGH":

   • YOU: Naming God

   • WHO: Identifying what God has done for us in the past

   • DO: Imploring God to respond to our present need

   • THROUGH: Offering our prayer through Jesus

Teacher Note

If little time remains, you may use the collects as the prayer to begin the next class session. Otherwise, proceed now, using the prayers to conclude this class session.

For example, a collect based on the sample mind map the class generated about the good shepherd might read: "[YOU] God, our faithful shepherd, you always desire what is best for us, your people. [WHO] You patiently respond to our every need and guide us to the right path when we are lost or confused. [DO] Draw near to those people who cry out today for your tender care, especially those who struggle with addiction, mental illness, or unemployment. Lighten their burdens, refresh their spirits, and strengthen them to persevere through all of life's struggles. [THROUGH] We ask this, as we ask all things, in the name of the one who called himself the Good Shepherd, Jesus, our Lord and brother. Amen."

9. **Allow** about 10 minutes for the students to work in their groups to write their collects. Remind them that their mind maps should provide the raw material for this task.

10. **Ask** each group to choose one member who will read the collect aloud. Then gather the class together in the large group. Identify the five students who will offer the collects aloud, and determine the order in which this will occur. Light a candle, or otherwise call the students to a prayerful, reflective attitude.

11. **Introduce** the prayer by reminding the students that this learning experience has enabled them to explore deeply several of the key metaphors and symbols John uses to present the person of Jesus, the Divine Son of God. Explain that sharing the collects in a meditative atmosphere will help everyone to continue to enter into the profound meaning of John's symbolic language.

Teacher Note

If you do not have a chime, you may light five small candles instead. Light the first candle and offer the first collect; then, after a full minute of silence, light the second candle, and so forth.

12. **Begin** by sounding the chime. Invite the first person to offer his or her collect, followed by about a minute of silence. Sound the chime again as a signal for the second person to offer his or her collect, again followed by a minute of silence. Repeat this process until all five collects have been offered. Finish with a final chime and an "Amen."

13. **Conclude** by emphasizing that good metaphors and symbols are not limited to only one correct meaning. Rather, they lend themselves to myriad interpretations, as each person brings his or her unique perspective to the task of exegesis. Explain that John has therefore given us a great gift: as we study, pray with, and reflect on the variety of images, metaphors, and symbols woven throughout his Gospel, we have the opportunity to deepen our understanding of Jesus, to grow in our relationship with him, and to cultivate our life of prayer and spirituality.

Understand

Step 9

Facilitate a critical examination of selected passages from John's Gospel that have often been misinterpreted as anti-Semitic.

1. **Prepare** by downloading and printing the following documents, one copy per student:

   - *Declaration on the Relation of the Church to Non-Christian Religions* (*Nostra Aetate,* 1965) (Vatican Council II)
   - *Guidelines and Suggestions for Implementing the Conciliar Declaration "Nostra Aetate"* (The Holy See, Commission for Religious Relations with the Jews, 1974)
   - "The Bible, the Jews, and the Passion," a 2004 article by Dr. Eugene J. Fisher, then associate director of the Secretariat for Ecumenical and Interreligious Affairs of the USCCB

   Although the students will read only one document, make copies of all three for each student to have for reference. Also download and make copies of the handout "The Gospel of John and Anti-Semitism" (Document #: TX002279). Ask the students to bring their Bibles for this class session. Make biblical or theological dictionaries available.

2. **Begin** by providing the students with the following historical and theological background information. Direct them to take notes.

   ➤ Recall that John's Gospel was the last of the four canonical Gospels to be written, between AD 90 and 100. Also recall that Jesus was Jewish, as were his first followers. These early believers were "Jewish Christians": they understood their faith in Jesus to be a natural extension and deepening of their Jewish identity. In proclaiming faith in Jesus as the Messiah, or the Christ, they did *not* renounce their Judaism.

➤ However, by the time John's Gospel was written, the early believers were facing a critical moment. Christianity was beginning to evolve into a new religion, separate and distinct from Judaism. Therefore, the people who had been Jewish Christians needed to make a decision: return to Judaism—leaving behind their newfound faith in Christ—or renounce Judaism and become Christian. It was no longer possible to engage in both religious traditions with integrity.

➤ John's Gospel was written with this situation as the backdrop. Biblical scholars believe that many passages in this Gospel reflect the tension between Jews and Christians at this time. For example, references to being "expelled from the synagogue" (such as 9:22 and 12:42) indicate that by the late first century, people who professed belief in Jesus were in fact being ousted from the Jewish community. Similarly, passages that speak of a division (in Greek, *schisma*) among the people (such as 7:43 and 9:16) reflect the break, or schism, occurring between Jews and Christians at the time this Gospel was written.

➤ Because of this historical situation, John's Gospel often depicts Jewish people in an unfavorable light. It is crucial to understand that this portrayal reflects the historical situation in which this Gospel was written. It does *not* reflect the current teaching of the Church regarding Judaism.

➤ Unfortunately, even in relatively recent times, many passages in John's Gospel have often been misinterpreted as anti-Semitic, as encouraging hatred toward and discrimination against Jewish people. Careful examination of these passages, along with relevant Church documents on this topic, can help to correct these misunderstandings.

Teacher Note

You may want to explain to your students that Fisher was an associate director for Jewish-Catholic relations of the USCCB Secretariat for Ecumenical and Interreligious Affairs from 1977 to 2007.

3. **Distribute** the three documents you downloaded and photocopied. Organize the students into groups of three students (or four students, if needed due to class size), and direct the groups to designate each person in the group as number 1, 2, or 3. If some groups have four members, there will be one duplicate number in the group. Tell the groups that the students who are number 1 will read *Relation of the Church to Non-Christian Religions*; students who are number 2 will read *Guidelines and Suggestions for Implementing "Nostra Aetate"*; and students who are number 3 will read the article by Fisher.

4. **Allow** about 15 minutes for the students to finish reading their assigned document. You may wish to have them highlight or annotate their document, indicating areas of the document with which they agree, those with which they disagree, and those they find confusing. Biblical or theological dictionaries may also aid reading comprehension.

5. **Direct** each group to appoint a timekeeper. Ask each member of the group to take at least 2 but not more than 3 minutes to share the contents of his

or her document with the group, noting key points of information, what stood out, what was surprising, and questions. The other members of the group should take brief notes.

6. **Distribute** the handout "The Gospel of John and Anti-Semitism" (Document #: TX002279), and assign each group one of the passages from John's Gospel listed on the handout. More than one group may work on the same passage. Have the students work in their groups to understand the passage and to complete the hand-out. Circulate among the groups to offer assistance as needed. Allow 15 to 20 minutes for the groups to work.

> **Teacher Note**
>
> If little time remains, you may pause at this point and continue this learning experience during the next class session.

7. **Draw** the class back together, and invite each group to share its findings, as time permits. Emphasize how the principles put forward in these documents can and should inform our approach to these difficult and problematic texts from John's Gospel. Be sure to mention the following specific points if they do not come up in the discussion:

   • *Relation of the Church to Non-Christian Religions* represented a monumental shift in Catholic theology: it removed the charge of deicide (literally, "God-killing") that for centuries had been levied against all Jews of every time and place. The document states that the Jewish authorities "pressed for the death of Christ" (4), but that not all Jews of that time nor all Jews of subsequent generations can be held responsible for Jesus' execution.

   • The *Guidelines and Suggestions* document explains that John's Gospel often uses the phrase *the Jews,* when what is likely meant is Jewish *leaders,* not all Jews. This document suggests that when John's Gospel is publicly proclaimed in liturgy, translating this phrase as "the leaders of the Jews" or "the adversaries of Jesus" may be more accurate and less problematic.

   • The article by Fisher draws particular attention to the many pitfalls of presenting or depicting Jesus' Passion and death, whether in the liturgies of Holy Week, in Passion plays, or in film. Great care must be taken not to portray these events in a way that is explicitly or implicitly anti-Semitic.

8. **Conclude** by reminding the students that, unfortunately, anti-Semitism is not simply a historical curiosity. In recent history, anti-Semitism made possible the slaughter of six million Jews in the Holocaust. Point out that it is particularly tragic when Christian Scripture is misused to support this type of ideology. Explain that good scholarship, thorough research, and responsible exegesis can help to avoid this.

Step 10

Make sure the students are all on track with their final performance tasks, if you have assigned them.

If possible, devote 50 to 60 minutes for the students to ask questions about the tasks and to work individually or in their small groups.

1. **Remind** the students to bring to class any work they have already prepared so that they can work on it during the class period. If necessary, reserve the library or media center so the students can do any book or online research. Download and print extra copies of the handouts "Final Performance Task Options for Unit 5" (Document #: TX002273) and "Rubric for Final Performance Tasks for Unit 5" (Document #: TX002274). Review the final performance task options, answer questions, and ask the students to choose one if they have not already done so.

2. **Provide** some class time for the students to work on their performance tasks. This then allows you to work with the students who need additional guidance with the project.

Step 11

Provide the students with time to complete and reflect on their chart of the four Gospels.

1. **Ask** the students to bring their copies of the unit 3 handout "Chart of the Gospels" (Document #: TX002245) for this class session. At this point, this chart should be complete except for the column on John.

2. **Tell** the students that today they will complete the final column in their chart, the one on the Gospel of John. As in prior units, emphasize that the students are not to simply copy this information from the student book. Rather, they are expected to begin with the student book and to supplement with other information they learn in class and through research on their own. Help them to understand that in creating a personalized chart for themselves, they are building a valuable reference that they may use throughout this course.

3. **Allow** about 20 minutes for the students to complete the John column in class.

Teacher Note

You may assign this task as homework and begin this learning experience at substep 4.

4. **Invite** the students to look back at their completed charts. In the current unit and in the two prior units, they have gained a significant amount of knowledge about all four Gospels. They are now in a position not only to compare the Gospels from theological, literary, and historical perspectives but also to reflect on which Gospel speaks most profoundly to their own spirituality. Invite the students to consider these or similar questions to prompt their thinking:

   • Which Gospel speaks to my own heart most clearly?

   • Which Gospel inspires me to live my faith through both the joys and struggles of life?

   • Which Gospel seems to provide direction for my life?

   • Which Gospel do I feel most drawn to intellectually? spiritually? emotionally?

   • Which Gospel challenges me to be a more faithful disciple?

   • Which Gospel presents Jesus in the way that I can best relate to, as a true friend and Savior?

   Direct the students to select the one Gospel that appeals to them most, based on their reflection on these questions, and then to write a one- to two-paragraph reflection explaining their choice. Allow about 10 minutes for the students to write. You may wish to play quiet instrumental music to foster a prayerful atmosphere.

5. **Organize** the students into pairs. Allow about 10 minutes for the partners to share their reflections. Invite them to notice similarities and differences not only in which Gospel they chose but also in their rationales. For example, some students may have chosen the same Gospel, but for entirely different reasons. Direct the students to write a brief, two- or three-sentence addendum to their reflections that summarizes and comments on the key points of their conversation with their partner.

6. **Draw** the class back together, and use a show of hands to determine how many of your students chose each Gospel. Invite at least one student who chose each Gospel to share the basis for his or her choice. Comment as appropriate, noting interesting points of comparison and contrast among the students' remarks.

7. **Conclude** by telling the students that many people of faith throughout the centuries have had a favorite Gospel—one that truly nourished their spirits and challenged them to deeper, more faithful discipleship. As the students continue to develop their faith in the coming years, they may wish to notice whether their favorite Gospel shifts: that is, as they grow in maturity or come to understand their faith more deeply, a different Gospel portrait of Jesus may appeal to them. Emphasize that in the life of a person of faith—of any age—the four Gospels have been and will remain a privileged way of encountering the person of Jesus and growing in fidelity to the mission he shares with all those who believe.

Step 12

Provide the students with a tool to use for reflecting on what they learned in the unit and how they learned.

This learning experience will provide the students with an excellent opportunity to reflect on how their understanding of the Gospel of John has developed throughout the unit.

1. **Prepare** for this learning experience by downloading and printing the handout "Learning about Learning" (Document #: TX001159; see Appendix), one for each student. Ask the students to bring in the handout "The Gospel of John: Myths and Facts" (Document #: TX002272) that they worked on at the beginning of this unit.

2. **Distribute** the handout and give the students about 15 minutes to answer the questions quietly. For the question "How did your understanding of the subject matter change throughout the unit?" refer the students back to the handout "The Gospel of John: Myths and Facts" (Document #: TX002272) that they worked on at the beginning of the unit. Invite them to consider these questions:

   • Which fact is much clearer to you now than at the beginning of the unit? What learning experiences helped you to clarify or deepen your understanding?

   • Which myth could you now challenge and correct if you were to hear or read this incorrect information? What learning experiences equipped you for this task?

3. **Invite** the students to share any reflections they have about the content they learned as well as their insights into the way they learned.

4. **Direct** the students to keep this handout in a separate section of their folder or binder so that they can refer back to it at the conclusion of the course.

The Gospel of John: Myths and Facts

In the blank space next to each statement, write the word *myth* or *fact* to indicate which one you believe that statement to be.

1. _____ The Gospel of John has nothing in common with the synoptic Gospels.

2. _____ In the Gospel of John, Jesus is a divine being, not a human being.

3. _____ The Gospel of John emphasizes Jesus' divinity.

4. _____ The Gospel of John promotes hatred of and discrimination against Jewish people.

5. _____ John's account of the birth of Jesus is the basis for many popular Christmas traditions.

6. _____ The Gospel of John begins with a poem.

7. _____ In the Gospel of John, Jesus does not perform miracles.

8. _____ The Gospel of John uses more metaphors and symbolism than do the synoptic Gospels.

9. _____ The Gospel of John was written during a time of great turmoil and transition in the early Christian community.

10. _____ The Gospel of John is incomprehensible to most Catholics.

11. _____ Key texts from John's Gospel are used in the liturgies of Lent, Holy Thursday, and Good Friday.

12. _____ The Gospel of John was the last canonical Gospel written.

13. _____ John's Gospel follows the same basic structure as the synoptic Gospels.

14. _____ Many famous and well-loved passages in John's Gospel—like "I am the vine, you are the branches" (John 15:5), "I am the bread of life" (John 6:3), and "I am the way and the truth and the life" (John 14:6)—do not appear in the synoptic Gospels.

Document #: TX002272

Final Performance Task Options for Unit 5

Important Information for All Three Options

The following are the main ideas that you are to understand from this unit. They should appear in this final performance task so that your teacher can assess whether you learned the most essential content.

- The Gospel of John consists of a prologue, the Book of Signs, the Book of Glory, and an epilogue.

- John portrays Jesus as the Divine Son of God.

- The Gospel of John presents the person of Jesus through metaphors and symbolism.

- Careful exegesis of John's Gospel enables us to avoid any damaging anti-Semitic misinterpretations.

In addition to demonstrating understanding of these four main concepts of the unit, your final performance task must also contain or demonstrate the following:

- In-depth, substantial content appropriate for an upper-level high-school religious studies course

- Responsible and accurate use of Scripture

- Substantive content that creatively and accurately engages with and interprets the material of this unit

- Proper grammar, spelling, and diction

- A neat and well-organized presentation

Option 1: An Exegetical Paper

Choose one passage from the Gospel of John, approximately five to fifteen verses in length. Ask your teacher to approve the passage that you select. Then research and write a four- to five-page exegetical paper in which you interpret that passage. Use one of the exegetical methods you studied in unit 2, and consult at least three sources of information other than your textbook. Your paper should follow this structure:

- An introduction that situates the passage you have chosen within the broad context of the literary structure and theological emphases of John's Gospel

- An overview of the major topics or questions regarding the selected passage that your paper will explore

Document #: TX002273

- A explanation of the methodology you will use to interpret the passage—that is, literary, sociohistorical, or ideological

- At least three substantive body paragraphs in which you analyze the passage using the methodology you have chosen and present your interpretation

- A conclusion in which you apply your interpretation of the passage to some aspect of the world today: for example, a concern that many young people face, a problem that your school is encountering, or a pressing matter of national or international justice

- A bibliography

Option 2: A Triptych

A triptych is a painting or drawing with three side-by-side sections, all of which present different facets of a common theme. Generally, the image in the middle section of the triptych focuses the viewer's attention on a core or central aspect of that theme; the images on either side supplement, support, or broaden the viewer's understanding.

Use any artistic media to create a triptych that presents the first three sections of John's Gospel: the prologue, the Book of Signs, and the Book of Glory. Incorporate what you have learned about John's literary, theological, and Christological emphases into your triptych. To accompany your artistic work, write a one-page (minimum) explanation, including a justification for your arrangement of the images (that is, your rationale behind which image you placed in the middle and which ones you put on the sides).

Option 3: A Presentation at a Youth Conference on Monotheistic Religions

Your diocesan office of youth ministry is sponsoring a conference for teens who practice the world's three monotheistic religions: Judaism, Christianity, and Islam. The conference has been designed to promote understanding among these three religions and to cultivate an appreciation for both our common roots and our uniqueness. You have been invited to facilitate a one-hour session at this conference on the Gospel of John, in which you present basic information about the Gospel, with particular attention to the way in which it has been misused to cause harm and division or to foster hatred and intolerance. Write a detailed outline for your session, including the content you will present and the strategies you will use to engage a religiously diverse group of young people in an exploration of this Gospel. Be sure to include creative activities that enable the group to interact with Gospel texts, and with each other, in meaningful ways.

Rubric for Final Performance Tasks for Unit 5

Criteria	4	3	2	1
Assignment includes all items requested in the instructions.	Assignment includes all items requested, and they are completed above expectations.	Assignment includes all items requested.	Assignment includes over half of the items requested.	Assignment includes less than half of the items requested.
Assignment shows understanding of the following concept: *The Gospel of John consists of a prologue, the Book of Signs, the Book of Glory, and an epilogue.*	Assignment shows unusually insightful understanding of this concept.	Assignment shows good understanding of this concept.	Assignment shows adequate understanding of this concept.	Assignment shows little understanding of this concept.
Assignment shows understanding of the following concept: *John portrays Jesus as the Divine Son of God.*	Assignment shows unusually insightful understanding of this concept.	Assignment shows good understanding of this concept.	Assignment shows adequate understanding of this concept.	Assignment shows little understanding of this concept.
Assignment shows understanding of the following concept: *The Gospel of John presents the person of Jesus through metaphors and symbolism.*	Assignment shows unusually insightful understanding of this concept.	Assignment shows good understanding of this concept.	Assignment shows adequate understanding of this concept.	Assignment shows little understanding of this concept.
Assignment shows understanding of the following concept: *Careful exegesis of John's Gospel enables us to avoid any damaging anti-Semitic misinterpretations.*	Assignment shows unusually insightful understanding of this concept.	Assignment shows good understanding of this concept.	Assignment shows adequate understanding of this concept.	Assignment shows little understanding of this concept.
Assignment uses proper grammar, spelling, and diction.	Assignment has no grammar or spelling errors.	Assignment has one grammar or spelling error.	Assignment has two grammar or spelling errors.	Assignment has more than two grammar or spelling errors.
Assignment uses its assigned or chosen media effectively.	Assignment uses its assigned or chosen media in a way that greatly enhances it.	Assignment uses its assigned or chosen media effectively.	Assignment uses its assigned or chosen media somewhat effectively.	Assignment uses its assigned or chosen media ineffectively.
Assignment is neatly done.	Assignment not only is neat but is exceptionally creative.	Assignment is neatly done.	Assignment is neat for the most part.	Assignment is not neat.

Vocabulary for Unit 5

collect: A prayer offered by a person leading an assembly in communal prayer, on behalf of a group ("collecting" the group's thoughts and needs). It often follows the "YOU—WHO—DO—THROUGH" format.

I AM: God's name as revealed to Moses at the burning bush; repeated by Jesus in John's Gospel. John uses the I AM statements to teach the divinity of Jesus.

metaphor: A figure of speech in which a word or phrase that ordinarily designates one thing is used to designate another, making an implied comparison.

New Eve: A reference to Mary, "mother of all the living," emphasizing her role in the new creation brought about by Christ. It is because Mary is the New Eve that in statues she is often portrayed standing on a snake, which represents the Devil in the Book of Genesis.

schism: A major break that causes division.

symbol: An object or action that points to another reality and leads us to look beyond our senses to consider a deeper mystery.

Document #: TX002275

Exploring John's Christology

1. Circle the passage that your group has been assigned.

   John 1:35–51   John 2:1–11   John 3:1–15   John 4:4–42   John 6:1–15

2. Read the passage carefully. Use biblical or theological dictionaries to look up words you don't understand.

3. Using the critical questioning method, write questions on your passage, following the critical questioning strategy. Write three questions for each level (for a total of nine questions). You don't need to answer the questions in writing, but be sure you can answer them aloud if asked. Write your questions in the blank space provided.

Document #: TX002276

4. When you form a new group with students who have read the other passages, use a new sheet of paper to take brief notes on each of the other four passages.

5. Compare your level 3 questions with those of your new group members. What similarities and differences do you notice among these questions? Write some brief observations here.

6. Drawing on your observations regarding your level 3 questions, and considering all five passages together, how would you describe John's Christology? In other words, how is Jesus presented in this Gospel? What aspects of his identity, personality, mission, and power are emphasized? What aspects are downplayed? What portrait of Jesus emerges from these passages? Work together to write responses to these questions.

Document #: TX002276

Old Testament Themes and Images in John's Prologue

1. Circle the passage that your group has been assigned:

   Genesis 1:1—2:4a   Proverbs 8:22–36   Wisdom 7:22b—8:1   Exodus 25:8–22

   Exodus 40:34–38   1 Kings 8:10–13 and 27–30

2. Read the passage carefully. Use biblical or theological dictionaries to look up words you don't understand.

3. Using your own words, write a two-sentence summary of this passage.

4. Where in the footnotes to John's prologue is this Old Testament passage referenced? In what ways is this passage related to the particular verse or section of the prologue that the footnote addresses?

5. In what ways is this passage connected with the overall theological emphases of the prologue?

Document #: TX002277

6. How does reading the Old Testament passage in its original context help you to better understand the theological and Christological points John is making in the prologue?

7. Why do you think John alludes to the Old Testament so frequently in the prologue? What effect do you think this would have had on those early believers who first heard or read this Gospel?

8. Discuss together how reading an Old Testament passage side by side with John's prologue helps to shed light on the meaning of the prologue. Then create an image that expresses the connection between the two passages. Rather than creating two images (one for each passage), create a single image that captures the relationship and commonality between the two passages. Use the bottom of this paper to sketch out your ideas, and then copy your image onto the newsprint you have been given.

Analyzing Artistic Depictions of the Book of Glory

1. Circle the passage from John's Gospel that your group has been assigned:

   - Jesus washing the disciples' feet: 13:1–17

   - the Beloved Disciple and the women at the foot of the cross: 19:25–27

   - piercing of Jesus' side: 19:31–37

   - appearance to Mary Magdalene at the empty tomb: 20:11–18

   - doubting Thomas: 20:24–29

2. Read the passage together carefully.

3. Find four artistic depictions of your group's Gospel story. Use the following Web sites:

   - *www.textweek.com* (look for the link to "art index," then search by Scripture reference or topic)

   - *www.wga.hu* (type a topic into the "text" box of the search engine)

   - *www.artcyclopedia.com* (click "browse artists by subject," then click on "religious art")

4. Choose four images that are substantially different from one another. Ways that images can be different include the following:

   - time periods

   - styles of art

   - countries of origin

   - artists

   - realistic / abstract

   - cultures

   - media (painting, sculpture, and so on.)

5. Organize all four images into one PowerPoint presentation; store this on a USB drive. Be sure to enlarge the images on the slides so that they are easily seen when projected in the classroom.

6. Prepare a presentation using the following questions as a guide to study and analyze each image. Write your answers on the newsprint provided. Asterisks on a question indicate that you must answer it. Choose several from among the others as you prepare your presentation.

- *What is the title of the piece? (Indicate if it is "untitled.")

- *Where is the piece located? (For example, is it in a museum or church? It is fine to say "unknown.")

- *Who is the artist? (It is fine to say "anonymous/unknown.")

- *When (approximately) was it created?

- *How accurately does the image depict the biblical story on which it is based? What, if anything, is missing? What has been added?

- How are the characters in the image depicted? With what emotions? What attitude is reflected in their body positioning? Are they static or in motion?

- In what medium (for example, oil, pen and ink, fresco) was the piece created?

- How would you describe the mood of the image? Notice color, shapes, forms, textures, and lines.

- How does the image use light and shadow? What dramatic emphasis is created?

- What do you think the artist wants the viewer to focus on?

- How does the image depict the passage of time? For example, is it a snapshot of a single moment, or does it depict many moments at once?

- *What spiritual, theological, or Christological message or meaning does the image convey?

- *To what extent does the image capture the particular themes and emphases of John's Gospel?

7. After you have studied and analyzed your images, discuss together the following questions, and write your answers on the newsprint for your presentation.

- How are the images you chose similar to or different from one another, with regard to mood, focus, style, and so on?

- Which image appeals to your group the most? Why?

- Which image do you think best captures the unique literary style and theological approach of John's Gospel?

- How would *you* create an image of this Gospel story? How would your work be different from that of the artists you have seen?

Using your PowerPoint and the notes you wrote on the butcher paper, you will present your images and share your analysis with the class in a 5-minute presentation.

The Gospel of John and Anti-Semitism

1. Circle the passage that your group has been assigned:

    John 5:18–47   John 6:32–59   John 7:11–36   John 8:31–59   John 18:28—19:16

2. Read the passage carefully. Use biblical or theological dictionaries to look up words you don't understand.

3. Describe the context of your assigned passage. For example, who is speaking, and to whom? Where is the passage set? What happens just before this passage, and what happens just afterward?

4. How would you characterize the tone of this passage?

5. Find and copy three specific quotes in this passage that portray the Jewish people in an unfavorable light.

6. How can one or more of the documents your group has read help you to understand this passage more accurately (that is, in a way that does not promote anti-Semitism)? Use at least two specific quotes from one or more of the documents to support your view.

Document #: TX002279

Unit 5 Test

Part 1: True or False

Write *true* or *false* in the space next to each statement.

1. _____ The Gospel of John has nothing in common with the synoptic Gospels.

2. _____ In the Gospel of John, Jesus is a divine being, not a human being.

3. _____ The Gospel of John emphasizes Jesus' divinity.

4. _____ The Gospel of John promotes hatred of and discrimination against Jewish people.

5. _____ John's account of the birth of Jesus is the basis for many popular Christmas traditions.

6. _____ The Gospel of John begins with a poem.

7. _____ In the Gospel of John, Jesus does not perform miracles.

8. _____ The Gospel of John uses more metaphors and symbolism than do the synoptic Gospels.

9. _____ The Gospel of John was written during a time of great turmoil and transition in the early Christian community.

10. _____ The Gospel of John is incomprehensible to most Catholics.

11. _____ Key texts from John's Gospel are used in the liturgies of Lent, Holy Thursday, and Good Friday.

12. _____ The Gospel of John was the last canonical Gospel written.

13. _____ John's Gospel follows the same basic structure as the synoptic Gospels.

14. _____ Many famous and well-loved passages in John's Gospel—like "I am the vine, you are the branches" (John 15:5), "I am the bread of life" (John 6:3), and "I am the way and the truth and the life" (John 14:6)—do not appear in the synoptic Gospels.

Part 2: Fill-in-the-Blank

Use the word bank to fill in the blanks in the following sentences. (*Note:* There are two extra terms in the word bank.)

Word Bank

water	Thomas	Bethlehem
blood	Peter	Samaritan
wine	Mary Magdalene	hymn
Nicodemus	Cana	Messiah

- In John's Gospel, Jesus' first sign is turning 1. _____ into 2. _____ at the wedding feast at 3. _____.

- The Pharisee whom Jesus teaches about being "born from above" is named 4. _____.

- Jesus meets a 5. _____ woman at a well and reveals himself to her as the 6. _____.

- The prologue to John's Gospel is a poem, likely used by early Christians as a liturgical 7. _____.

- When the side of the crucified Jesus is pierced, 8. _____ and water flow out of the wound.

- At the empty tomb, the Risen Christ commissions 9. _____ to share the Good News of the Resurrection with the other disciples.

- The Risen Christ invites 10. _____ to faith by urging him to touch Jesus' wounds.

Document #: TX002280

Part 3: Essay

Respond to the following with two to three substantial paragraphs.

1. Explain the structure of John's Gospel, including how each of the first three sections (excluding the epilogue) contributes to John's literary and theological approach to presenting the person of Jesus.

2. Why has the Gospel of John often been misinterpreted as anti-Semitic? How can we use responsible exegesis and the teachings of the Church to challenge these misinterpretations?

3. What is John's Christology? What literary tools does he use in presenting Jesus in this way?

Document #: TX002280

Unit 5 Test Answer Key

Part 1: True or False

1. False
2. False
3. True
4. False
5. False

6. True
7. False
8. True
9. True
10. False

11. True
12. True
13. False
14. True

Part 2: Fill-in-the-Blank

1. water
2. wine
3. Cana
4. Nicodemus

5. Samaritan
6. Messiah
7. hymn
8. blood

9. Mary Magdalene
10. Thomas

Part 3: Essays

1. The unique structure of John's Gospel consists of a prologue, a Book of Signs, and a Book of Glory, plus an epilogue that was added after the Gospel was completed. The prologue is a poem that the early Christians probably used as a liturgical hymn. As such, it circulated independently of the rest of the Gospel; sometime before the Gospel's completion, it was added to the beginning as a kind of overture. The prologue clearly introduces John's "high" Christology, that is, a Christology that emphasizes Jesus' divinity. In it, Jesus is presented as the Divine Son of God, the preexistent Word who was made flesh at a particular point in human history. To portray Jesus in this way, John draws on various Old Testament ideas, including the first Creation story in Genesis, the figure of Wisdom, and the idea of God's glory: the same glory that once filled the tabernacle and the Temple is now fully present in the person of Jesus.

   In the Book of Signs, Jesus performs seven miracles (which John calls signs, *semeion* in Greek). Those who witness the signs with an open heart, mind, and spirit are moved to greater faith in Jesus: they come to understand his identity more clearly and grow in their commitment to a life of discipleship. In contrast, those who are closed even to the possibility of faith sometimes develop greater hostility toward Jesus and his disciples as a result of the signs. The signs begin with Jesus' turning water into wine at the wedding feast at Cana and end with his raising Lazarus from the dead. Neither of these signs has a clear parallel in the synoptic Gospels.

   The Book of Glory recounts the story of Jesus' final days, beginning with the Last Supper and ending with the post-Resurrection appearances. It emphasizes the movement toward Jesus' "hour," when he will be "lifted up" on the cross in glory. Although the general trajectory of Jesus' arrest, trial, suffering, death, and Resurrection is similar to the narrative presented in the synoptic Gospels, the Book of Glory contains many unique elements. These include Jesus' washing of the disciples' feet at the Last Supper, the mysterious figure known as the Beloved Disciple, the piercing of Jesus' side, and the post-Resurrection appearances to Mary Magdalene and Thomas.

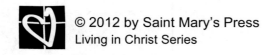© 2012 by Saint Mary's Press
Living in Christ Series

2. The Gospel of John has often been misinterpreted as anti-Semitic because in it Jesus frequently engages in vigorous debate and argument with Jewish leaders. There are also many references to "the Jews" conspiring to kill Jesus and to throw those who believed in him out of the synagogue.

Responsible exegesis can help us to understand such passages more accurately. First, biblical scholars maintain that many references to "the Jews" would actually be more accurately translated as "Jewish leaders." This helps us to remember that Jesus' disputes were not with the Jewish people as a whole (which would not make sense anyway, because he himself was Jewish), but rather with some of the Jewish leaders and teachers of his time period. Second, we must recall that John's Gospel was the last canonical Gospel to be written, approximately AD 90–100. By this point, Christianity had evolved into its own religion, separate from Judaism. Jesus' early followers, who had identified themselves as Jewish Christians, had to make the painful decision either to leave their Jewish roots behind and fully embrace Christianity, or else return to Judaism and reject their newfound faith in Jesus. This caused much tumult and upheaval within families, communities, and synagogues. Thus much of the tension and negativity surrounding "the Jews" in John's Gospel reflects these historical circumstances in which the Gospel was written.

The teachings of the Church can also shed light on the apparent anti-Semitism in John's Gospel. In the Vatican Council II document *Declaration on the Relation of the Church to Non-Christian Religions (Nostra Aetate),* the Church formally rejected the charge of deicide—God-killing—that had been levied against Jews for centuries. This shift in Jewish-Christian relations must inform any interpretation of a Gospel passage in which Jews are mentioned. Later Church documents, including the *Guidelines and Suggestions for Implementing "Nostra Aetate,"* have emphasized the need to pay careful attention to the way in which the Gospel of John, especially the Passion narrative, is read, used, and taught—especially, but not exclusively, in the liturgy. In translation, proclamation, preaching, art, and creative enactment, great care must be taken to avoid portraying the Jewish people in a negative light, either explicitly or implicitly.

3. Like all the canonical Gospels, John presents Jesus as both human and divine. However, he emphasizes Jesus' divinity, portraying him as the Divine Son of God, preexistent from all eternity and in full control of his saving mission on earth. One literary tool that supports this Christology is the "I AM" statements (in Greek, *ego eimi*). Sometimes the phrase "I AM" stands alone; other times, it is completed with a phrase. In either case, the "I AM" statements are used to support John's "high Christology" by alluding to God's appearance to Moses at the burning bush, in which God revealed the Divine Name to be "I am who I am." In other passages, John sometimes presents Jesus self-identifying as divine, as in his conversations with Nicodemus and the Samaritan woman at the well.

The signs, John's word for Jesus' miracles, reflect his divinity, not only in the acts themselves but also in the deepened faith they evoke in those who witness them with open minds and hearts. Finally, Jesus' divinity is clearly evident throughout the Book of Glory. Unlike the synoptic accounts of the Passion, the Jesus of John's Gospel experiences no agony in the garden, no fear or anxiety, and no sense of having been abandoned by God. Rather, he remains in full control of his emotions and actions until he draws his final breath, proclaiming, "It is finished."

Document #: TX002281

Unit 6

The Acts of the Apostles

Overview

In this unit the students continue their progress through the New Testament by engaging in close study of the Acts of the Apostles. By presenting biographical information about Paul, this unit also provides important background the students will need for their study of Paul's letters in unit 7.

Key Understandings and Questions

Upon completing this unit, the students will have a deeper understanding of the following key concepts:

- The Acts of the Apostles presents an ideal vision of the early Christian community.
- The Acts of the Apostles recounts the expansion of the Apostles' ministry to include the Gentiles.
- The Acts of the Apostles recounts the Apostles' missionary activities "to the ends of the earth."
- Paul was instrumental in the growth of the early Christian community.

Upon completing the unit, the students will have answered the following questions:

- How does the Acts of the Apostles describe the early Christian community?
- What was the significance of the Apostles' mission as recounted in the Acts of the Apostles?
- What was the mission of the Apostles?
- What role did Paul play in the growth of the early Christian community?

How Will You Know the Students Understand?

The following resources will help you to assess the students' understanding of the key concepts covered in this unit:

- handout "Final Performance Task Options for Unit 6" (Document #: TX002287)
- handout "Rubric for Final Performance Tasks for Unit 6" (Document #: TX002288)
- handout "Unit 6 Test" (Document #: TX002295)

Student Book Articles

This unit draws on articles from *The New Testament: The Good News of Jesus Christ* student book and incorporates them into the unit instruction. Whenever the teaching steps for the unit require the students to refer to or read an article from the student book, the following symbol appears in the margin: (📖). The articles covered in the unit are from "Section 2: The Synoptic Gospels and the Acts of the Apostles," and are as follows:

- "Witness to Christ in Jerusalem (Acts of the Apostles, Chapters 1–7)" (article 25)
- "Witness to Christ in Judea and Samaria (Acts of the Apostles, Chapters 8–12" (article 26)
- "Witness to Christ to the Ends of the Earth (Acts of the Apostles, Chapters 13–28" (article 27)

The Suggested Path to Understanding

This unit in the teacher guide provides you with one learning path to take with the students, to enable them to begin their study of the Acts of the Apostles. It is not necessary to use all the learning experiences, but if you substitute other material from this course or your own material for some of the material offered here, check to see that you have covered all relevant facets of understanding and that you have not missed knowledge or skills required in later units.

Step 1: Preassess what the students already know about the Acts of the Apostles by conducting a "chalk talk" session.

Step 2: Follow this assessment by presenting to the students the handouts "Final Performance Task Options for Unit 6" (Document #: TX002287) and "Rubric for Final Performance Tasks for Unit 6" (Document #: TX002288).

Step 3: Present a basic introduction to the Acts of the Apostles, and then invite the students to begin reading Acts using the practice of Sustained Silent Reading (SSR).

Step 4: Guide the students in examining key texts in which the Acts of the Apostles presents an ideal vision of the early Christian community.

Step 5: Facilitate the students' creation of a large map of the ancient Mediterranean world that can be used as a reference for the remainder of the course.

Step 6: Guide the students in discovering more about the cities of the Roman Empire in which the Apostles first preached the Good News to both Jews and Gentiles.

 Step 7: Lead the students in exploring the mission of the Apostle Peter through a close reading of the first half of the Acts of the Apostles.

 Step 8: Introduce the mission of the Apostle Paul through a close reading of the second half of the Acts of the Apostles.

 Step 9: Present information regarding Paul's missionary journeys that the students will apply in several creative ways.

 Step 10: Make sure the students are all on track with their final performance tasks, if you have assigned them.

 Step 11: Provide the students with a tool to use for reflecting on what they learned in the unit and how they learned.

Background for Teaching This Unit

Visit *smp.org/LivinginChrist* for additional information about these and other theological concepts taught in this unit:

- "Paul's Cultural Context" (Document #: TX002282)
- "The Acts of the Apostles" (Document #: TX001061)

The Web site also includes information on these and other teaching methods used in the unit:

- "Chalk Talk" (Document #: TX002283)
- "Using the Jigsaw Process" (Document #: TX001020)
- "Sustained Silent Reading" (Document #: TX002237)

Scripture Passages

Scripture is an important part of the Living in Christ series and is frequently used in the learning experiences for each unit. The Scripture passages featured in this unit are as follows:

- Acts 2:42–47 (communal life of the early believers)
- Acts 4:32–37 (the early Christians holding all things in common)
- Acts 3:1–26 (cure of a beggar at the Temple)
- Acts 5:1–11 (Ananias and Sapphira)
- Acts 8:4–25 (Simon the magician and the mission in Samaria)

- Acts 9:1–22 (Paul's conversion and journey to Damascus)
- Acts 13:4—14:28 (Paul's first missionary journey)
- Acts 15:40—18:23 (Paul's second missionary journey)
- Acts 16:11–40 (the conversion of Lydia; Paul's imprisonment in Philippi)
- Acts 17:1–9 (Paul in Thessalonica)
- Acts 18:1–11 (Paul in Corinth)
- Acts 19:1—21:40 (Paul's third missionary journey)
- Acts 19:23–40 (the riot of the silversmiths in Ephesus)
- Acts 27:1—28:16 (Paul's final journey)
- Acts 28:11–31 (Paul in Rome)

Vocabulary

The student book and the teacher guide include the following key terms for this unit. To provide the students with a list of these terms and their definitions, download and print the handout "Vocabulary for Unit 6" (Document #: TX002289), one for each student.

elder	Hebrews
eunuch	Hellenists
Gentile	presbyter

Learning Experiences

Explain

Step 1

Preassess what the students already know about the Acts of the Apostles by conducting a "chalk talk" session.

1. **Prepare** by reviewing the method article "Chalk Talk" (Document #: TX002283). Organize space and materials for the chalk talk: newsprint and markers, board space and markers or chalk, or an interactive white board. If your class size is small to medium (no larger than approximately twenty students), plan to conduct the chalk talk as one large group. If your class is larger than twenty students, plan to divide the class into two or three groups of ten to fifteen students each. Each group will need a large piece of newsprint or a section of board space, along with markers or chalk, one for each student. Draw a circle in the middle of each piece of paper or section of board space on which the students will work; in the middle of this circle, write "The Acts of the Apostles."

2. **Begin** by introducing the focus of this new unit: the Acts of the Apostles. Explain that, as in prior units, you would like to see what the students already know about the new topic, as well as what questions they have.

3. **Explain** the logistics of the chalk talk procedure:

   ➤ Chalk talk is a silent learning experience. Once it begins, you must remain silent until I announce that the learning experience has concluded.

   ➤ Anyone may participate in the chalk talk at any time by writing a comment or question on the paper or board. As more comments and questions are written, you may comment on the comments, drawing connecting lines to illustrate the flow of ideas.

   ➤ You may write whatever ideas you have about the topic, even if those ideas are not fully formed, or even if you are not sure whether they are correct.

4. **Distribute** materials and begin the chalk talk. If the students seem unsure at the beginning, you may write an initial thought or two to prompt them, such as "the Apostle Paul" or "the Apostle Peter" or "relationship to Luke's Gospel." You may add information at other points during the chalk talk as well, or you may choose simply to observe, saving your comments for the conclusion of the exercise. Allow the chalk talk to proceed for at least 5 minutes, and longer if it seems worthwhile. Because there may be extended periods in which the students simply look at the chalk talk and consider what else to write, be wary of stopping the exercise prematurely.

5. **Allow** the students to step back and examine the finished product at the conclusion of the chalk talk exercise. Invite general observations with the following questions:

   • To what extent are you surprised by how much you, as a class, already know about the Acts of the Apostles?

   • What are your most pressing questions about the Acts of the Apostles?

   • *(If your students did the chalk talk in small groups)* What similarities and differences do you notice among the chalk talks?

   Affirm your students' prior knowledge of the Acts of the Apostles by pointing out examples of correct information on the chalk talk. You may also wish to indicate examples of incorrect or incomplete information, assuring the students that these will be corrected as the unit proceeds.

6. **Save** the chalk talk so that you can refer to it throughout the unit, especially at the conclusion. If your students used an interactive white board, save the chalk talk using the software that accompanies this equipment. If your students used a standard white board or chalk board, take a digital photograph of the chalk talk before you erase it. If they used newsprint, save this, perhaps hanging it in the classroom as a visual point of reference.

7. **Refer** to the chalk talk throughout the unit as appropriate, correcting mistakes on it or elaborating on points that were not fully developed. Alternatively, you may wish to refer back to it only at the unit's conclusion, as the students reflect on all that they have learned about the Acts of the Apostles.

Step 2

Follow this assessment by presenting to the students the handouts "Final Performance Task Options for Unit 6" (Document #: TX002287) and "Rubric for Final Performance Tasks for Unit 6" (Document #: TX002288).

Teacher Note

Remind the students to choose their final performance task in accordance with any course requirements you may have established. In addition, if you are offering the semester-long portfolio project to your students (perhaps as part or all of their final exam), explain that students who wish to assemble a portfolio must choose option 1.

Teacher Note

You will want to assign due dates for the performance tasks.

If you have done these performance tasks, or very similar ones, with students before, place examples of this work in the classroom. During this introduction explain how each is a good example of what you are looking for, for different reasons. This allows the students to concretely understand what you are looking for and to understand that there is not only one way to succeed.

This unit provides you with three ways to assess that the students have a deep understanding of the most important concepts in the unit: writing an exegetical paper, creating an illustrated children's book, or developing a series of prayer experiences based on theological themes found in the Acts of the Apostles. Refer to "Using Final Performance Tasks to Assess Understanding" (Document #: TX001011) and "Using Rubrics to Assess Work" (Document #: TX001012) at *smp. org/LivinginChrist* for background information.

1. **Prepare** by downloading and printing the handouts "Final Performance Task Options for Unit 6" (Document #: TX002287) and "Rubric for Final Performance Tasks for Unit 6" (Document #: TX002288), one of each for each student.

2. **Distribute** the handouts. Give the students a choice as to which performance task to work on and add more options if you so choose.

3. **Review** the directions, expectations, and rubric in class, allowing the students to ask questions. You may want to say something to this effect:

   ➤ If you wish to work alone, you may choose option 1 or 2. If you wish to work with a partner, you may choose option 2 or 3. If you wish to work with a group of three or four, you may choose option 3 only.

   ➤ Near the end of the unit, you will have one full class period to work on the final performance task. However, keep in mind that you should be working on, or at least thinking about, your chosen task throughout the unit, not just at the end.

4. **Explain** the types of tools and knowledge the students will gain throughout the unit so that they can successfully complete the final performance task.

5. **Answer** questions to clarify the end point toward which the unit is headed. Remind the students as the unit progresses that each learning experience builds the knowledge and skills they will need in order to show you that they understand the Acts of the Apostles.

 Understand   ## Step 3

Present a basic introduction to the Acts of the Apostles, and then invite the students to begin reading Acts using the practice of Sustained Silent Reading (SSR).

1. **Prepare** by downloading the PowerPoint "Introducing the Acts of the Apostles" (Document #: TX002285) and arranging for the use of an LCD projector in your classroom. If needed, download and make extra copies of the unit 3 handout "Sustained Silent Reading Log Instructions" (Document #: TX002244). Ask the students to bring their Bibles to class.

2. **Begin** by explaining to the students that the Acts of the Apostles is a unique book in the New Testament and that some basic background information as this unit begins will be helpful for their study.

3. **Present** the PowerPoint "Introducing the Acts of the Apostles" (Document #: TX002285). Direct the students to take notes. Supplement the information on the slides with the "notes" appearing in the PowerPoint or with other information you deem relevant and appropriate.

4. **Direct** the students to get out their Bibles and Sustained Silent Reading (SSR) logs. Distribute copies of the handout "Sustained Silent Reading Log Instructions" (Document #: TX002244) to any student who needs one. Review these instructions with the students, and remind them of your expectations regarding the SSR log (for example, keeping it in a separate section of their binder or notebook), including your procedure for collecting and assessing this work.

5. **Tell** the students to begin reading the Acts of the Apostles during today's SSR session, keeping in mind the background information they learned from the PowerPoint presentation. Allow them to read for 15 minutes. Near the end of this time, remind them to make an entry in their SSR log.

6. **Provide** the students with a brief stretch break after SSR before continuing with the day's lesson.

> **Teacher Note**
>
> Consistently including a 15-minute SSR session in every subsequent class session will enable your students to read the Acts of the Apostles in its entirety during this unit and, more broadly, to cultivate the discipline of careful, reflective reading.

Article
25

Step 4

Guide the students in examining key texts in which the Acts of the Apostles presents an ideal vision of the early Christian community.

1. **Prepare** by gathering newsprint and markers.

2. **Assign** the students to read article 25, "Witness to Christ in Jerusalem (Acts of the Apostles, Chapters 1–7)," as well as the introductory material for the Acts of the Apostles found in the student book, as preparation for this learning experience. Ask the students to bring their Bibles for this class discussion.

3. **Begin** by organizing the students into pairs. Assign half of the pairs Acts 2:42–47 and the other half Acts 4:32–37. Explain that these brief passages give us information about life in the early Christian community in Jerusalem. After the pairs read the passage they have been assigned, ask them to write notes that respond to this question:

   • What vision of the early Christian community does this text present? For example, what are the community's characteristics, practices, and values?

   Give the pairs about 10 minutes to work.

4. **Invite** two or three pairs who worked on each of the two passages to share their findings with the class. List important points on the board, including, but not limited to, the following characteristics and practices of the early Christian community:

   • living communally, sharing material possessions
   • selling property to support the common good, especially supporting those in need
   • communal prayer, including celebration of the Eucharist ("the breaking of the bread")
   • a focus on the leadership of the Apostles as teachers and witnesses
   • continued practice of Jewish worship ("meeting together in the temple area")
   • a joyful spirit ("exultation" and "praising God")
   • a growing community that welcomes new members
   • unity ("one heart and mind")

5. **Pose** this question to the class:

   • Do you think that this vision was always fully and perfectly realized?

   It may be obvious to the students that the answer is no. To make this clear, have the students read aloud together the story of Ananias and

Sapphira (Acts 5:1–11). This passage may be most engaging if read in parts, with students taking the roles of the narrator, Peter, and Sapphira.

6. **Explain** to the students that, although the untimely deaths of Ananias and Sapphira may trouble us, this passage helps us to understand that not everyone in the early Christian community lived up to the ideal vision presented in Acts, chapters 2 and 4. The vision shows us what this early community strove for and worked toward—even though they sometimes fell short, both as individuals and as a community. Remind the students of the concept of "now and not yet" presented in unit 3 as a characteristic of the Reign of God. Explain that the ideal vision of the early Christian community that the Acts of the Apostles offers is similar. At the time that these texts were written, the beautiful vision presented in Acts, chapters 2 and 4, was "now," that is, "realized," to some extent. However, as Acts, chapter 5, demonstrates, that vision was also "not yet" *fully* realized.

7. **Direct** the students to have a brief conversation with their partners about this question:

   • Why do you think it is important to have an ideal vision—for ourselves or for a group of which we are a part—even if we do not always live up to it?

   After allowing 2 to 3 minutes for conversing, solicit responses from the class. Responses may include the following:

   • An ideal vision shows us what is possible if we work hard and make sacrifices to achieve our goals.

   • An ideal vision motivates us to do better or to improve our behavior or choices.

   • An ideal vision can be a tool for evaluating ourselves and monitoring our progress.

   • An ideal vision can refocus us on our priorities and commitments, especially when we may have gotten distracted or off track.

   • An ideal vision can challenge us to be more faithful to our values.

8. **Direct** the pairs of students to merge with one or two other pairs near them, to form groups of four to six students. Each group should then choose one community on which to focus for the remainder of this learning experience. It is best if each group chooses a different community. Possibilities include the following:

   • family
   • school
   • city or town
   • parish
   • youth group
   • sports team

- club
- group of friends
- class in school (such as juniors or seniors)
- student council officers
- retreat leaders

Everyone in the group need not belong to the community on which the group chooses to focus, but everyone should have at least some degree of familiarity with that community.

9. **Distribute** newsprint to the groups, and direct each group to write a paragraph in which it identifies and expresses an ideal vision of its chosen community. The vision should take into account the example of Jesus, the values of the Gospel, and even the lives of the early Christians in the Acts of the Apostles, as imperfect as they were. From this Christian perspective, what practices, behaviors, attitudes, and values should characterize the ideal family, school, team, and so on? The students may follow the general format and length of Acts 2:42–47 or Acts 4:32–37 as they write. Allow about 15 minutes for the groups to write their paragraphs and to copy them onto newsprint to post in the classroom.

10. **Allow** the students the opportunity to take a "gallery tour" to view the work of the groups. Encourage the students to pay particular attention to the ideal visions of the communities to which they themselves belong. To what extent do their attitudes and actions contribute to the realization of that ideal vision? To what extent do they detract from it?

11. **Remind** the students that the vision presented in the Acts of the Apostles, although idyllic, can inspire us to strive to live the Gospel with greater fidelity in every community of which we are a part. Acts shows us what is possible, when we are open to the presence of the Risen Christ and to the power of the Holy Spirit.

Step 5

Facilitate the students' creation of a large map of the ancient Mediterranean world that can be used as a reference for the remainder of the course.

1. **Prepare** by downloading and printing "Key Places in the Acts of the Apostles" (Document #: TX002290). Make enough copies of the map so that an equal number of students will work on each of the four quadrants. You will also need four large pieces of approximately 3-x-2-foot newsprint or poster board. The exact dimensions are not crucial as long as all four pieces are the same size. Gather markers, as well as other art supplies, such as glue, yarn, cotton balls, glitter, ribbon, small pieces of fabric, and wooden sticks.

Prepare resources that will allow the students to conduct some brief, basic research in class about the region on which their small groups will focus. This can be accomplished in one or more of the following ways:

- having printed resources available in your classroom, such as biblical dictionaries and atlases
- having four computers (one per group) with Internet access available in your classroom
- taking all students to the computer lab for a 20-minute research session
- sending selected students (two or three from each group) to the computer lab for a 20-minute research session

Alternatively, you could assign this research component as homework the previous night.

2. **Introduce** this learning experience with these or similar remarks:

   ➤ As mentioned in the PowerPoint presentation at the beginning of this unit, one important way in which the Acts of the Apostles differs from other books of the New Testament is the extent to which geography plays an important role in the events it describes.

   ➤ As you learned in the presentation, Acts recounts the spread of the Christian message from Jerusalem "to the ends of the earth" (Acts 1:8).

   ➤ It is important that we try to understand what "the ends of the earth" meant for these early Christians—remembering that they had a much more limited knowledge of the world than we do today.

   ➤ As we read about the Apostles' travels during the missionary campaign years—especially Paul's three missionary journeys and his final journey to Rome—we want to understand clearly the distance and geography they traversed.

   ➤ Today we'll work closely with a map of the ancient Mediterranean world and, in the process, create a visual aid to which we can refer throughout the remainder of this unit.

3. **Organize** the class into four groups, each of which will be assigned one of the four quadrants of the map. Give each group one of the four pieces of newsprint or poster board. Explain that the group will use the poster board to create a larger version of the section of the map they have been assigned. This larger version must have the following characteristics:

   - *to scale:* Tell the students they must carefully measure where to place the various locations on their newsprint or poster board. Explain that the quadrants will be joined together, so they must be to scale.

- *enhanced* and *three-dimensional:* Invite the students to use the art supplies you have provided to indicate the location of rivers, forests, mountains, other geographical features, and important landmarks. For example, a piece of blue ribbon may indicate a river, wooden sticks colored green may indicate a forest, and glitter may indicate a sandy coastline. Cotton balls could be sheep grazing on a hillside.

- *informed by research:* Ask the students to consult the print or online research sources to which they have access to get ideas about what to include on the map. For example, they may find that they want to draw the Temple in Jerusalem or the Parthenon in Athens.

Allow at least 30 minutes for the groups to complete their section of the map.

Teacher Note

Depending on the size of the groups, suggest that the groups organize into subgroups to focus on particular aspects of their task: for example, some group members could conduct research, several more could plot out the map on the poster board, and others might prepare the various objects to be glued onto the map.

4. **Post** the four finished quadrants together on the wall so that they form a large, complete map of the ancient Mediterranean world. After allowing time for the students to admire one another's work, review the following information with them, and ask them to find the boldfaced locations on the map:

   ➤ The Acts of the Apostles begins in and around **Jerusalem**, with the Ascension of Jesus and the sending of the Holy Spirit at Pentecost.

   ➤ Later, the Christian mission spreads to other cities in **Judea** (such as **Joppa** and **Caesarea**) and to **Samaria**.

   ➤ Paul, who is from the city of **Tarsus**, has an encounter with the Risen Christ as he is traveling to **Damascus**.

   ➤ The missionary campaign then extends north to **Seleucia** and **Antioch**, and west to the island of **Cyprus**, to **Iconium** (in **Galatia**), and to **Perga** (in **Pamphylia**).

   ➤ Paul's subsequent missionary journeys take him still farther west, into the cities of Asia Minor (for example, **Troas** and **Ephesus**) and Europe (for example, **Philippi**, **Thessalonica**, **Athens**, and **Corinth**).

   ➤ Paul makes his final journey to **Rome**, which for this time period was truly "the ends of the earth." By the time of Paul's death, the early Christian community had spread the Gospel message throughout much of the known world.

5. **Conclude** by pointing out that the students have created a valuable study aid to which they can refer throughout the unit. As they read the Acts of the Apostles, especially during SSR sessions, encourage them to consult the map as needed to visualize the geographical setting of Acts and the distances that the Apostles traveled to preach the Good News.

6. **Display** the map in the classroom at least for the remainder of this unit. The students will add to it during the learning experience on Paul's missionary journeys.

Articles
26, 27

 Step 6

Guide the students in discovering more about the cities of the Roman Empire in which the Apostles first preached the Good News to both Jews and Gentiles.

1. **Prepare** by ensuring that most or all students will have access to computers with Internet access during this class session. Gather art supplies, such as construction paper, newsprint, and markers. Download and print the handout "Cities of the Roman Empire, First Century AD" (Document #: TX002291), one for each student.

2. **Assign** the students to read article 26, "Witness to Christ in Judea and Samaria (Acts of the Apostles, Chapters 8–12)," and article 27, "Witness to Christ to the Ends of the Earth (Acts of the Apostles, Chapters 13–28)," in the student book as preparation for this learning experience.

3. **Begin** by inviting the students to reexamine the map they created during the prior class session. Remind them that virtually the entire area on that map was part of the Roman Empire. Share this basic information about the Roman Empire:

   ➤ The Roman *Republic* began around 500 BC and gradually expanded to become the Roman *Empire* around 44 BC, when Julius Caesar rose to power.

   ➤ Successive emperors expanded the empire's territory north into Britain, west to the Atlantic Ocean, south into the deserts of Africa, and east to the Euphrates River.

   ➤ The people of these various regions were diverse in language, religion, and way of life. Yet the influence of Roman values, culture, and social norms was felt throughout the empire, even in far-flung Judea, where Christianity began.

   ➤ This was the world into which the Apostles sought to bring the Christian message, first to Jews and then to Gentiles.

   Tell the students that they will learn more about this world, and the Apostles' mission, by investigating cities of the Roman Empire in which key events in the Acts of the Apostles took place.

4. **Organize** the class into eight groups. Distribute the handout "Cities of the Roman Empire, First Century AD" (Document #: TX002291). Assign each group one of the eight cities listed at the top of the handout.

5. **Have** the students begin to conduct Internet research on their assigned city. You may wish to supplement online resources with biblical dictionaries, atlases, and other printed materials. As you guide and assist the students, ensure that they focus on the correct historical time period (the first century AD). Also assure them that their research need not be comprehensive. Rather, they are simply trying to get a snapshot of life in that city during the time of the Acts of the Apostles. Therefore they do not necessarily need to answer every question listed on the handout. Allow 25 to 30 minutes for the students to conduct their research. As they finish, have them move on to the next steps on the handout: reading the passage from Acts that is set in their assigned city and preparing the advertisement for their city.

> **Teacher Note**
>
> If time is limited, you may assign completion of the advertisement as homework and plan time for the student presentations during the following class session.

6. **Have** the students present their findings to the class, including the following information:

- a synopsis of the information they found in their research
- a reading or summary of the Scripture passage
- an explanation of their advertisement

7. **Comment** as appropriate during or following the student presentations. You may wish to make the following points if the students do not make them:

➤ As the Acts of the Apostles begins in Jerusalem, we can see that the Apostles are preaching only to other Jews. Examples include Peter's speeches at Pentecost and in the Temple area after healing the beggar.

➤ As Acts continues, the Apostles bring the Gospel message to the Samaritans. Recall that the Samaritans, despite sharing a common religious heritage with the Jews, were often hated and misunderstood by the Jews. Yet they accept the Word of God (see Acts 8:14).

➤ Eventually, the Apostles preach the Gospel to the Gentiles, offering them the same Baptism that had been offered to the Jews and Samaritans. This is a significant development in the early Church, for it allows the Apostles the freedom to travel far and wide, sharing the Good News with all who are open to it, regardless of their religious background. Christianity would never have grown into a global religion without this change.

➤ The Acts of the Apostles tells us that many of the predominantly Gentile cities to which the Apostles traveled—like Thessalonica and Corinth—did have synagogues. This indicates that Jews and Gentiles coexisted in these cities and that, therefore, the Apostles could preach to both groups.

➤ In various parts of Acts, we see evidence of religious pluralism in the Roman Empire, for example, the practices of magic and fortune-telling and the worship of gods and goddesses (such as the cult of the goddess Artemis at Ephesus). It is into this incredibly diverse, complex world that the Apostles courageously brought the Gospel message, often at great risk to themselves.

8. **Conclude** by noting that these past two learning experiences have focused on the *world* in which the Apostles preached the Good News. The next two learning experiences will focus on the *people* who engaged in that ministry of preaching, most notably Peter and Paul.

 Interpret

Step 7

Lead the students in exploring the mission of the Apostle Peter through a close reading of the first half of the Acts of the Apostles.

1. **Prepare** by downloading and printing the handout "The Apostles Peter and Paul" (Document #: TX002292). The students will need the handout for this learning experience, as well as the next. Ask the students to bring their Bibles for this class session.

2. **Begin** by referring back to the chalk talk that the students created during the preassessment for this unit. Post the newsprint, or project the digital photograph for the students to see. Draw their attention to any information on the chalk talk regarding the Apostle Peter. Ask if the students remember any other facts about Peter from the New Testament, especially Gospel stories such as when Jesus gives him the keys to the Kingdom of Heaven in Matthew, his denials of Jesus in all four of the Passion narratives, and his seaside conversation with the Risen Christ in the Gospel of John. Help the students to understand that the Peter in the Acts of the Apostles is the same person: the Peter who denied that he even knew Jesus in the Gospels emerges in Acts as a key leader in the early Christian community.

3. **Ask** the students to count off by six. Assign each numbered group two chapters of Acts that prominently feature the Apostle Peter: chapters 1–2, 3–4, 5–6, 8–9, 10–11, and 12 and 15. Ask the students to use today's SSR session to read their assigned chapters individually, taking notes so that they can share what they learn about Peter with their classmates. Allow enough time for the students to finish their assigned SSR reading.

> **Teacher Note**
>
> You may assign this reading as homework, so that the students will arrive for class having already read their two chapters.

4. **Use** the jigsaw process to organize the students into groups of six people, in which each group member has read different chapters in the Acts of the Apostles. Beginning with chapter 1 and proceeding in order, ask the students to share within their groups the content of what they read, with particular attention to the Apostle Peter. What does Peter do and say in these chapters that gives us insight into both his personality and his mission? Direct the students to take notes on their group members' remarks. Allow about 15 minutes for this process.

5. **Distribute** the handout "The Apostles Peter and Paul" (Document #: TX002292). Have the students work in their groups to respond to the questions, based on what they have learned about Peter from their reading and discussion of the first half of Acts. Because the students will use this same handout for their study of Paul in the next learning experience, instruct them to write their responses on a separate piece of paper. Explain that each member of the group should record the group's responses, because all students will need to refer back to these notes. Allow 10 to 15 minutes for the groups to work.

6. **Draw** the class back together, and invite volunteers from each small group to share with the class their group's responses to the questions. As a portrait of Peter's leadership in the early Church begins to emerge from the students' responses, help them to understand how we can see our own mission to preach and act in the name of the Risen Lord reflected in the life and witness of Peter.

7. **Direct** the students to keep their notes on Peter and also to keep their copies of the handout "The Apostles Peter and Paul" (Document #: TX002292). Explain that they will need both for the next learning experience, which will focus on Paul, the other pillar of the early Church.

Step 8

Introduce the mission of the Apostle Paul through a close reading of the second half of the Acts of the Apostles.

1. **Prepare** by downloading and making copies of the handout "Peter and Paul Venn Diagram" (Document #: TX002293), as well as extra copies of the handout "The Apostles Peter and Paul" (Document #: TX002292). Ask the students to bring their Bibles for this class session.

2. **Begin** by referring back to the chalk talk that the students created during the preassessment for this unit. Post the newsprint, or project the digital photograph for the students to see. Draw their attention to any information on the chalk talk regarding the Apostle Paul. Ask if the students remember any other facts about Paul from the New Testament, perhaps information

they have learned in this course or in other religious studies courses, heard in a homily, or encountered in another venue.

3. **Ask** the students to count off by seven. Assign each number to groups of chapters of Acts that prominently feature the Apostle Paul: chapters 13–14, 16–17, 18–19, 20–21, 22–23, 24–25, and 26–28. Ask the students to use today's SSR session to read their assigned chapters individually, taking notes so that they can share what they learn about Paul with their classmates. Allow enough time for the students to finish their assigned reading.

Teacher Note

You may assign this reading as homework, so that the students will arrive for class having already read their assigned section.

4. **Use** the jigsaw process to organize the students into groups of seven people, in which each group member has read a different section in the Acts of the Apostles. Beginning with chapter 13 and proceeding in order, ask the students to share within their groups the content of what they read, with particular attention to the Apostle Paul. What does Paul do and say in these chapters that gives us insight into both his personality and his mission? Direct the students to take notes on their group members' remarks. Allow about 20 minutes for this process.

5. **Ask** the students to locate their copies of the handout "The Apostles Peter and Paul" (Document #: TX002292). Make extra copies available for students who may have misplaced theirs. Have the students work in their groups to respond to the questions, based on what they have learned about Paul from their reading and discussion of the second half of Acts. Remind them to use a separate sheet of paper for their responses. Explain that each member of the group should record the group's responses, because all students will need to refer back to these notes. Allow 10 to 15 minutes for the groups to work.

6. **Draw** the class back together, and invite volunteers from each small group to share their group's responses to the questions with the class. As a portrait of Paul's leadership in the early Church begins to emerge from the students' responses, help them to understand how instrumental Paul was to the growth of Christianity. His willingness to travel extensively (in an age when travel brought at best discomfort and at worst great danger), to minister courageously, and to extend the Gospel message to all people, both Jews and Gentiles, definitively shaped the community that over time became the Church.

7. **Distribute** the handout "Peter and Paul Venn Diagram" (Document #: TX002293). Direct the students to locate their notes on Peter from the previous learning experience. Ask the students to work either alone or with a partner to complete the Venn diagram, using their notes on both Peter and Paul. Tell them to write items that Peter and Paul have in common in the middle section, where the circles overlap; the students will write items unique to each person on the appropriate side of each circle. It is most

helpful if these latter items are written as corresponding points of contrast. For example, on the Peter side, students may write "was a follower of the earthly Jesus"; and then on the Paul side they would write "had an encounter with the Risen Christ." Allow about 10 minutes for the students to work.

8. **Gather** the class back together, and invite two or three students to reproduce their Venn diagrams on the board. Invite comments and questions as appropriate.

9. **Assign** a reflective writing assignment as homework. Direct the students to choose either Peter or Paul and write two short paragraphs, one in response to each of the following questions:

   - What was the significance of his (Peter's or Paul's) mission for the early Church? In other words, how did his mission shape the early Church in profound and lasting ways?

   - How does his mission give us, as the contemporary Church, an example to emulate?

10. **Conclude** by telling the students that in the next learning experience, they will continue their study of Paul by focusing on his missionary journeys.

Step 9

Present information regarding Paul's missionary journeys that the students will apply in several creative ways.

1. **Prepare** by downloading the PowerPoint "The Missionary Journeys of the Apostle Paul" (Document #: TX002286) and arranging for the use of an LCD projector in your classroom. Download and print the handout "Paul's Missionary Journeys" (Document #: TX002294), one for each student. Gather construction paper, four different colors of yarn, scissors, markers, and other art supplies.

> **Teacher Note**
>
> You may wish to remind the students that Paul also wrote Epistles, or letters, in the course of his travels. These will be the focus of the next unit.

2. **Begin** by reviewing basic information about the Apostle Paul from the previous learning experience. Remind the students in particular that Paul traveled extensively throughout the known world during the years of the missionary campaign. Today's learning experience will allow the students to become more familiar with the details of the travels Paul undertook to preach the Gospel.

3. **Present** the PowerPoint "The Missionary Journeys of the Apostle Paul" (Document #: TX002286). Direct the students to take notes, but advise them that they do not need to write down every detail (such as specific chapters and verses of Acts, or every city Paul visits). Assure the students that they will not need to remember the precise routes of all of Paul's journeys and that this overview has been designed simply to give them a flavor for Paul's commitment to preaching the Gospel, a commitment that brought him and his companions to the ends of the earth.

4. **Organize** the students into four groups. Distribute the handout "Paul's Missionary Journeys" (Document #: TX002294), and assign each group one of Paul's four journeys as listed on the handout. Have the students work in these groups to complete the three tasks regarding their group's assigned journey, as explained on the handout. Allow at least 30 minutes for the groups to complete these tasks. Depending on the size of the groups, you may wish to have the groups divide into subgroups to complete all three tasks in a timely fashion.

5. **Draw** the class back together, and invite the groups to present their travel brochures and postcards to their classmates. Offer comments and respond to questions as needed. Also examine the classroom map together, helping the students to understand both the routes and the distances Paul traveled.

6. **Direct** the students to reflect on all they have learned about the Apostle Paul in this unit, especially in this learning experience and the prior one. Tell them that their study of Paul will continue in the next unit, and ask them to respond to the following questions on a piece of paper:

   - What is one important fact you have learned about Paul during this unit?
   - What is one question you still have about any aspect of Paul's life, work, ministry, or importance to the ancient or contemporary Church?

   Collect these papers as the students leave the classroom.

> **Teacher Note**
>
> Although the maps of Paul's missionary journeys that appear in the student book are similar to those included in the PowerPoint, students may find it helpful to refer to their student books during the presentation so that they can examine the maps more closely.

> **Teacher Note**
>
> If little time remains in this class session, you may allow the students to complete the travel brochure and postcard as homework and present these during the next class session.

Step 10

Make sure the students are all on track with their final performance tasks, if you have assigned them.

If possible, devote 50 to 60 minutes for the students to ask questions about the tasks and to work individually or in their small groups.

1. **Remind** the students to bring to class any work they have already prepared so that they can work on it during the class period. If necessary, reserve the library or media center so the students can do any book or online research. Download and print extra copies of the handouts "Final Performance Task Options for Unit 6" (Document #: TX002287) and "Rubric for Final Performance Tasks for Unit 6" (Document #: TX002288). Review the final performance task options, answer questions, and ask the students to choose one if they have not already done so.

2. **Provide** some class time for the students to work on their performance tasks. This then allows you to work with the students who need additional guidance with the project.

Step 11

Provide the students with a tool to use for reflecting on what they learned in the unit and how they learned.

This learning experience will provide the students with an excellent opportunity to reflect on how their understanding of the Acts of the Apostles has developed throughout the unit.

1. **Prepare** for this learning experience by downloading and printing the handout "Learning about Learning" (Document #: TX001159; see Appendix), one for each student. Make the chalk talk from the unit preassessment available for the students to examine; that is, post the sheets of newsprint, or project the digital photographs of the chalk talk.

2. **Distribute** the handout and give the students about 15 minutes to answer the questions quietly. For the question "How did your understanding of the subject matter change throughout the unit?" refer the students back to the chalk talk. Invite them to consider these additional questions:

   • What is one example of an item on the chalk talk that you now understand more deeply than before? What learning experiences helped you to develop this understanding?

   • What is one example of an item on the chalk talk that you now know is incorrect or incomplete? What learning experiences enabled you to clarify or correct these inaccuracies?

3. **Invite** the students to share any reflections they have about the content they learned as well as their insights into the way they learned.

4. **Direct** the students to keep this handout in a separate section of their folder or binder so that they can refer back to it at the conclusion of the course.

Final Performance Task Options for Unit 6

Important Information for All Three Options

The following are the main ideas that you are to understand from this unit. They should appear in this final performance task so that your teacher can assess whether you learned the most essential content:

- The Acts of the Apostles presents an ideal vision of the early Christian community.

- The Acts of the Apostles recounts the expansion of the Apostles' ministry to include the Gentiles.

- The Acts of the Apostles recounts the Apostles' missionary activities "to the ends of the earth."

- Paul was instrumental in the growth of the early Christian community.

In addition to demonstrating understanding of these four main concepts of the unit, your final performance task must also contain or demonstrate the following:

- In-depth, substantial content appropriate for an upper-level high-school religious studies course

- Responsible and accurate use of Scripture

- Substantive content that creatively and accurately engages with and interprets the material of this unit

- Proper grammar, spelling, and diction

- A neat and well-organized presentation

Option 1: An Exegetical Paper

Choose one passage from the Acts of the Apostles, approximately five to fifteen verses in length. Ask your teacher to approve the passage that you select. Then, research and write a four- to five-page exegetical paper in which you interpret that passage. Use one of the exegetical methods you studied in unit 2, and consult at least three sources of information other than your student book. Your paper should follow this structure:

- An introduction that situates the passage you have chosen within the broad context of the literary, historical, and theological emphases of the Acts of the Apostles

- An overview of the major topics or questions regarding the selected passage that your paper will explore

- A explanation of the methodology you will use to interpret the passage—that is, literary, sociohistorical, or ideological

- At least three substantive body paragraphs in which you analyze the passage using the methodology you have chosen and present your interpretation

- A conclusion in which you apply your interpretation of the passage to some aspect of the world today: for example, a concern that many young people face, a problem that your school is encountering, or a pressing matter of national or international justice

- A bibliography

Option 2: A Children's Book

Write and illustrate a children's book about the Acts of the Apostles that is directed at fourth graders in a Catholic elementary school. Your book must be neatly bound and visually appealing, and it must consist of at least ten pages of material, including at least six original illustrations.

Option 3: A Series of Prayer Experiences

Your parish youth group has chosen to spend the next four meetings reading, studying, and praying with the Acts of the Apostles. You have been asked to plan the opening prayer experiences for all four meetings. Each prayer experience is expected to last about 15 minutes and to focus on one particular theological or spiritual theme found in the Acts of the Apostles. Potential themes include community, unity, inclusivity, mission, the power of the Holy Spirit, and fidelity to God in the midst of struggle. Write detailed outlines of these four prayer experiences, including the following elements:

- the passage or passages from the Acts of the Apostles to be proclaimed

- music selections

- ritual elements

- written collects (prayers) to begin and end the experience (in YOU-WHO-DO-THROUGH format)

- items needed to create a prayerful environment, such as candles or incense

- any other supplies needed to engage the group and draw them into a prayerful frame of mind

On the due date, you will conduct one of your four prayer experiences for the class.

Rubric for Final Performance Tasks for Unit 6

Criteria	4	3	2	1
Assignment includes all items requested in the instructions.	Assignment includes all items requested, and they are completed above expectations.	Assignment includes all items requested.	Assignment includes over half of the items requested.	Assignment includes less than half of the items requested.
Assignment shows understanding of the following concept: *The Acts of the Apostles presents an ideal vision of the early Christian community.*	Assignment shows unusually insightful understanding of this concept.	Assignment shows good understanding of this concept.	Assignment shows adequate understanding of this concept.	Assignment shows little understanding of this concept.
Assignment shows understanding of the following concept: *The Acts of the Apostles recounts the expansion of the Apostles' ministry to include the Gentiles.*	Assignment shows unusually insightful understanding of this concept.	Assignment shows good understanding of this concept.	Assignment shows adequate understanding of this concept.	Assignment shows little understanding of this concept.
Assignment shows understanding of the following concept: *The Acts of the Apostles recounts the Apostles' missionary activities "to the ends of the earth."*	Assignment shows unusually insightful understanding of this concept.	Assignment shows good understanding of this concept.	Assignment shows adequate understanding of this concept.	Assignment shows little understanding of this concept.
Assignment shows understanding of the following concept: *Paul was instrumental in the growth of the early Christian community.*	Assignment shows unusually insightful understanding of this concept.	Assignment shows good understanding of this concept.	Assignment shows adequate understanding of this concept.	Assignment shows little understanding of this concept.
Assignment uses proper grammar and spelling.	Assignment has no grammar or spelling errors.	Assignment has one grammar or spelling error.	Assignment has two grammar or spelling errors.	Assignment has more than two grammar or spelling errors.
Assignment uses its assigned or chosen media effectively.	Assignment uses its assigned or chosen media in a way that greatly enhances it.	Assignment uses its assigned or chosen media effectively.	Assignment uses its assigned or chosen media somewhat effectively.	Assignment uses its assigned or chosen media ineffectively.
Assignment is neatly done.	Assignment not only is neat but is exceptionally creative.	Assignment is neatly done.	Assignment is neat for the most part.	Assignment is not neat.

Document #: TX002288

Vocabulary for Unit 6

elder: A person appointed to have authority in governing a local church.

eunuch: An emasculated man. Such men were excluded from the assembly of the Lord (see Deuteronomy 23:1).

Gentile: A non-Jewish person. In Scripture the Gentiles were those outside the covenant, those who did not know how to fulfill God's will. Without this knowledge, they could not be in right relationship with God, and so were considered "unholy" or "unclean." In the New Testament, Saint Paul and other evangelists reached out to the Gentiles, baptizing them into the family of God.

Hebrews: In some New Testament writings, Hebrew-speaking Jewish Christians.

Hellenists: Greek-speaking Jewish Christians.

presbyter: A synonym to *elder* in the Acts of the Apostles and an alternative word for *priest* today.

Key Places in the Acts of the Apostles

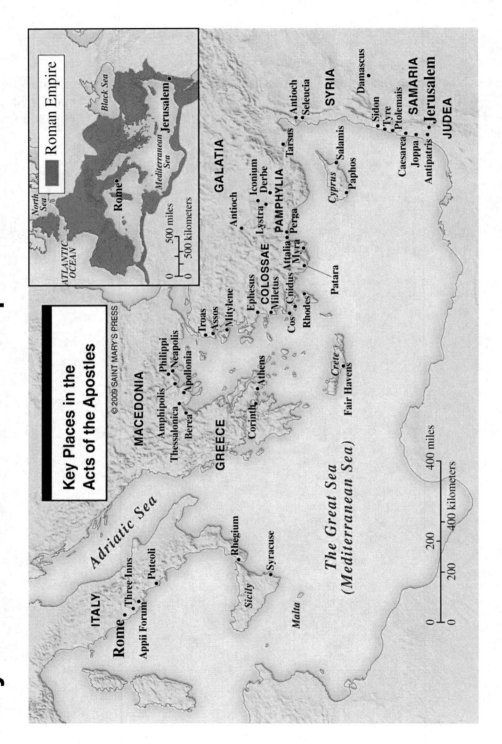

Key Places in the
Acts of the Apostles

Key Places in the Acts of the Apostles

Document #: TX002290

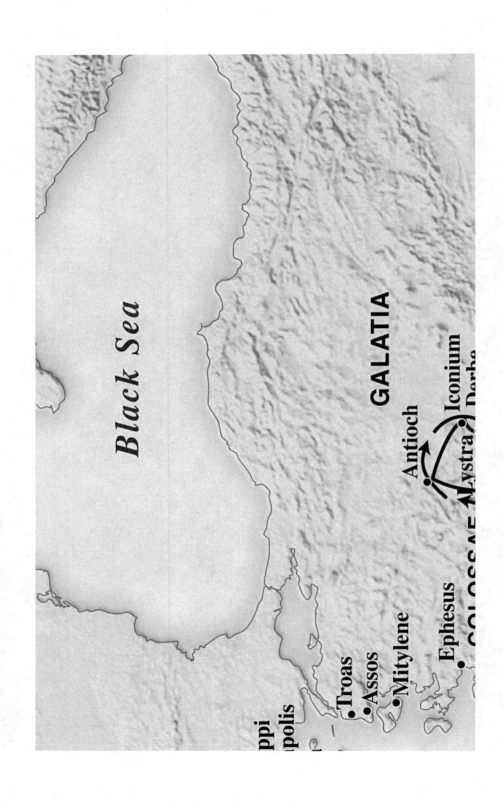

Document #: TX002290

Syracuse

Malta

The Great Sea (Mediterranean Sea)

Crete

Fair Havens

© 2012 by Saint Mary's Press
Living in Christ Series

Document #: TX002290

COLOSSAE

Miletus

Cos · Cnidus Attalia · Myra

Rhodes ·

PAMPHYLIA

Tarsus

Perga

Patara

Antioch

Seleucia

SYRIA

Damascus

Salamis

Cyprus

Paphos

Sidon

Tyre

Ptolemais

SAMARIA

Caesarea ·

Joppa ·

Antipatris · · Jerusalem

JUDEA

Cities of the Roman Empire, First Century AD

1. Circle the city your group has been assigned. Note that each city is listed with an accompanying Scripture passage from the Acts of the Apostles.

   Jerusalem (3:1–26)   Samaria (8:4–25)   Damascus (9:1–22)   Philippi (16:11–40)

   Thessalonica (17:1–9)   Corinth (18:1–11)   Ephesus (19:23–40)   Rome (28:11–31)

2. Using the Internet, conduct some basic research about your assigned city at the time described in the Acts of the Apostles (the first century AD, approximately 30–60). Take notes on a separate piece of paper. Use the following questions to guide your research:

   - What was the population of the city?

   - What different religious groups lived there? For example, Jews, Gentiles, pagan groups, or others.

   - On what was the economy of the city based? For example, trade, shipbuilding, agriculture, other things. How might the city have been economically or politically useful to the larger enterprise of the Roman Empire?

   - What were the city's notable geographic features?

   - What languages were spoken in the city?

   - What else was notable about the city? For example, any particular landmarks, customs, traditions, or events.

   - How does learning more about this city help you to recognize both the challenges and the value of the Apostles' ministry there?

3. Read the passage from Acts that features your assigned city (see the list above). How does this passage enhance your understanding of what first-century life was like in this city and of the Apostles' mission there? Take notes on a separate piece of paper.

4. Using the information you have found from both your research and Scripture, prepare an advertisement for your city that encourages people from other parts of the first-century Roman Empire to move or visit there. Your advertisement may take the form of a one-page magazine or newspaper ad, a billboard, or a bumper sticker. It should include a slogan or catchphrase that captures some important information about your city, as well as at least one illustration. Use the back of this paper to sketch out your ideas before using the art materials provided to create your ad.

© 2012 by Saint Mary's Press
Living in Christ Series

Document #: TX002291

The Apostles Peter and Paul

Working in your small group, answer the following questions on a separate piece of paper. You will use these same questions for your study of both Peter and Paul.

1. What is he (Peter or Paul) like as a person? For example, what are his characteristics and traits? What can you ascertain about his personality and values?

2. In what actions does he engage? For example, teaching, preaching, healing, traveling, other activities.

3. What key theological ideas does he put forward both in his formal speeches and in informal, one-on-one conversations?

4. How does he refer to, allude to, or otherwise draw on the Old Testament in his speeches?

5. What struggles or challenges does he face in his ministry of sharing the Good News? How does he respond to these difficulties?

6. How would you describe his style of leadership? For example, how does he make decisions, resolve conflicts, or settle controversial issues?

7. As contemporary disciples, what can we learn from his example?

Document #: TX002292

Peter and Paul Venn Diagram

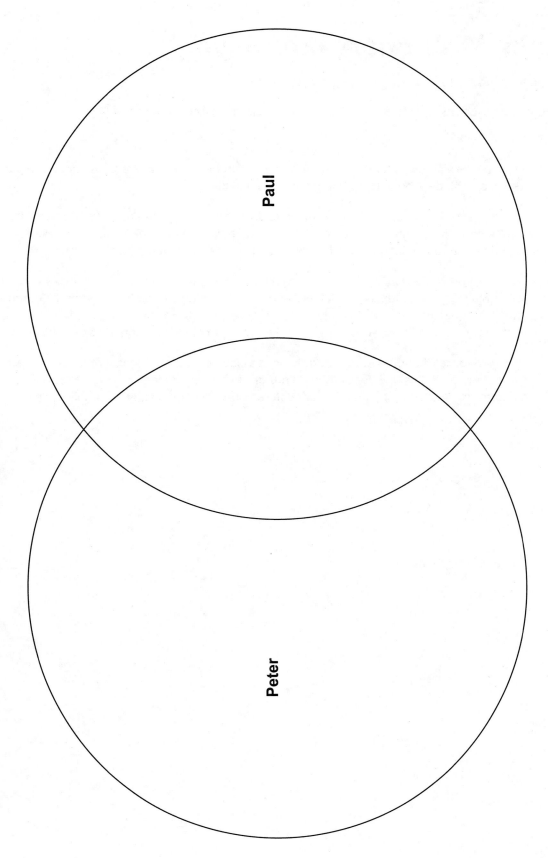

Paul

Peter

© 2012 by Saint Mary's Press
Living in Christ Series

Paul's Missionary Journeys

1. Circle the journey that your group has been assigned:

Journey 1: Acts 13:4—14:28

Journey 2: Acts 15:40—18:23

Journey 3: Acts 19:1—21:40

Journey 4: Acts 27:1—28:16

2. Complete the following three tasks with regard to the journey you have been assigned. Use your class notes, Bible, and student book to gather information and ideas.

- Create a travel brochure in which Paul advertises this journey, seeking to recruit additional companions to join him. Include written information and illustrations about cities and sites that will be visited, potential hazards that may be encountered, and the benefits of participation.

- Create a postcard in which someone who has accompanied Paul on this journey writes home to her or his friends and family to tell them about the trip. Has the trip been memorable, fun, dangerous, exciting, or some combination of these things? Follow the typical format of a postcard, that is, a picture on one side and a message of several sentences on the other.

- Use yarn to plot the route of this journey on the classroom map that you and your classmates created earlier in this unit. Be sure that your group is using a different color of yarn than the other groups are using, so that the four different journeys are clearly distinguishable on the map.

© 2012 by Saint Mary's Press
Living in Christ Series

Document #: TX002294

Unit 6 Test

Part 1: Multiple Choice

Write your answers in the blank spaces at the left.

1. _____ The Acts of the Apostles is considered to be "part 2" of which Gospel?

   A. Mark
   B. Matthew
   C. Luke
   D. John

2. _____ Acts was written around _____.

   A. 10 BC
   B. AD 30
   C. AD 65
   D. AD 85

3. _____ The events described in Acts occurred in the sociohistorical setting of _____.

   A. the Babylonian Exile
   B. the reign of Alexander the Great
   C. the Roman Empire
   D. the Persian Empire

4. _____ Paul had an encounter with the Risen Lord when he was traveling on the road to _____.

   A. Jerusalem
   B. Damascus
   C. Rome
   D. Thessalonica

5. _____ Paul's first European convert was _____.

   A. Peter
   B. Barnabus
   C. Phoebe
   D. Lydia

6. _____ The Acts of the Apostles begins with _____.

    A. Jesus' Resurrection
    B. Jesus' Ascension
    C. Pentecost
    D. Paul's first missionary journey

7. _____ According to Acts, Paul's final journey ends in the city of _____.

    A. Rome
    B. Philippi
    C. Jerusalem
    D. Joppa

8. _____ According to Acts, the preaching of the Christian message _____.

    A. begins with the Gentiles and expands to the Jews
    B. begins with the Samaritans and expands to the Romans
    C. begins with the Jews and expands to the Gentiles
    D. none of the above

9. _____ Challenges and struggles Paul faced in the course of his missionary journeys include _____.

    A. imprisonment
    B. being shipwrecked
    C. being expelled from inhospitable or unreceptive cities
    D. all of the above

10. _____ The Acts of the Apostles is often called _____.

    A. the Gospel of the Truth
    B. the Gospel of Jesus
    C. the Gospel of the Holy Spirit
    D. the Gospel of the Gentiles

11. _____ The missionary journeys of the Apostle Paul center on this geographic feature:

    A. the Mediterranean basin
    B. the Swiss Alps
    C. Mount Ararat
    D. the Roman coliseum

12._____ According to Acts, which two key people emerge as significant leaders in the early Christian community?

    A. Mary and Martha
    B. Silas and Barnabas
    C. Gaius and Philip
    D. Peter and Paul

Part 2: Essay

Respond to the following with two or more substantial paragraphs.

1. Describe the communal life of the early Christians as recounted in the Acts of the Apostles. How do we know that this description was an ideal vision that was not always fully lived out? How can ideal visions in general, and this ideal vision in particular, shape our values and priorities today?

2. What information does the Acts of the Apostles give us regarding the missionary campaign of the early Christians? In your response, include the following information about this campaign:

- general setting and some specific places visited

- intended audiences

- key people

- challenges

3. Discuss the life and ministry of the Apostle Paul. Why is he considered to have been so important to the life and growth of the early Church?

Document #: TX002295

Unit 6 Test Answer Key

Part 1: Multiple Choice

1.	C	**5.**	D	**9.**	D
2.	D	**6.**	B	**10.**	C
3.	C	**7.**	A	**11.**	A
4.	B	**8.**	C	**12.**	D

Part 2: Essay

1. As recounted in the Acts of the Apostles, the early Christians lived a communal life in which they shared their material possessions freely with one another. They sold their property to support the common good, laying the proceeds from such sales at the feet of the Apostles, to be distributed to all as needed. They also prayed together, both through their continued practice of Jewish prayer and their celebration of the Eucharist, sometimes referred to in Acts as the breaking of the bread. They lived in joy and unity, constantly praising God and welcoming new believers.

The story of Ananias and Sapphira helps us to understand that Acts' presentation of the early Christian community was an ideal vision that was not always completely followed. Ananias and Sapphira sold a piece of property but kept some of the purchase price for themselves. When Peter questioned them about this, they lied. This indicates that, although the early Christians may have constantly striven to live a vision of equality, justice, and peace, they were not always successful in doing so.

Even though an ideal vision is just that—an ideal—it can still have an important effect on our values and priorities. It can show us what is possible if we work hard and make sacrifices to achieve our goals. It can motivate us to improve our behavior and be a tool for evaluating ourselves and monitoring our progress. It can refocus us on our priorities and commitments, challenging us to be more faithful to our values when we may have gotten distracted or off track. In particular, the ideal vision of the early Christian community presented in the Acts of the Apostles challenges us to imagine the possibility of a group of people who are completely united with one another and with the Lord Jesus. It can motivate us to make choices more in line with such an ideal: to share our resources generously, to commit ourselves to prayer, and to work for the common good of all people, especially those most in need.

2. The Acts of the Apostles recounts many key aspects of the missionary campaign of the early Christians, which occurred from approximately AD 30 to 65, that is, before the writing of the Gospels. It describes how the preaching of the Gospel began in Jerusalem, with Jesus' Ascension and the outpouring of the Holy Spirit at Pentecost. The Apostles, with Peter and Paul most prominent among them, then brought that message to the surrounding cities and towns of Judea and to Samaria. Finally, Paul expanded the reach of the Apostles' ministry by undertaking three missionary journeys (plus one final journey to Rome) to preach the Gospel. Accompanied at various times by companions such as Barnabas, John (also called Mark), Silas, and Timothy, he traveled throughout the Mediterranean world, including Asia Minor, Europe, and the islands of Cyprus, Crete, and Malta.

This geographic expansion of the Gospel message "to the ends of the earth" (represented by Rome) mirrors the expansion of the target audience for this message. In the beginning, the Apostles preached

Document #: TX002296

only to Jews and those considering conversion to Judaism—usually beginning their work in the synagogues of the cities and towns they visited. With the geographic expansion of the Apostles' mission came an accompanying expansion to a Gentile (non-Jewish) audience. This expansion, though controversial at the time, was a watershed event in Christian history. Christianity would never have developed into a global religion without this crucial first step of expanding the missionary campaign beyond a Jewish audience.

Throughout the missionary campaign, the Apostles faced various challenges and struggles. People—both Jews and Gentiles—who were unreceptive to the Gospel message persecuted the Apostles, arresting them, beating them, imprisoning them, or expelling them from a particular city or town. The Apostles also had to contend with the difficulties of travel in the first-century world: inclement weather, floods, shipwrecks, and simple physical exhaustion.

3. Paul, also known as Saul, initially persecuted followers of Jesus. However, his encounter with the Risen Lord on the road to Damascus prompted him to shift his views completely: the one who began as a persecutor of this new religious movement became one of its most ardent devotees. Paul is sometimes called "the Apostle to the Gentiles" because his three missionary journeys (and fourth final journey) solidified the idea that the Christian message was meant for everyone, not just for Jews.

In the course of his missionary journeys, Paul visited many key cities and towns in the Mediterranean world, including those of Asia Minor (such as Antioch and Ephesus) and Europe (such as Athens, Corinth, Philippi, and Rome). He sought to establish Christian communities in each of these areas, communities with whom he remained in contact via his Epistles, or letters, some of which are still preserved for us today in the New Testament.

Unit 7

The Pauline and Deutero-Pauline Letters

Overview

In this unit the students continue their progress through the New Testament by engaging in close study of the Pauline and Deutero-Pauline letters.

Key Understandings and Questions

Upon completing this unit, the students will have a deeper understanding of the following key concepts:

- First-century letters, including Paul's, follow a specific format and have recognizable characteristics.
- Many of Paul's letters respond to specific problems that the early Christian communities were facing.
- In his letters, Paul presents a vision of the Church as Christ's own Body, animated by the Holy Spirit.
- In his letters, Paul helps the early Christian community to understand the saving effect of their faith in Jesus.

Upon completing the unit, the students will have answered the following questions:

- What are the format and characteristics of first-century letters?
- How does Paul try to support the early Christian communities?
- What is the ecclesiology of First Corinthians?
- According to Romans, how are we saved?

How Will You Know the Students Understand?

The following resources will help you to assess the students' understanding of the key concepts covered in this unit:

- handout "Final Performance Task Options for Unit 7" (Document #: TX002300)
- handout "Rubric for Final Performance Tasks for Unit 7" (Document #: TX002301)
- handout "Unit 7 Test" (Document #: TX002305)

Student Book Articles

This unit draws on articles from *The New Testament: The Good News of Jesus Christ* student book and incorporates them into the unit instruction. Whenever the teaching steps for the unit require the students to refer to or read an article from the student book, the following symbol appears in the margin: (📖). The articles covered in the unit are from "Section 4: The Letters of Paul," and are as follows:

- "Overview of the New Testament Letters" (article 36)
- "Paul's Letters Compared to the Acts of the Apostles" (article 37)
- "The Form and Characteristics of Paul's Letters" (article 38)
- "First Corinthians: Responding to Community Problems" (article 39)
- "The Eucharist and Resurrection in First Corinthians" (article 40)
- "Second Corinthians" (article 41)
- "Justification by Faith in Romans and Galatians" (article 42)
- "Christians, Law, and Conscience" (article 43)
- "Love of Others" (article 44)
- "First Thessalonians" (article 45)
- "Philippians" (article 46)
- "Philemon" (article 47)

The Suggested Path to Understanding

This unit in the teacher guide provides you with one learning path to take with the students, to enable them to begin their study of the Pauline and Deutero-Pauline letters. It is not necessary to use all the learning experiences, but if you substitute other material from this course or your own material for some of the material offered here, check to see that you have covered all relevant facets of understanding and that you have not missed knowledge or skills required in later units.

 Step 1: Preassess what the students already know about the Pauline and Deutero-Pauline letters by doing an inner circle / outer circle pair share.

 Step 2: Follow this assessment by presenting to the students the handouts "Final Performance Task Options for Unit 7" (Document #: TX002300) and "Rubric for Final Performance Tasks for Unit 7" (Document #: TX002301).

 **Step 3:** Continue the practice of Sustained Silent Reading (SSR).

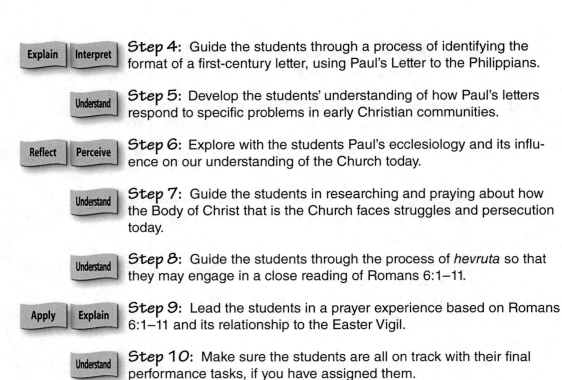

Explain **Interpret** **Step 4:** Guide the students through a process of identifying the format of a first-century letter, using Paul's Letter to the Philippians.

Understand **Step 5:** Develop the students' understanding of how Paul's letters respond to specific problems in early Christian communities.

Reflect **Perceive** **Step 6:** Explore with the students Paul's ecclesiology and its influence on our understanding of the Church today.

Understand **Step 7:** Guide the students in researching and praying about how the Body of Christ that is the Church faces struggles and persecution today.

Understand **Step 8:** Guide the students through the process of *hevruta* so that they may engage in a close reading of Romans 6:1–11.

Apply **Explain** **Step 9:** Lead the students in a prayer experience based on Romans 6:1–11 and its relationship to the Easter Vigil.

Understand **Step 10:** Make sure the students are all on track with their final performance tasks, if you have assigned them.

Reflect **Step 11:** Provide the students with a tool to use for reflecting on what they learned in the unit and how they learned.

Background for Teaching This Unit

Visit *smp.org/LivinginChrist* for additional information about these and other theological concepts taught in this unit:

- "Introduction to the Letters" (Document #: TX001062)
- "The Church as the Body of Christ and Sacrament" (Document #: TX001521)
- "Pauline and Deutero-Pauline Letters" (Document #: TX002297)

The Web site also includes information on these and other teaching methods used in the unit:

- "Written Conversations" (Document #: TX001328)
- "*Hevruta*: Learning Together" (Document #: TX001321)
- "Sustained Silent Reading" (Document #: TX002237)

Scripture Passages

Scripture is an important part of the Living in Christ series and is frequently used in the learning experiences for each unit. The Scripture passages featured in this unit are as follows:

- Romans 14:1–11 (do not judge)
- 1 Corinthians 11:17–33 (abuse of the Eucharist)
- 1 Corinthians 19:14–33 (eating meat sacrificed to idols)
- 2 Corinthians 11:1–15 (false apostles)
- 1 Thessalonians 4:1–8 (call to holiness)
- Galatians 5:13–26 (be of service)
- Philippians, chapters 1–4 (imitating Christ)
- Philemon, chapters 7–20 (plea for Onesimus)

Vocabulary

The student book and the teacher guide include the following key terms for this unit. To provide the students with a list of these terms and their definitions, download and print the handout "Vocabulary for Unit 7" (Document #: TX002302), one for each student.

Body of Christ	libation
civil disobedience	ministry
civil law	praetorium
conscience	pseudonymous
Jerusalem collection	Torah
justification	

Learning Experiences

| Explain | **Step 1** |

Preassess what the students already know about the Pauline and Deutero-Pauline letters by doing an inner circle / outer circle pair share.

1. **Prepare** by selecting a fun and upbeat song to play during parts of this learning experience. Because it is simply a cue to move, the song should have a good tempo and should not be something well known by the students. You will need a CD or MP3 player.

2. **Begin** by introducing the focus of this new unit: the Pauline and Deutero-Pauline letters. Explain that, as in prior units, you would like to see what the students already know about the new topic, as well as what questions they have.

3. **Separate** the students into two equal groups. Clear a space in the middle of your classroom. Have the first group stand in a circle, facing out, while the other group stands in a circle around them facing in. Each student should face a partner. Explain to the students that as they hear the music played, they should walk in a circle: students in both circles should move to their left, facing each other. When the music stops, the students should be in front of a new partner. Tell them that they will then receive further directions. Begin playing the music.

4. **Stop** the music after approximately 15 seconds. Tell the students that those in the inner circle will have 30 seconds to respond to the following question, while their partners in the outer circle are to listen only.
   - What do you know about the Apostle Paul?

5. **Play** the music again after the allotted time has passed. After a few seconds, pause the music again, and tell the students in the outer circle to share with their current partner what they know about the following:
   - Which books of the New Testament did Paul write?

6. **Continue** this process, ensuring that you alternate between having the inner circle and the outer circle respond. Tell the students that they can add to the information they have heard from a previous partner in addition to answering the question asked. Use the following questions for each subsequent round, or you may choose to add your own:
   - What else do you know about how or why Paul wrote these books?
   - What do you know about how Paul portrays the Church?

- What else do you know about Paul's understanding of Christ and how we are saved?

7. **Invite** the students to share with the class something they *heard* from another person, regardless of whether it is right or wrong. As students share what they have heard, take a moment to clarify any blatant misinformation.

8. **Direct** the students to return to their seats and spend a few minutes responding to the following:

    - What have you learned about the Apostle Paul through this learning experience? Name three things you learned.

    - What questions do you have about Paul and his writing? Name two things you would like to learn about or explore in the course of this unit.

    Allow 2 to 3 minutes for the students to respond.

9. **Tell** the students to turn to a partner to share their responses. Time permitting, invite volunteers to share their responses with the class.

Understand

Step 2

Follow this assessment by presenting to the students the handouts "Final Performance Task Options for Unit 7" (Document #: TX002300) and "Rubric for Final Performance Tasks for Unit 7" (Document #: TX002301).

This unit provides you with three ways to assess that the students have a deep understanding of the most important concepts in the unit: writing an exegetical paper, writing a letter from Paul today, and developing a mockup of Paul's social networking page. Refer to "Using Final Performance Tasks to Assess Understanding" (Document #: TX001011) and "Using Rubrics to Assess Work" (Document #: TX001012) at *smp.org/LivinginChrist* for background information.

1. **Prepare** by downloading and printing the handouts "Final Performance Task Options for Unit 7" (Document #: TX002300) and "Rubric for Final Performance Tasks for Unit 7" (Document #: TX002301), one of each for each student.

2. **Distribute** the handouts. Give the students a choice as to which performance task to work on and add more options if you so choose.

> **Teacher Note**
>
> Remind the students to choose their final performance task in accordance with any course requirements you may have established. In addition, if you are offering the semester-long portfolio project to your students (perhaps as part or all of their final exam), explain that the students who wish to assemble a portfolio must choose option 1.

3. **Review** the directions, expectations, and rubric in class, allowing the students to ask questions. You may want to say something to this effect:

   ➤ If you wish to work alone, you may choose option 1 or 2. If you wish to work with a group of three or four, you may choose option 3 only.

   ➤ Near the end of the unit, you will have one full class period to work on the final performance task. However, keep in mind that you should be working on, or at least thinking about, your chosen task throughout the unit, not just at the end.

4. **Explain** the types of tools and knowledge the students will gain throughout the unit so that they can successfully complete the final performance task.

5. **Answer** questions to clarify the end point toward which the unit is headed. Remind the students as the unit progresses that each learning experience builds the knowledge and skills they will need in order to show you that they understand the Pauline and Deutero-Pauline letters.

Step 3

Continue the practice of Sustained Silent Reading (SSR).

Articles 36, 37

1. **Prepare** by downloading and making extra copies, if needed, of the unit 3 handout "Sustained Silent Reading Log Instructions" (Document #: TX002244). Review these instructions with the students, and remind them of your expectations regarding the SSR log (for example, keeping it in a separate section of their binder or notebook), including your procedure for collecting and assessing this work.

2. **Assign** the students to read article 36, "Overview of the New Testament Letters," and article 37, "Paul's Letters Compared to the Acts of the Apostles," in the student book as preparation for beginning their SSR of Paul's letters.

3. **Tell** the students to begin reading First Corinthians during today's SSR session. Allow them to read for 15 minutes. Near the end of this time, remind them to make an entry in their SSR log.

4. **Provide** the students with a brief stretch break after SSR before continuing with the day's lesson.

Step 4

Guide the students through a process of identifying the format of a first-century letter, using Paul's Letter to the Philippians.

Articles
38, 46

1. **Prepare** by downloading the PowerPoint "The Format of a First-Century Letter" (Document #: TX002299) and arranging for the use of an LCD projector. Create or find online examples of the following forms of personal communication: a text message, an e-mail, a college acceptance letter, a postcard from a relative on vacation, a birthday card from someone's grandmother. You can photocopy and post these on the board or on poster paper around the room, or you can make digital images and project them.

2. **Assign** the students to read article 38, "The Form and Characteristics of Paul's Letters," and article 46, "Philippians," in the student book as preparation for this learning experience. Ask the students to bring their Bibles to class.

3. **Begin** by directing the students' attention to the examples of personal communication that you have posted, or project the digital images of the samples one by one. Invite volunteers to read each example and identify what kind of personal communication it is (e.g., text message, e-mail, birthday card). As volunteers identify each form of communication, ask the class:

   ➤ What enables us to distinguish these kinds of communication so easily? What helps us to know what kind of communication this is?

   Student responses might include the format of the communication, the appearance (as in the case of an e-mail), or grammar, spelling, punctuation, and syntax (as in the case of a text message).

4. **Explain** to the students that the indicators they have named are some characteristics that help us to identify the form, or genre, of a written communication. When we can identify the form of a text, we can then glean further information or ask more questions of the text.

Teacher Note

You may want to ask for further examples of different genres to help the students understand the concept more clearly.

5. **Tell** the students that the letters of Paul likewise have a distinct form that distinguishes them from other genres. Present the PowerPoint "The Format of a First-Century Letter" (Document #: TX002299). The "notes" for slides 2, 3, and 4 include directions for student reading and sharing; the students will need their Bibles.

6. **Ask** the students, following the presentation, to consider the following:

   • How can the structure of a letter help to convey meaning?

   Remind the students that the structure of writing helps to identify a particular form or genre. The form is a kind of support that helps to express meaning.

7. **Conclude** this learning experience by assigning the following as homework. Direct the students each to write a letter from the community of Philippi to Paul, using the structure of a first-century letter. Their letters can be written in response to Paul's Letter to the Philippians, or they can be the communication that preceded his letter.

Articles 39, 41, 43, 44, 45, 47

 Understand

Step 5

Develop the students' understanding of how Paul's letters respond to specific problems in early Christian communities.

1. **Prepare** by downloading and printing the handout "Paul's Response to the Early Christian Communities" (Document #: TX002303), one for each student. Gather resource materials for the students, including biblical commentaries, dictionaries, and encyclopedias.

2. **Assign** the students to read article 39, "First Corinthians: Responding to Community Problems"; article 41, "Second Corinthians"; article 43, "Christians, Law, and Conscience"; article 44, "Love of Others"; article 45, "First Thessalonians"; and article 47, "Philemon"; in the student book as preparation for this learning experience. Ask the students to bring their Bibles to class.

3. **Begin** by reminding the students that many of Paul's letters respond to specific problems early Christian communities were facing. Ask the students to recall the specific problem addressed in Paul's Letter to the Philippians, based on their examination of Philippians during the previous learning experience. Tell the students that they will now have an opportunity to explore particular problems or issues addressed by Paul in some of his letters.

Teacher Note

In Philippians Paul addresses a conflict between two women who are members of the community: Euodia and Syntyche. We do not know the nature of the problem, but we do know that it was serious enough to disrupt the life of the community and therefore to attract Paul's attention.

4. **Organize** the students into seven small groups. Distribute the handout "Paul's Response to the Early Christian Communities" (Document #: TX002303), and review the directions with the class. Assign each group one of the passages listed on the handout. Encourage the groups to use their student books and other references to better understand their assigned passage. Allow groups to work for approximately 15 minutes.

5. **Tell** the students that they will continue working in their groups to act out the problem addressed by Paul in their assigned passage, as well as the solution he offers. They can do so from the perspective of Paul, of the intended recipients, of an outsider, or of some combination of these. Explain that although the students can use modern language references and their imagination, they should be true to the text and avoid any interpretation at this point. The idea is to convey the basic information of the text without having every group read each text. Allow them 5 to 7 minutes to prepare to enact their passage.

6. **Gather** the class back together, and invite each group to enact its assigned passage. As each passage is enacted, write the passage, the problem, and the possible solution on the board for reference.

7. **Lead** a general discussion about the problems Paul addresses. In particular, ask the students to consider these questions:

   • To what extent are these particular problems bound by the culture and time of the ancient Mediterranean world?

   • What similar or parallel problems or issues face the world today?

   • How might the solutions Paul offers be implemented to address these problems today?

   • Paul's counsel and insight were sought and heeded by these early communities. To whom do you turn for counsel and insight when you face conflicts or problems?

   • What might we learn from these early communities and from Paul about how to handle conflict?

8. **Conclude** this learning experience by reminding the students that through his letters, Paul supported early Christian communities across great distances. We have learned a great deal about the development of early communities and the struggles and questions they faced because of Paul's response to them.

Step 6

Explore with the students Paul's ecclesiology and its influence on our understanding of the Church today.

1. **Prepare** by reviewing the method article "Written Conversations" (Document #: TX001328) at *smp.org/LivinginChrist.* Download and print the handout "Models of the Church Chart" (Document #: TX002323), one for each student. Gather markers and five large pieces of poster paper. Ask the students to bring their Bibles to class. On the board write the following questions:

   1. With what images does Paul describe the Church?

   2. What can you tell about Paul's priorities or concerns from this passage?

   3. To what extent do these images appeal to you and your understanding of the Church?

2. **Begin** by explaining to the students that Paul articulates a particular ecclesiology in 1 Corinthians, chapter 12, that has significantly influenced how we understand the Church today. Remind the students that Paul was writing before the formal establishment or structures of the Church as we know it. The early Christian community was still developing and trying to figure out who and what it was.

3. **Read** 1 Corinthians, chapter 12, as a class.

4. **Organize** the students into pairs. Direct each student to write a response to the first question for 3 minutes. Tell the students that they must remain silent during this time and must write for the entire 3 minutes. They may write words, phrases, or complete sentences; make connections and inferences; put forward ideas and musings; and even pose further questions.

5. **Have** the partners exchange their papers after the allotted time has passed. Ask the students to read what their partner has written and then take another 3 minutes to write a response. Repeat this procedure once, twice, or even three more times, depending on the students' ability to write in silence. Explain that the pairs may begin to address the second and third questions when they are ready and as they deem suitable in the course of their written conversation. Once they have exchanged papers for the last time, invite the students to discuss their written conversation out loud with their partners for 2 to 3 minutes.

> **Teacher Note**
>
> You may want to remind the students of the definition of *ecclesiology:* "This word (from the Greek *ekklēsia,* meaning 'assembly,' and *logos,* meaning 'word') refers to the study of the *Church,* the *Christian assembly.* Ecclesiology is the area of *theology* that studies the origins, *nature,* structure, and purpose of the Church" (*Saint Mary's Press® Glossary of Theological Terms*).

> **Teacher Note**
>
> You may choose to assign this passage as homework before this learning experience.

6. **Invite** volunteers to share with the class any insights, ideas, questions, or areas of agreement or disagreement that emerged through this process.

7. **Organize** the class into five different groups. Distribute the handout "Models of the Church Chart" (Document #: TX002323), one to each student. Assign each group one of the models from the handout: institution, mystical body / communion, herald, servant, or sacrament. Direct them to discuss the following in their groups:

   - How is Paul's ecclesiology (as expressed in 1 Corinthians, chapter 12) reflected in this particular model of the Church?

   - In what way does this model stand in contrast to the ecclesiology Paul presents?

8. **Distribute** poster paper, markers, and other art supplies to each group. Tell the students that they will now create an image that shows the model they have read and discussed, as well as its relationship to Paul's writing. Allow approximately 10 minutes for groups to create this image or symbol. Remind the students that they will post these images around the room, and tell them that everyone in the group should be able to explain the meaning of the image.

9. **Have** the groups post their images around the room after the allotted time. Invite each group to briefly summarize their model of the Church and explain the image for this model, as well as its relationship to Paul's writing. As each group presents, invite other students to offer observations and insights about the models. In particular, ask them to consider which model most closely resembles Paul's ecclesiology as stated in 1 Corinthians, chapter 12, as well as what model most appeals to them and why.

10. **Conclude** by assigning a journal entry as homework to answer this question:

    - Where is Paul's vision of the Church being carried out in the school, the parish, or the world?

Teacher Note

As an extra-credit assignment, you might encourage the students to take one of the "Models of the Church" surveys on Quizfarm.com.

Article
40

Step 7

Guide the students in researching and praying about how the Body of Christ that is the Church faces struggles and persecution today.

1. **Prepare** by gathering the following simple materials for a prayer experience: a few long pieces of fabric and a candle. The pieces of fabric should be long enough to allow you to create a cross on the floor in the middle of the classroom or chapel. Do the following preliminary research related to the planned prayer experience to identify topics that you will assign to the students during this learning experience:

   - If your school is sponsored by a religious order, research where its members are ministering. (For example, if your school is sponsored by the Sisters of Mercy, you might have the students research South Africa, the Philippines, Guyana, or Peru.)

   - If your school is diocesan, find out whether the diocese has a formal relationship with a diocese in the developing world. (For example, if you are in the Diocese of Cleveland, you could have your students research the diocese's relationship with El Salvador.)

   To vary the research options for each group, you may choose to have the students focus on particular areas of a given country, or you might also assign surrounding countries. Download and print the handout "The Body of Christ" (Document #: TX002304), one for each student. Finally, reserve the computer lab (if necessary), or arrange to bring in equipment so students have Internet access.

2. **Assign** the students to read article 40, "The Eucharist and Resurrection in First Corinthians," in the student book as preparation for this learning experience. Ask the students to bring their Bibles to class.

3. **Begin** by reminding the students that Paul's ecclesiology is rooted in the image of the Body of Christ. He uses this language not only to refer to Jesus' Body and Blood present in the Eucharist but also to explain how the Church is both diverse and unified. Remind the students that as members of the Body of Christ, we should have equal concern for other members of the Body who may be struggling or suffering in some way. Explain that the students will have an opportunity to research some area of the world where the Body of Christ is struggling.

4. **Organize** the class into groups of three. Distribute the handout "The Body of Christ" (Document #: TX002304) to each student. Assign to each group one of the issues, areas of the world, or groups of people you have prepared. Allow 15 to 20 minutes for the groups to do their research.

5. **Assign** to each group one of the following topics for the next part of the learning experience. More than one group can be assigned to any topic.
   - the hands of Christ
   - the feet of Christ
   - the eyes of Christ
   - the heart of Christ
   - the voice of Christ

   Explain that each group will write a prayer on behalf of the people it has learned about through this research. The prayer should focus on how the groups hope to be Christ's hands, feet, eyes, heart, or voice in the world. The prayers they write should include two elements:
   - what they observe happening to Christ's Body in the world
   - how they hope to be Christ's Body in the world

   Provide this example for the students:

   ➤ We see Christ's Body suffering in the world when we see so many people in our city who are homeless or hungry or who are just struggling to get by. We hope to be Christ's eyes by not looking away from or ignoring someone who is suffering. We pray for the courage to look at them, smile, and let them know they are not invisible.

   Allow approximately 5 minutes for the groups to prepare their prayers.

6. **Place** the fabric in the shape of a cross on the floor in the center of the room, and gather the students around the fabric cross. Call the students to quiet as you begin the prayer. Explain that they will pray with a variation of a prayer written by Saint Teresa of Ávila.

   In the name of the Father, and of the Son, and of the Holy Spirit. Amen.
   Christ has no body now but yours.
   No hands, no feet, no eyes, no heart, no voice on earth but yours . . .

   Yours are the hands: [Have the "hands" groups share their prayers.]
   ALL: We are the Body of Christ.
   Yours are the feet: [Have the "feet" groups share their prayers.]
   ALL: We are the Body of Christ.
   Yours are the eyes: [Have the "eyes" groups share their prayers.]
   ALL: We are the Body of Christ.
   Yours are the heart: [Have the "heart" groups share their prayers.]
   ALL: We are the Body of Christ.
   Yours are the voice: [Have the "voice" groups share their prayers.]

   WE are his Body, the Body of Christ.

We ask this through Christ, our Lord.
Amen.

In the name of the Father, and of the Son, and of the Holy Spirit.
Amen.

Article
42

Step 8

Guide the students through the process of hevruta so that they may engage in a close reading of Romans 6:1–11.

1. **Prepare** by downloading and printing the handout "Using *Hevruta*" (Document #: TX002324), one for each student. Review the method article "*Hevruta*: Learning Together" (Document #: TX001321) at *smp.org/ LivinginChrist*.

2. **Assign** the students to read article 42, "Justification by Faith in Romans and Galatians," in the student book as preparation for this learning experience. Ask the students to bring their Bibles to class.

3. **Begin** by telling the students that Paul's Letter to the Romans has greatly influenced the lives of people throughout history:

   ➤ As a young man who was bound for success and fame, Saint Augustine was prompted by an inner voice to pick up the Letter to the Romans and read. From that moment forward, his life was changed, and he in turn significantly affected Western Christianity.

   ➤ When Martin Luther was a young monk, his close reading of Romans led him to change his understanding of justification by faith and God's grace.

   ➤ Saint Teresa of Ávila, a great mystic from Spain, was comforted by the Letter to the Romans and was reminded of God's great love for us.

   ➤ John Wesley, a cleric of the Church of England and founder of the Methodist Church in the 1700s, was profoundly influenced by hearing a reading of Romans. He shifted the focus of his ministry and preached about God's free grace.

4. **Explain** that the students will have an opportunity to read in greater depth one section of Paul's Letter to the Romans to understand more fully the effect of this Epistle. Tell the students that to explore the significance of this letter, they will use an ancient Jewish method of studying text called *hevruta*. The basic concepts of *hevruta* are as follows:

   • *Hevruta* is a Hebrew word that means "friendship," "connection," or "partner."

- It is an ancient Jewish method of studying a text with a partner: the two people work together to understand the text's essential ideas and the questions it raises.

- *Hevruta* is based on the idea that no one person has a complete understanding of anything: we need one another if we are to find the truth.

- *Hevruta* is student-driven learning, which means that the responsibility for learning is placed on the student, with the teacher there to guide and assist.

5. **Distribute** the handout "Using *Hevruta*" (Document #: TX002324), and read the steps aloud with the students. Once you have explained the basic concepts of *hevruta*, direct the students to form pairs and begin the process outlined on the handout, reading Romans 6:1–11. Circulate around the room to answer any questions and ensure that the students are on task. Allow approximately 20 minutes for pairs to engage in the process.

6. **Draw** the class back together, and invite the students to share the insights derived from this process. In the course of the discussion, ask the students the following questions:

   - Why do you think this letter, and this passage in particular, has profoundly affected the lives of people such as Augustine, Martin Luther, Teresa of Ávila, and John Wesley?

   - What significance does this reading have for us and our understanding of Baptism, sin, and grace?

7. **Conclude** this learning experience by reminding the students that, as Paul tells us, through the Sacrament of Baptism, we die to sin and receive a new life in Jesus Christ. Through his death and Resurrection, Jesus has overcome death and we, in turn, are no longer enslaved by sin. God's grace and forgiveness abound.

Apply | Explain

Step 9

Lead the students in a prayer experience based on Romans 6:1–11 and its relationship to the Easter Vigil.

1. **Prepare** by gathering the following symbols of the Easter season that will be used as part of the prayer: a bowl or pitcher of water, oil in a vase or glass bowl, and a large candle (representing fire).

2. **Begin** by explaining to students that Romans 6:1–11—which they read closely through the process of *hevruta* in the previous learning experience—is one of the readings at the Easter Vigil. Remind the students that

at the Easter Vigil, the catechumens are fully initiated into the Catholic Church. Make the following points:

➤ The passage from Romans is most appropriate for this occasion because it captures the essence of what is happening in the Rite of Christian Initiation.

➤ Through the Sacrament of Baptism, we participate in the Paschal Mystery. We share in the death of Christ and therefore escape sin's grasp and power over us.

➤ This does not mean that we no longer are capable of sin. Rather, it means that we try to live our lives in and for God, experiencing God's abundant mercy, forgiveness, and grace when we do sin, and seeking to live into the fullness of Resurrection in the future.

Tell the students that they will have an opportunity to further explore the meaning of Romans 6:1–11 as it relates to the Easter Vigil and their own faith. In particular, they will use three symbols of the Easter Vigil—water, oil, and fire—as part of their reflection.

3. **Organize** the students into six groups, and assign two groups to each symbol (water, oil, and fire). Explain that each group will prepare an aspect of the prayer experience based on its symbol, as follows:

Teacher Note

If the students are finding it difficult to make the connection between these symbols and conversion, refer them to resources such as *Saint Mary's Press® Essential Bible Dictionary.* If you have access to the Internet, the students can also consult the *Catholic Encyclopedia* online.

- Water (group 1): Write a statement of two or more sentences that explains the relationship between water and conversion.

- Water (group 2): Write a prayer that incorporates the imagery of water to ask God for the ability to be open to continual conversion.

- Oil (group 1): Write a statement of two or more sentences that explains the relationship between oil and conversion.

- Oil (group 2): Write a prayer that incorporates the imagery of oil to ask God for the ability to be open to continual conversion.

- Fire (group 1): Write a statement of two or more sentences that explains the relationship between fire and conversion.

- Fire (group 2): Write a prayer that incorporates the imagery of fire to ask God for the ability to be open to continual conversion.

Allow approximately 10 minutes for the groups to work.

4. **Draw** the class back together. Place the three symbols, along with a Bible opened to Romans 6:1–11, on a table or another space designated for prayer. Remind the students that each group will share its statements and prayers as part of this experience. The groups may choose to read their statements and prayers out loud as a group, or each group may designate one member to read the group's part aloud.

5. **Invite** the students to pause in silence as you light the candle and begin the prayer:

> In the name of the Father, and of the Son, and of the Holy Spirit. Amen.
>
> *(Read Romans 6:1–11. Pause for a moment of silence.)*
>
> Loving God, through our Baptism, we participate in the death and Resurrection of Jesus and are, thus, freed from the bonds of sin and open to the path of new life.
>
> Through the symbol of water, we are reminded . . .
>
> *(Water [group 1] reads its statement.)*
>
> We pray . . .
>
> *(Water [group 2] reads its prayer.)*
>
> Through the symbol of oil, we are reminded . . .
>
> *(Oil [group 1] reads its statement.)*
>
> We pray . . .
>
> *(Oil [group 2] reads its prayer.)*
>
> Through the symbol of fire, we are reminded . . .
>
> *(Fire [group 1] reads its prayer.)*
>
> We pray . . .
>
> *(Fire [group 2] reads its prayer.)*
>
> We ask this through Christ our Lord. Amen.

6. **Maintain** the quiet of the prayer, and direct the students to spend the next several minutes writing a journal entry in response to the following question:

   • How might this passage from Romans affect us if we truly believe what it says?

   Time permitting, you may choose to invite the students to share their responses with a partner or with the class.

Step 10

Make sure the students are all on track with their final performance tasks, if you have assigned them.

If possible, devote 50 to 60 minutes for the students to ask questions about the tasks and to work individually or in their small groups.

1. **Remind** the students to bring to class any work they have already prepared so that they can work on it during the class period. If necessary, reserve the library or media center so the students can do any book or online research. Download and print extra copies of the handouts "Final Performance Task Options for Unit 7" (Document #: TX002300) and "Rubric for Final Performance Tasks for Unit 7" (Document #: TX002301). Review the final performance task options, answer questions, and ask the students to choose one if they have not already done so.

2. **Provide** some class time for the students to work on their performance tasks. This then allows you to work with the students who need additional guidance with the project.

Step 11

Provide the students with a tool to use for reflecting on what they learned in the unit and how they learned.

This learning experience will provide the students with an excellent opportunity to reflect on how their understanding of the Pauline and Deutero-Pauline letters has developed throughout the unit.

1. **Prepare** for this learning experience by downloading and printing the handout "Learning about Learning" (Document #: TX001159; see Appendix), one for each student. You may also wish to write on the board or a piece of poster paper (or project through the LCD projector) these questions from the preassessment learning experience in step 1:

   • What do you know about the Apostle Paul?

   • Which books of the New Testament did Paul write?

   • What else do you know about how or why Paul wrote these books?

   • What do you know about how Paul portrays the Church?

   • What else do you know about Paul's understanding of Christ and how we are saved?

2. **Distribute** the handout and give the students about 15 minutes to answer the questions quietly. For the question, "How did your understanding of the subject matter change throughout the unit?" invite them to consider the questions from the preassessment.

3. **Invite** the students to share any reflections they have about the content they learned as well as their insights into the way they learned.

4. **Direct** the students to keep this handout in a separate section of their folder or binder so that they can refer back to it at the conclusion of the course.

Final Performance Task Options for Unit 7

Important Information for All Three Options

The following are the main ideas that you are to understand from this unit. They should appear in this final performance task so that your teacher can assess whether you learned the most essential content.

- First-century letters, including Paul's, follow a specific format and have recognizable characteristics.

- Many of Paul's letters respond to specific problems that the early Christian communities were facing.

- In his letters, Paul presents a vision of the Church as Christ's own Body, animated by the Holy Spirit.

- In his letters, Paul helps the early Christian community to understand the saving effect of their faith in Jesus.

In addition to demonstrating understanding of these four main concepts of the unit, your final performance task must also contain or demonstrate the following:

- In-depth, substantial content appropriate for an upper-level high-school religious studies course

- Responsible and accurate use of Scripture

- Substantive content that creatively and accurately engages with and interprets the material of this unit

- Proper grammar, spelling, and diction

- A neat and well-organized presentation

Option 1: An Exegetical Paper

Choose one passage from one of the Pauline or Deutero-Pauline letters, approximately five to fifteen verses in length. Ask your teacher to approve the passage you select. Then research and write a four- to five-page exegetical paper in which you interpret that passage. Use one of the exegetical methods you studied in unit 2, and consult at least three sources of information other than your student book. Your paper should follow this structure:
- an introduction that situates the passage you have chosen within the broad context of the literary, historical, and theological emphases of the Pauline or Deutero-Pauline letters

- an overview of the major topics or questions regarding the selected passage that your paper will explore

- a explanation of the methodology you will use to interpret the passage—that is, literary, sociohistorical, or ideological

- at least three substantive body paragraphs in which you analyze the passage using the methodology you have chosen and present your interpretation

- a paragraph explaining the relationship of the passage to Paul's vision of the Church, as well as how it may convey the significance of the saving effect of faith in Jesus

- a conclusion in which you apply your interpretation of the passage to some aspect of the world today: for example, a concern that many young people face, a problem that your school is encountering, or a pressing matter of national or international justice

- a bibliography

Option 2: A Letter from Paul Today

Write your own Pauline letter, four to five pages in length. Your letter should follow the same format as a letter of Paul and should address a substantive issue or problem in your school, your city or town, the nation, or another country. Just as in Paul's letters, your letter should include an ecclesiology that speaks to the particular problem or issue. Finally, your letter should include research that elaborates on the issue or problem. Attach a bibliography to your letter.

Option 3: Create a Mockup of a Social Networking Page for Paul

In this group option, you will create a mockup of a social networking page for Paul that elaborates on his life, ministry, and letters. Include information about the communities to whom his letters were addressed and the issues with which they struggled and to which Paul responded. You may use a word-processing program or layout program to create the mockup of the page. The mockup should include original content and pictures that your group creates. Although you may use humor, all posts should be relevant to the topic of Paul and his letters.

Rubric for Final Performance Tasks for Unit 7

Criteria	4	3	2	1
Assignment includes all items requested in the instructions.	Assignment includes all items requested, and they are completed above expectations.	Assignment includes all items requested.	Assignment includes over half of the items requested.	Assignment includes less than half of the items requested.
Assignment shows understanding of the following concept: *First-century letters, including Paul's, follow a specific format and have recognizable characteristics.*	Assignment shows unusually insightful understanding of this concept.	Assignment shows good understanding of this concept.	Assignment shows adequate understanding of this concept.	Assignment shows little understanding of this concept.
Assignment shows understanding of the following concept: *Many of Paul's letters respond to specific problems that the early Christian communities were facing.*	Assignment shows unusually insightful understanding of this concept.	Assignment shows good understanding of this concept.	Assignment shows adequate understanding of this concept.	Assignment shows little understanding of this concept.
Assignment shows understanding of the following concept: *In his letters, Paul presents a vision of the Church as Christ's own Body, animated by the Holy Spirit.*	Assignment shows unusually insightful understanding of this concept.	Assignment shows good understanding of this concept.	Assignment shows adequate understanding of this concept.	Assignment shows little understanding of this concept.
Assignment shows understanding of the following concept: *In his letters, Paul helps the early Christian community to understand the saving effect of their faith in Jesus.*	Assignment shows unusually insightful understanding of this concept.	Assignment shows good understanding of this concept.	Assignment shows adequate understanding of this concept.	Assignment shows little understanding of this concept.
Assignment uses proper grammar and spelling.	Assignment has no grammar or spelling errors.	Assignment has one grammar or spelling error.	Assignment has two grammar or spelling errors.	Assignment has more than two grammar or spelling errors.
Assignment uses its assigned or chosen media effectively.	Assignment uses its assigned or chosen media in a way that greatly enhances it.	Assignment uses its assigned or chosen media effectively.	Assignment uses its assigned or chosen media somewhat effectively.	Assignment uses its assigned or chosen media ineffectively.
Assignment is neatly done.	Assignment not only is neat but is exceptionally creative.	Assignment is neatly done.	Assignment is neat for the most part.	Assignment is not neat.

Document #: TX002301

Vocabulary for Unit 7

Body of Christ: A term that when capitalized designates Jesus' Body in the Eucharist, or the entire Church, which is also referred to as the Mystical Body of Christ.

civil disobedience: Deliberate refusal to obey an immoral demand from civil authority or an immoral civil law.

civil law: Law pertaining to the state and its citizens as distinct from the Church.

conscience: The "interior voice," guided by human reason and Divine Law, that leads us to understand ourselves as responsible for our actions, and prompts us to do good and avoid evil. To make good judgments, one needs to have a well-formed conscience.

Jerusalem collection: The collection for the poor in Jerusalem that Paul thought was extremely important and agreed to support.

justification: God's action of bringing a sinful human being into right relationship with him. It involves removal of sin and the gift of God's sanctifying grace to renew holiness.

libation: The pouring out of a precious liquid as an offering to the Lord.

ministry: Based on a word for "service," a way of caring for and serving others and helping the Church fulfill her mission. *Ministry* refers to the work of sanctification performed by those in Holy Orders through the preaching of God's Word and the celebration of the Sacraments. It also refers to the work of the laity in living out their baptismal call to mission through lay ministries, such as that of lector or catechist.

praetorium: The palace of the governor of a Roman province.

pseudonymous: Written by one person but attributed to another as a way of honoring an esteemed predecessor.

Torah: A Hebrew word meaning "law," referring to the first five books of the Old Testament.

Paul's Response to the Early Christian Communities

1. Circle the passage that has been assigned to your group:

   1 Thessalonians 4:1–8 (call to holiness)

   1 Corinthians 11:17–33 (abuse of the Eucharist)

   1 Corinthians chapter 8 (eating meat sacrificed to idols)

   2 Corinthians 11:1–15 (false apostles)

   Galatians 5:13–26 (be of service)

   Philemon, verses 7–20 (plea for Onesimus)

   Romans 14:1–11 (do not judge)

2. Read your assigned passage.

3. With the members of your group, discuss the following questions, and record your group's responses on a separate piece of paper. You may use the student book, as well as other resources, to help you understand more fully the problem being addressed.

   • To whom is Paul writing in your assigned passage?

   • What problem is Paul addressing in his letter?

   • Does he propose a solution to this problem? What solution does he offer?

Models of the Church Chart

Model	Institution
Key Words	teach, sanctify, govern Magisterium The Church authority comes from Apostolic Tradition.
Signs and Functions	Pope, bishops, priests *Catechism of the Catholic Church* Canon Law diocesan directories
Members	all who formally recognize themselves in relationship to an official Church community and Church teachings
Connection to Jesus	Matthew 16:13–20
Early Church	Acts of the Apostles 6:1–7

Model	Mystical Body / Communion
Key Words	People of God fellowship unity and diversity of gifts in community Christ is the Head Church is the Body
Signs and Functions	prayer groups intimate relationship
Members	all who share in the Body of Christ through the grace of the Holy Spirit
Connection to Jesus	John 15:5
Early Church	Acts of the Apostles 4:32–37

Model	Herald
Key Words	Word of God conversion witness salvation
Signs and Functions	Bible studies evangelization missions media
Members	all who give witness to their life in Christ and see the Word of God as key
Connection to Jesus	Matthew 28:16–20
Early Church	Acts of the Apostles 2:37–41

Model	Servant
Key Words	service to the world dialogue liberation justice peace prophetic
Signs and Functions	hospitals Saint Vincent de Paul Society Catholic Campaign for Human Development Habitat for Humanity Catholic Relief Services
Members	all who serve the needs of others as Christ did "Whatever you did for one of these least brothers of mine, you did for me." (Matthew 25:40)
Connection to Jesus	John 13:3–15
Early Church	Acts of the Apostles 5:12–16

© 2012 by Saint Mary's Press
Living in Christ Series

Document #: TX002323

Model	Sacrament
Key Words	grace nourished by the Sacraments "Be what you have received."
Signs and Functions	liturgy light and salt for the world (to be a sign of Christ) communal prayer source of grace
Members	all who share in the liturgical life of the Church so as to be transformed by grace to be a sign of Christ in the world
Connection to Jesus	Luke 21:19–20
Early Church	Acts of the Apostles 2:42–47

Chart adapted from notes provided by Dr. Philip Verhalen, STL, based on *Models of Church,* by Avery Dulles, SJ. Garden City, NY: Doubleday, 1974.

© 2012 by Saint Mary's Press
Living in Christ Series   Document #: TX002323

The Body of Christ

Your teacher will assign a specific issue, area of the world, or group of people that your group will research. Write the information in the space provided.

- What area of the world are you researching?

- What hardships or struggles are the people in that area facing at this time?

  Briefly describe the situation.

- What particular struggles is the Church, the Body of Christ, facing at this time?

- What concrete things can we do to alleviate the suffering or struggle of people in the area you researched?

Using *Hevruta*

Read these instructions carefully as your teacher reviews them with you in class:

- Sit face-to-face with your partner.

- Use your "twelve-inch" voice: this ensures that your partner, but not the whole class, will hear you.

- Take turns reading the assigned text slowly and *aloud*. As you hear the words, silently note anything that jumps out at you: this could be a word or phrase you do not understand; something that seems problematic, disturbing, or inconsistent; something that moves you or touches you; or something you either agree or disagree with.

- You and your partner take turns posing questions to each other about the text. Explore what answers to your questions the text provides, and what answers your partner may come up with. Some questions may not have easy answers, and some questions may have no answers at all—in *hevruta* that's okay!

If you're stuck on what kinds of questions to ask, consider these three broad categories:

1. *What does the text say?* On a really basic level, what is this text about? How do you know? What words or ideas are repeated in this text?

2. *What does the text mean?* What is the deeper message that comes across in this text? Do you agree with this message? Why or why not? What metaphors or symbols do you see in the text?

3. *What does the text mean to you?* How does this text relate to your own life? What have you experienced that is similar to something you see in this text? What could this text teach you?

Be sure to write down your questions and answers in a notebook or on a sheet of paper so you remember them and can share them with the class later.

Unit 7 Test

Part 1: Fill-in-the-Blank

Use the word bank to fill in the outline of Paul's letters, identifying the subsections of each part of a typical Pauline letter in order of appearance.

Word Bank

theological discussion
ethical admonition
formal greeting
thanksgiving
conclusion

doxology or prayer
recipient
individual greetings
thesis statement
sender

personal postscript
initial exhortation
practical matters

Beginning

1.

2.

3.

4.

Body

1.

2.

3.

4.

Conclusion

1.

2.

3.

4.

5.

Document #: TX002305

Part 2: Matching

Match each term in column 1 with a description from column 2. Write the letter that corresponds to your choice in the space provided.

Column 1

1. _____ Body of Christ

2. _____ civil disobedience

3. _____ civil law

4. _____ conscience

5. _____ Jerusalem collection

6. _____ justification

7. _____ libation

8. _____ ministry

9. _____ praetorium

10. _____ pseudonymous

11. _____ Torah

Column 2

A. The pouring out of a precious liquid as an offering to the Lord.

B. The collection for the poor in Jerusalem that Paul thought was extremely important and agreed to support.

C. The "interior voice," guided by human reason and Divine Law, that leads us to understand ourselves as responsible for our actions, and prompts us to do good and avoid evil. To make good judgments, one needs to have a well-formed conscience.

D. A term that when capitalized designates Jesus' Body in the Eucharist, or the entire Church, which is also referred to as the Mystical Body of Christ.

E. God's action of bringing a sinful human being into right relationship with him. It involves removal of sin and the gift of God's sanctifying grace to renew holiness.

F. Based on a word for "service," a way of caring for and serving others and helping the Church to fulfill its mission. It refers to the work of sanctification performed by those in Holy Orders through the preaching of God's Word and the celebration of the Sacraments. It also refers to the work of the laity in living out their baptismal call to mission through lay ministries, such as that of lector or catechist.

G. Law pertaining to the state and its citizens as distinct from the Church.

H. Written by one person but attributed to another as a way of honoring an esteemed predecessor.

I. A Hebrew word meaning "law," referring to the first five books of the Old Testament.

J. The palace of the governor of a Roman province

K. Deliberate refusal to obey an immoral demand from civil authority or an immoral civil law.

© 2012 by Saint Mary's Press
Living in Christ Series

Document #: TX002305

Part 3: Essay

Respond to the following with at least one substantial paragraph.

1. How did Paul try to support the early Christian communities? Give specific examples from one of his letters.

2. What is Paul's ecclesiology as explained in 1 Corinthians, chapter 12? In what way is his understanding of Church appealing to you? In what way do you disagree with his vision of Church?

Document #: TX002305

Unit 7 Test Answer Key

Part 1: Fill-in-the-Blank

Beginning

1. sender
2. recipient
3. formal greeting
4. thanksgiving

Body

1. initial exhortation
2. thesis statement
3. theological discussion
4. ethical admonition

Conclusion

1. conclusion
2. practical matters
3. individual greetings
4. personal postscript
5. doxology or prayer

Part 2: Matching

1. D
2. K
3. G
4. C

5. B
6. E
7. A
8. F

9. J
10. H
11. I

Part 3: Essay

1. Through his letters Paul offers counsel regarding specific situations. In the example of the Letter to the Philippians, Paul addresses a conflict between two women of the community, Euodia and Syntyche. From his letter, we do not know the specifics of the conflict; however, we do know that this conflict has caused enough of a problem for the community that it somehow has come to Paul's attention. Paul simply urges them to come to a mutual understanding and to rejoice in their unity in Christ. *(Student answers will vary if they choose other letters to support their response.)*

2. Paul's vision of the early Church is exemplified in his image of the Body of Christ. He uses this language not only to refer to Jesus' Body and Blood present in the Eucharist but also to explain how the Church is both diverse and unified. As members of the Body of Christ, we should have equal concern for other members of the Body who may be struggling or suffering in some way. He uses this metaphor to help the early community understand that every member of the community has an important role and no one should be looked down upon. *(Student answers to the personal questions will vary.)*

Document #: TX002306

Unit 8

Late First-Century Writings

Overview

As the students conclude their study of the New Testament, they will examine several key examples of late first-century writings: the Book of Revelation, the Letter to the Hebrews, the pastoral epistles, and the catholic epistles.

Key Understandings and Questions

Upon completing this unit, the students will have a deeper understanding of the following key concepts:

- The Book of Revelation was written at a time in which the early Christian communities faced persecution.
- The Book of Revelation uses the conventions of apocalyptic literature, including symbolism, crisis imagery, and visions.
- The Letter to the Hebrews presents a Christology that draws on the tradition of the ancient Israelite priesthood.
- The pastoral epistles, which are attributed to Paul, and the catholic epistles address the various needs and situations of the early Christians.

Upon completing the unit, the students will have answered the following questions:

- How does sociohistorical criticism help us to interpret the Book of Revelation?
- How does literary criticism help us to interpret the Book of Revelation?
- What is the Christology of the Letter to the Hebrews?
- How did the pastoral epistles and the catholic epistles support the early Christians?

How Will You Know the Students Understand?

The following resources will help you to assess the students' understanding of the key concepts covered in this unit:

- handout "Final Performance Task Options for Unit 8" (Document #: TX002313)
- handout "Rubric for Final Performance Tasks for Unit 8" (Document #: TX002314)
- handout "Unit 8 Test" (Document #: TX002321)

Student Book Articles

This unit draws on articles from *The New Testament: The Good News of Jesus Christ* student book and incorporates them into the unit instruction. Whenever the teaching steps for the unit require the students to refer to or read an article from the student book, the following symbol appears in the margin: (📖). The articles covered in the unit are from "Section 3: The Johannine Writings," and "Section 5: Later Letters," and are as follows:

- "The Conventions of Apocalyptic Literature" (article 32)
- "Symbolic Language in the Book of Revelation" (article 33)
- "An Overview of Revelation" (article 34)
- "Eternal Truths of Revelation" (article 35)
- "Ephesians" (article 48)
- "Colossians" (article 49)
- "Second Thessalonians" (article 50)
- "The Pastoral Letters" (article 51)
- "Christ the High Priest" (article 52)
- "Exhortations to Faithfulness" (article 53)
- "The Letter of James" (article 54)
- "The Letters of First and Second Peter, and Jude" (article 55)
- "The Letters of John" (article 56)

The Suggested Path to Understanding

This unit in the teacher guide provides you with one learning path to take with the students, to enable them to begin their study of the Book of Revelation, the pastoral epistles, and the catholic epistles. It is not necessary to use all the learning experiences, but if you substitute other material from this course or your own material for some of the material offered here, check to see that you have covered all relevant facets of understanding and that you have not missed knowledge or skills required in later units.

 Step 1: Preassess what the students already know about the late first-century writings of the New Testament by having them complete a crossword puzzle.

 Step 2: Follow this assessment by presenting to the students the handouts "Final Performance Task Options for Unit 8" (Document #: TX002313) and "Rubric for Final Performance Tasks for Unit 8" (Document #: TX002314).

Step 3: Present an overview of the late first-century writings of the New Testament, and then invite the students to begin reading these texts using the practice of Sustained Silent Reading (SSR).

 Step 4: Guide the students in exploring how and why the Book of Revelation was written in symbolic language, or code, and provide them with an opportunity to interpret a chapter from this book.

 Step 5: Use the method of literary criticism to facilitate the students' examination of the Book of Revelation as apocalyptic literature.

 Step 6: Facilitate the students' exploration of the Christology of the Letter to the Hebrews within the broad context of the diversity of New Testament Christologies.

 **Step 7:** Conduct a brief overview of the pastoral epistles and the catholic epistles.

 Step 8: Make sure the students are all on track with their final performance tasks, if you have assigned them.

 Step 9: Provide the students with a tool to use for reflecting on what they learned in the unit and how they learned.

Background for Teaching This Unit

Visit *smp.org/LivinginChrist* for additional information about these and other theological concepts taught in this unit:

- "Christian Persecutions in the Roman Empire" (Document #: TX002307)
- "Revelation: A New Testament Apocalypse" (Document #: TX002308)

The Web site also includes information on this and other teaching methods used in the unit:

- "Sustained Silent Reading" (Document #: TX002237)

Scripture Passages

Scripture is an important part of the Living in Christ series and is frequently used in the learning experiences for each unit. The Scripture passages featured in this unit are as follows:

- Revelation, chapter 4 (vision of worship in the heavenly court)
- Revelation, chapter 5 (the scroll and the lamb)
- Revelation, chapter 6 (the first six seals)
- Revelation, chapter 7 (the 144,000 elect)
- Revelation, chapter 12 (the woman and the dragon)
- Revelation, chapter 13 (the two beasts)
- Revelation, chapter 16 (the seven bowls)
- Revelation, chapter 17 (the destruction of Babylon the harlot)
- Revelation, chapter 20 (the thousand-year reign of Christ)
- Revelation, chapter 21 (the new Heaven, the new earth, and the new Jerusalem)
- Hebrews 2:14–18 (Jesus' death frees us from sin and death)
- Hebrews 4:14—5:10 (Jesus, the great High Priest)
- Hebrews 7:23–28 (Jesus' priesthood and the Levitical priesthood of ancient Israel)
- Hebrews, chapter 9 (Jesus as the mediator of a new covenant)
- Hebrews 10:1–10 (Jesus' one, perfect sacrifice)

Vocabulary

The student book and the teacher guide include the following key terms for this unit. To provide the students with a list of these terms and their definitions, download and print the handout "Vocabulary for Unit 8" (Document #: TX002315), one for each student.

. . . .

apocalyptic literature	Levitical priests
apostate	martyr
crisis imagery	New Jerusalem
Dispersion (Diaspora)	prophet
end times	salvation
expiation	Septuagint
Holy of Holies	vision

Learning Experiences

Explain

Step 1

Preassess what the students already know about the late first-century writings of the New Testament by having them complete a crossword puzzle.

Teacher Note

As you begin this unit, note that the appendix includes directions and a handout for conducting a final course synthesis with students after this unit. If you choose that option, be sure to schedule this unit to allow adequate time.

1. **Prepare** by downloading and printing the first page of the handout "Crossword Puzzle: Late First-Century New Testament Writings" (Document #: TX002312), one for each student. For your reference, print a single copy of the second page with the answer key. Gather green, yellow, and red markers, one of each color for each student.

2. **Congratulate** the students on reaching the eighth unit of this course. Inform them that this final unit will enable them to explore selected writings of the New Testament that were written in the late first century. Invite them to demonstrate the extent of their prior knowledge of this topic by completing a crossword puzzle comprising various key words and concepts.

3. **Distribute** the handouts to the students, and give them about 10 minutes to work individually on completing the puzzle. They should do the best they can, inferring answers even if they are not sure. You may wish to give them the hint that some of the answers to certain items actually appear in the clues for other items.

4. **Invite** the students to consult briefly with someone near them to get any answers they may have missed. Then go over the crossword in the large group to ensure that all students have accurate responses.

5. **Ask** the students to examine the list of clues more closely. Hand out the markers, ensuring that each student has one of each color. Ask the students to work individually to determine their level of familiarity with the word or concept behind each clue and then to use the markers to code each clue as follows:

   - green: The student knows the concept very well and can explain it to others.
   - yellow: The student is somewhat familiar with the concept but perhaps lacks some knowledge.
   - red: The student is not at all familiar with the concept.

Some concepts—like "good" or "seven"—will be generally familiar to the students, but ask them to code the clues based on their familiarity with these concepts as they apply to late first-century New Testament writings. Allow about 5 minutes for this process.

6. **Direct** the students to focus on the concepts they coded yellow or red and to now seek out the knowledge of their classmates to gain further information about at least one of these concepts. Explain that each student should find another student who can tell her or him some additional information about one or more of these concepts—more information than is given in the clues themselves. Ask the students to record this information on the back of the handout. Allow 5 to 10 minutes for the students to circulate and gather information.

7. **Draw** the class back together, and invite several volunteers to share the additional information they gleaned from their classmates. Tell the students that as they study the late first-century New Testament writings—namely, the Book of Revelation, the Letter to the Hebrews, the pastoral epistles, and the catholic epistles—they will build on, enhance, and deepen this prior knowledge.

8. **Direct** the students to keep their handouts in their binders or folders so that they may refer back to them at the end of the unit.

 Understand

Step 2

Follow this assessment by presenting to the students the handouts "Final Performance Task Options for Unit 8" (Document #: TX002313) and "Rubric for Final Performance Tasks for Unit 8" (Document #: TX002314).

This unit provides you with three ways to assess that the students have a deep understanding of the most important concepts in the unit: writing an exegetical paper, writing and producing an episode of a Catholic radio talk show, or designing a Bible game show. Refer to "Using Final Performance Tasks to Assess Understanding" (Document #: TX001011) and "Using Rubrics to Assess Work" (Document #: TX001012) at *smp.org/LivinginChrist* for background information.

1. **Prepare** by downloading and printing the handouts "Final Performance Task Options for Unit 8" (Document #: TX002313) and "Rubric for Final Performance Tasks for Unit 8" (Document #: TX002314), one of each for each student.

> **Teacher Note**
>
> Remind the students to choose their final performance task in accordance with any course requirements you may have established. In addition, if you are offering the semester-long portfolio project to your students (perhaps as part or all of their final exam), explain that the students who wish to assemble a portfolio must choose option 1.

2. **Distribute** the handouts. Give the students a choice as to which performance task to work on and add more options if you so choose.

3. **Review** the directions, expectations, and rubric in class, allowing the students to ask questions. You may want to say something to this effect:

   ➤ If you wish to work alone, you must choose option 1. If you wish to work with a partner or with a group or three or four, you may choose option 2 or 3.

   ➤ Near the end of the unit, you will have one full class period to work on the final performance task. However, keep in mind that you should be working on, or at least thinking about, your chosen task throughout the unit, not just at the end.

4. **Explain** the types of tools and knowledge the students will gain throughout the unit so that they can successfully complete the final performance task.

5. **Answer** questions to clarify the end point toward which the unit is headed. Remind the students as the unit progresses that each learning experience builds the knowledge and skills they will need in order to show you that they understand the late first-century writings of the New Testament.

Teacher Note

You will want to assign due dates for the performance tasks.

If you have done these performance tasks, or very similar ones, with students before, place examples of this work in the classroom. During this introduction explain how each is a good example of what you are looking for, for different reasons. This allows the students to concretely understand what you are looking for and to understand that there is not only one way to succeed.

Step 3

Present an overview of the late first-century writings of the New Testament, and then invite the students to begin reading these texts using the practice of Sustained Silent Reading (SSR).

1. **Prepare** by downloading the PowerPoint "Overview of Late First-Century New Testament Writings" (Document #: TX002310) and arranging for the use of an LCD projector in your classroom. If needed, download and print extra copies of the unit 3 handout "Sustained Silent Reading Log Instructions" (Document #: TX002244). Ask the students to bring their Bibles to class.

2. **Begin** by telling the students that this final unit will allow them to explore a variety of New Testament writings composed during the last decades of the first century. Because these writings differ widely both in genre and in content, they will find it helpful to begin with an overview. In addition, explain that a general review of the contents of the New Testament will enable the

students to understand better how these late first-century writings fit into the New Testament's overall structure.

3. **Present** the PowerPoint "Overview of Late First-Century New Testament Writings" (Document #: TX002310). Direct the students to take notes. Supplement the material on the slides with other information you deem relevant or appropriate.

4. **Invite** any questions or comments after the presentation, reminding the students that this has been simply a brief overview of the unit. You may also wish to reassure them that they will not be reading all of the writings discussed in this unit; rather, each student will read Revelation, Hebrews, and one to three of the pastoral epistles and catholic epistles.

5. **Direct** the students to get out their Bibles and Sustained Silent Reading (SSR) logs. Distribute copies of the handout "Sustained Silent Reading Log Instructions" (Document #: TX002244) to any student who needs one. Review these instructions with the students, and remind them of your expectations regarding the SSR log (for example, keeping it in a separate section of their binder or notebook), including your procedure for collecting and assessing this work.

6. **Tell** the students to begin reading the Book of Revelation during today's SSR session. You may wish to alert them to the fact that the Book of Revelation is difficult material, because it is filled with language and images that, on the surface, may seem obscure or fanciful. Affirm their efforts to begin reading the book on their own, and assure them that subsequent learning experiences in this unit will help them to understand its meaning more fully. Allow them to read for 15 minutes. Near the end of this time, remind them to make an entry in their SSR log. Explain that after they finish reading the Book of Revelation during the SSR sessions, they should begin reading the Letter to the Hebrews.

7. **Provide** the students with a brief stretch break after SSR before continuing with the day's lesson.

> **Teacher Note**
>
> Consistently including a 15-minute SSR session in every subsequent class session will enable your students to read the Book of Revelation and the Letter to the Hebrews in their entirety during this unit and, more broadly, to cultivate the discipline of careful, reflective reading.

Articles
33, 34

Step 4

Guide the students in exploring how and why the Book of Revelation was written in symbolic language, or code, and provide them with an opportunity to interpret a chapter from this book.

1. **Prepare** by downloading the PowerPoint "The Book of Revelation: Message to a Persecuted Community" (Document #: TX002311) and arranging for the use of an LCD projector in your classroom. Gather newsprint or construction paper. Make available any resources for biblical research, such as *Saint Mary's Press® Essential Bible Dictionary.*

2. **Assign** the students to read article 33, "Symbolic Language in the Book of Revelation"; article 34, "An Overview of Revelation"; and the introductory material about the Book of Revelation found in the student book as preparation for this learning experience. Ask the students to bring their Bibles to class.

3. **Begin** with a brief brainstorming session centered on this question:

   • What do you know about African American spirituals?

   Start with a 2-minute pair share. Then draw the class back together, and record on the board facts the students know. Points you could mention, if the students do not, include the following:

   • These songs were sung by enslaved African Americans, often while working in the fields on plantations in the U.S. South.

   • Singing was permitted because it enabled the plantation owner to know the slaves' location.

   • Because most slaves were illiterate (it was illegal to teach a slave to read or write), the songs were sung from memory and were passed on as an oral tradition.

   • The songs' lyrics often expressed faith in God's protection or belief in a better life in Heaven.

   • They were often sung in a "call and response" style.

   • Several well-known examples of African American spirituals include "Swing Low, Sweet Chariot," "Wade in the Water," and "This Train Is Bound for Glory."

   • African American spirituals were a major influence on the American tradition of Gospel music.

4. **Explain** to the students that the lyrics of many African American spirituals, although literally and overtly about religious matters, were also coded messages about the Underground Railroad, the system of transporting escaped slaves to freedom in the North. Share with the students these words and phrases commonly used in the spirituals, along with the meaning of these symbols:

   - "wade in the water": directed escaped slaves to travel along the riverbank or across a body of water, so that search dogs would be thrown off their scent
   - "train or chariot": the Underground Railroad
   - "glory": freedom
   - "Jordan River": Ohio River or Mississippi River
   - "steal away to Jesus": come to a meeting of slaves planning an escape or revolt
   - "Canaan": the North
   - "drinking gourd": the Big Dipper, a constellation that pointed the way north
   - "band of angels": Underground Railroad "conductors" or workers

   Help the students to understand why it would have been crucial for slaves to communicate with one another in this type of symbolic language, making these or similar points:

   ➤ Coded or symbolic language enabled the slaves to share information about escape plans, escape routes, and the Underground Railroad without the slave owners' knowledge.

   ➤ To the slave owners who overhead these songs, the slaves were simply singing religious music infused with seemingly harmless biblical references.

   ➤ Among the slaves themselves, however, valuable and potentially life-saving information was being communicated.

5. **Share** with the students these observations:

   ➤ The situation of enslaved African Americans living in the southern United States during the nineteenth century closely parallels that of Christians living in the Roman Empire during the first and second centuries.

   ➤ Like the slaves, the Christians were not entirely free—in fact, they were frequently subjected to persecution, torture, and even death. Like the African American slaves, they needed a way to communicate with one another in a way that their Roman oppressors could not understand: that is, in symbols.

➤ A prime example of this type of early Christian literature is the Book of Revelation. Because it was composed during a time when the early Christians faced persecution, it was written using symbolism that the Christians would understand but the Romans would not.

Tell the students that the following PowerPoint presentation will enable them to better understand the historical, political, and social context in which the Book of Revelation was written and prepare them for the experience of interpreting a chapter from it.

6. **Present** the PowerPoint "The Book of Revelation: Message to a Persecuted Community" (Document #: TX002311). Direct the students to take notes. Supplement the material on the slides with other information you deem relevant or appropriate.

7. **Invite** comments and questions from the students after the presentation. You may wish to tell them that if they take a Church history course, they will learn much more detail about the challenges and struggles that the early Christians faced. However, the basic information from this presentation should be enough to help them study the Book of Revelation.

8. **Organize** the class into five groups. Assign each group one of the following chapters from the Book of Revelation: 5, 7, 13, 16, and 21. Ask each group to read its assigned chapter and then interpret it—that is, determine the meaning of the chapter that the early Christians, but not the Romans, would have understood. To analyze the symbols, the students should refer to their student books, any footnotes in their Bibles, and any other tools of biblical research you have made available in the classroom. Suggest that the students pay particular attention to numbers, colors, and images—like a lamb, a scroll, a seal, horns, or eyes—that carry symbolic or coded meaning. Ask the students to locate six to ten examples of symbolic language in their assigned chapters. Allow about 15 minutes for the groups to complete this task.

9. **Ask** the groups to use the examples they found to create a handbook for understanding their chapter. Explain that each entry should include the original, literal language from Revelation and then provide its meaning for the early Christians. Some entries may also include illustrations. Read aloud the following example of an entry for Revelation 5:6:

> ***Original language:*** *a lamb that had been slain, with seven horns and seven eyes*
>
> ***Encoded meaning:*** *The lamb is Jesus, who has been crucified and raised. The number 7 symbolizes perfection; the horns symbolize power; and the eyes symbolize knowledge or wisdom. Therefore, Jesus is all-powerful and all-knowing; in other words, he is God.*
>
> ***Illustration:*** *This entry may include an illustration of the lamb.*

Allow about 15 minutes for the students to construct their handbooks. Point out that the books may be created as actual little books, using construction paper, or can be simply sketched out on newsprint.

10. **Have** each group share its handbook with the class. Help the students notice how many symbols, images, and motifs recur throughout the Book of Revelation. Point out that once the students have examined the symbolism of one or two chapters, they can more easily understand the rest of the book.

> **Teacher Note**
> If time is short, students may complete this as homework.

11. **Remind** the students of the reason that the Book of Revelation was written in symbolic language or code: its audience was late first-century Christians facing persecution from Rome. Explain that during the next class session, the students will learn more about apocalyptic literature, a literary genre that often becomes popular within the context of persecution.

Articles 32, 35

Step 5

Use the method of literary criticism to facilitate the students' examination of the Book of Revelation as apocalyptic literature.

1. **Prepare** by downloading and making copies of the handout "Literary Features of Apocalyptic Writing" (Document #: TX002316), one for each student.

2. **Assign** the students to read article 32, "The Conventions of Apocalyptic Literature," and article 35, "Eternal Truths of Revelation," in the student book as preparation for this learning experience. Ask the students to bring their Bibles to class.

3. **Begin** by asking the students to recall the genre of the Book of Revelation: apocalyptic literature. As defined in the student book, this literary form uses dramatic elements and highly symbolic language to offer hope to people in crisis. Explain that much misinterpretation that has plagued the Book of Revelation has resulted from inattention to the unique features of this literary form. Inform the students that in this learning experience they will closely examine one section of the Book of Revelation, seeking examples of common literary features of apocalyptic writing.

4. **Ask** the students to gather back into the same five groups from the previous learning experience (step 4), and distribute copies of the handout "Literary Features of Apocalyptic Writing" (Document #: TX002316). Explain that each group will examine the same chapter it studied in the previous learning experience plus one additional chapter, as listed on the handout.

That is, the group that worked with chapter 5 will now study chapters 4 and 5; the group that worked with chapter 7 will now study chapters 6 and 7, and so forth.

Teacher Note

Because the Book of Revelation is so difficult to understand, the students' work in this learning experience is likely to be more productive if they return to a chapter with which they are already familiar.

5. **Review** the directions on the handout aloud, as well as the descriptions of the literary features that appear in the first column of the handout. Ask the groups to read their assigned chapters and then work to complete the table on the handout. Emphasize that they are unlikely to find an example of every literary feature in the two chapters on which they are focusing; they should simply find as many as they are able. Allow 20 to 25 minutes for the groups to complete this work.

6. **Draw** the class back together, and invite each group to share several examples of the literary features of apocalyptic writing it found in its assigned chapters. As each group shares, ask the other students to add some or all of these examples to their own handouts, especially for those literary features that did not appear in their own assigned chapters. This will allow each student to have a more complete picture of the many ways in which the Book of Revelation incorporates the features of apocalyptic writing.

Articles
52, 53

Step 6

Facilitate the students' exploration of the Christology of the Letter to the Hebrews within the broad context of the diversity of New Testament Christologies.

1. **Prepare** by downloading and printing one copy of the handout "New Testament Christologies" (Document #: TX002317), cutting along the dotted lines so that each student will have either a book of the New Testament or a New Testament Christology. You may need to use part or all of a second copy of the handout, depending on the size of your class. If you have an odd number of students, two students can share one slip of paper. Keep a copy for yourself as an answer key.

    Download and make copies of the handouts "Priests and Levites" (Document #: TX002318) and "The Tradition of the Ancient Israelite Priesthood and the Letter to the Hebrews" (Document #: TX002319), one of each for each student.

2. **Assign** the students to read article 52, "Christ the High Priest," and article 53, "Exhortations to Faithfulness," in the student book as preparation for this learning experience. Ask them to bring their Bibles to class.

3. **Begin** with a brief learning experience to help students review the diversity of New Testament Christologies. Tell the students that they will each receive a slip of paper on which is written either a book of the New Testament or a Christology of the New Testament. If they receive a book of the New Testament, they must find the person who has the corresponding Christology; if they receive a Christology, they must find the person who has the corresponding book. Distribute the slips of paper from the handout "New Testament Christologies" (Document #: TX002317), and allow 3 or 4 minutes for the students to find their partners.

4. **Ensure** that all the students have found their correct partners by briefly reviewing all the New Testament Christologies that appear on the handout "New Testament Christologies" (Document #: TX002317). Pose the following question for discussion:

   • Why is there such diversity in the Christologies of the New Testament?

   Remind the students that each New Testament author developed a portrayal of Jesus that suited the needs of the audience being addressed. These Christologies are not contradictory; rather, they simply highlight various aspects of Jesus' life, identity, and saving mission.

5. **Ask** the students to identify the one Christology from this introductory learning experience that they have not yet studied: that of the Letter to the Hebrews, which portrays Jesus as a great High Priest in the tradition of the ancient Israelite priesthood. Tell the students that the Christology of the Letter to the Hebrews will be the focus of today's class session.

> **Teacher Note**
>
> Have the students remain with the partners they have found in this introductory segment for the remainder of this learning experience.

6. **Ask** the students to recall, from the student book articles they read as homework, the primary barrier to understanding that modern-day readers of the Letter to the Hebrews encounter: lack of familiarity with the traditions and practices of the ancient Israelite priesthood, which centered on worship in the Temple in Jerusalem. Explain that to help the students understand this letter more fully, they will learn or review some basic information about the ancient Israelite priesthood.

7. **Distribute** copies of the handout "Priests and Levites" (Document #: TX002318). As the students read, invite them to underline or highlight words or concepts that they think may be particularly important for their study of the Letter to the Hebrews. Give the students about 10 minutes to read the handout quietly.

8. **Explain** that the students will now work with their partners to study several key traditions of the ancient Israelite priesthood and to examine how the author of the Letter to the Hebrews uses and interprets those traditions to present a unique Christology.

9. **Distribute** copies of the handout "The Tradition of the Ancient Israelite Priesthood and the Letter to the Hebrews" (Document #: TX002319).
   Explain that the first column lists seven key traditions of the ancient Israelite priesthood. Ask the students to work with their partners to write a brief
   description or definition of each tradition in the second column, using information from the handout "Priests and Levites" (Document #: TX002318),
   their student books, and any footnotes found in their Bibles. Then ask the
   pairs to look up the passages from the Letter to the Hebrews listed in the
   third column and to write a brief description for each passage, explaining
   how the author of this letter draws upon and reinterprets the corresponding
   tradition to present a unique Christology. When the pairs have completed
   the chart, invite them to respond to the question at the end of the handout "The Tradition of the Ancient Israelite Priesthood and the Letter to the
   Hebrews" (Document #: TX002319). Allow 20 to 25 minutes for the pairs to
   work.

10. **Draw** the class back together and review the handout, ensuring that all the
    students have correct responses. Ask volunteers to share answers to the
    question at the end of the handout. Be sure to highlight any of these impor-
    tant points that the students might have overlooked:

    - The author of the Letter to the Hebrews presents Jesus' death as
      a sacrifice for sin, one that, unlike the sacrifices offered daily in the
      Temple in Jerusalem, will never need to be repeated.

    - The author compares Jesus' entrance into the heavenly sanctuary with
      the high priest's annual entrance into the Holy of Holies on the Day of
      Atonement (Yom Kippur).

    - Unlike the power of the Levitical priests, whose priesthood ended with
      their deaths, Jesus' power to save us endures forever.

    - The worship and sacrifice offered by the priests of ancient Israel was
      based on the laws of the Torah, a manifestation of the first covenant
      God made with humanity—specifically, with Abraham, Sarah, and their
      descendants. Through his life, death, and Resurrection, Jesus has
      become the mediator of a new covenant, by which we receive redemp-
      tion, forgiveness of our sin, and eternal life.

11. **Transition** to an explanation of the homework assignment in these or simi-
    lar words:

    ➤ Now that your semester of studying the New Testament is nearly over,
      you have a firm grasp of the variety of Christologies present in its vari-
      ous books.

➤ Recall that every New Testament author endeavored to present a Christology that was understandable and compelling for the audience being addressed. For example, the author of the Letter to the Hebrews writes to an audience intimately familiar with the traditions of the ancient Israelite priesthood. A presentation of Jesus as a high priest would, therefore, have been persuasive and intriguing for them.

➤ If you were creating a Christology aimed at reaching young people today, what would it be? What portrayal of Jesus would be accessible, attractive, and meaningful? Furthermore, what would be the most effective way to communicate this Christology to a wide audience of young people? Would it be through creative spoken word, like a poetry slam? Through a video posted on YouTube? Through a social networking site, like Twitter or Facebook? Through a song?

➤ Your homework is to create your own Christology, and then to communicate that Christology in a way that would reach young people and move them to faith.

> **Teacher Note**
>
> You may wish to have the students complete this assignment with the same partner with whom they have worked during this learning experience, or you may allow them to work alone.

12. **Allow** time during the following class session for the students to present their Christologies. The class could vote on the one they believe would be most effective—both in content and in presentation—for drawing young people to a renewed faith in Jesus.

Apply **Explain**

Step 7

Conduct a brief overview of the pastoral epistles and the catholic epistles.

Articles
48, 49,
50, 51,
54, 55,
56

1. **Prepare** by downloading and printing the handout "The Pastoral and Catholic Epistles" (Document #: TX002320), one for each student.

2. **Assign** the students to read article 48, "Ephesians"; article 49, "Colossians"; article 50, "Second Thessalonians"; article 51, "The Pastoral Letters"; article 54, "The Letter of James"; article 55, "The Letters of First and Second Peter, and Jude"; and article 56, "The Letters of John"; in the student book as preparation for this learning experience. Ask the students to bring their Bibles to class.

3. **Begin** by pointing out that there are two categories of New Testament books that the students have not yet explored: the pastoral epistles and the catholic epistles.

> **Teacher Note**
>
> You may want to assign the student book articles a few days in advance to give the students enough time to complete the reading assignment.

Invite the students to recall the basic information about these books that they learned at the beginning of this unit:

➤ The pastoral epistles are 1 Timothy, 2 Timothy, and Titus. These are addressed to the pastors, or leaders, of various early Christian communities.

➤ Although the pastoral epistles have traditionally been attributed to Paul, their late date of composition (AD 90–100) makes it highly unlikely that Paul himself wrote them. Rather, one of Paul's followers or associates likely wrote in his name (or pseudonymously) as a way to honor him and evoke his authority.

➤ The catholic epistles are 1 and 2 Peter, Jude, James, and 1, 2, and 3 John. These are addressed to a universal, or "catholic," audience rather than to a single geographically specific Christian community.

➤ The earliest catholic epistle is probably 1 Peter, which may have been written as early as AD 70. The latest is 2 Peter, which was written between AD 100 and 125.

4. **Tell** the students that this learning experience will give them a brief overview of some of these writings. In particular, they will be asked to note the following:

• similarities and differences between these epistles and the Pauline epistles (that is, the epistles the students studied in unit 7)

• the ways in which the pastoral epistles and catholic epistles sought to address the concrete needs and situations of early Christian communities

• the relevance of these epistles for our lives of faith today

5. **Organize** the students into five groups. Distribute the handout "The Pastoral and Catholic Epistles" (Document #: TX002320). Explain that each group will read and study one, two, or three of the pastoral epistles or catholic epistles according to the assignments indicated on the handout. Assure the students that the groups reading two or three epistles are working with some of the shortest writings in the entire Bible.

6. **Use** today's SSR session to allow the students to individually read one or more of the epistles that their groups have been assigned. You may wish to allow slightly more time for SSR today (perhaps 20 or even 25 minutes) to ensure that most students will be able to finish at least one epistle. For each group assigned to two or three epistles, you may wish to assign one reading to each group member for this SSR, so that the group has collectively read all its assigned readings. Students who finish early could then move on to another of their group's assigned readings. For example, half the students in group 2 could start their SSR with 2 Timothy, and half could start with Titus.

7. **Direct** the students to work in their groups, after the SSR session concludes, to discuss questions A through D on the handout regarding the

pastoral or catholic epistles they have been assigned. Allow about 20 minutes for the students to complete this work in their groups. While they are working, write the letters *A, B,* and *C* down the left-hand side of the board (mirroring the handout), and write the numbers *1* through *5* across the top of the board, leaving room underneath for the corresponding groups to write their responses for questions A through C. You will use question D for the prayer experience at the end of this step.

8. **Direct** the students to write their responses to questions A, B, and C on the board under their corresponding group number. Then invite the class to examine the resultant matrix, noting similarities and differences among the pastoral and catholic epistles. Draw the students' attention to the many ways in which these texts that were written last in the New Testament canon sought to support, encourage, challenge, and provide practical advice to early Christian communities. Ask the students to take a few minutes to record notes from the other groups in the corresponding columns of their handout, for their own reference.

9. **Call** the students to quiet, perhaps lighting a candle or incense and playing soft music. Tell the students that the pastoral and catholic epistles, which were written to support early Christians in their lives of faith, can also support us today in our efforts to live as more faithful disciples. Ask the students to quiet their minds and open their hearts as they listen to the quotes their peers have selected from these writings.

> **Teacher Note**
>
> If little time remains, the following prayer experience may be used as the opening prayer for the next class session.

10. **Invite** each group to read, slowly and prayerfully, the quotes it selected from the pastoral and catholic epistles (i.e., its responses to question D on the handout). Allow a brief moment of silence after each quote. Once all the quotes have been read, conclude with your own spontaneous prayer. Ask the Holy Spirit to enliven your students' minds, hearts, and spirits, so that God's Word, dwelling securely within them, may find concrete expression in their loving acts of service, justice, and compassion.

 Understand

Step 8

Make sure the students are all on track with their final performance tasks, if you have assigned them.

If possible, devote 50 to 60 minutes for the students to ask questions about the tasks and to work individually or in their small groups.

1. **Remind** the students to bring to class any work they have already prepared so that they can work on it during the class period. If necessary, reserve the library or media center so the students can do any book or online research. Download and print extra copies of the handouts "Final

Performance Task Options for Unit 8" (Document #: TX002313) and "Rubric for Final Performance Tasks for Unit 8" (Document #: TX002314). Review the final performance task options, answer questions, and ask the students to choose one if they have not already done so.

2. **Provide** some class time for the students to work on their performance tasks. This then allows you to work with the students who need additional guidance with the project.

Step 9

Provide the students with a tool to use for reflecting on what they learned in the unit and how they learned.

This learning experience will provide the students with an excellent opportunity to reflect on how their understanding of the late first-century writings of the New Testament has developed throughout the unit.

1. **Prepare** for this learning experience by downloading and printing the hand-out "Learning about Learning" (Document #: TX001159; see Appendix), one for each student. Ask the students to bring their completed preassessment handout "Crossword Puzzle: Late First-Century New Testament Writings" (Document #: TX002312) with them to class.

2. **Distribute** the handout and give the students about 15 minutes to answer the questions quietly. For the question "How did your understanding of the subject matter change throughout the unit?" refer the students back to their completed crossword puzzle. Invite them to choose the one concept from each color-coded category (red, yellow, and green) that they learned the most about during this unit. For each of these, ask the students to consider what learning experiences were most helpful to them in gaining new knowledge and in clarifying, deepening, and expanding their existing knowledge.

3. **Invite** the students to share any reflections they have about the content they learned as well as their insights into the way they learned.

4. **Direct** the students to keep this handout in a separate section of their folder or binder so that they can refer back to it.

Crossword Puzzle: Late First-Century New Testament Writings

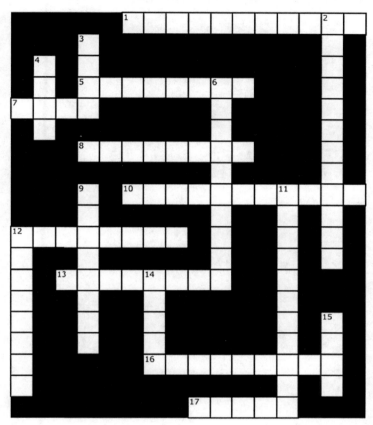

Across

1. A type or foreshadowing of Jesus the High Priest
5. The Israelites' living outside of Palestine after the Babylonian Exile
7. The Book of Revelation was written in symbolic language, or _____ so that Christians could understand its message but the Romans could not.
8. The four _____ of the Apocalypse
10. A type of literature well known from the first century BC to the second century AD, but less familiar to us today
12. Type of epistle in the New Testament directed to leaders of the early Church
13. Roman emperor who persecuted the Christians during his reign
16. A key to understanding the Book of Revelation
17. Number that symbolizes perfection

Down

2. Parts of the Letter to the Hebrews that encourage the early Christians to remain faithful
3. An example of a catholic epistle
4. What finally triumphs in the Book of Revelation
6. The last book in the Bible
9. Universal
11. Major problem that the early Christians faced
12. Christology of the Letter to the Hebrews
14. An example of a pastoral epistle
15. Image used for Jesus in the Book of Revelation

Document #: TX002312

Answer Key

Across
1. Melchizedek
5. Diaspora
7. code
8. horsemen
10. apocalyptic
12. pastoral
13. Domitian
16. symbolism
17. seven

Down
2. exhortations
3. Jude
4. good
6. Revelation
9. catholic
11. persecution
12. priestly
14. Titus
15. lamb

© 2012 by Saint Mary's Press
Living in Christ Series

Document #: TX002312

Final Performance Task Options for Unit 8

Important Information for All Three Options

The following are the main ideas that you are to understand from this unit. They should appear in this final performance task so that your teacher can assess whether you learned the most essential content.

- The Book of Revelation was written at a time in which the early Christian communities faced persecution.

- The Book of Revelation uses the conventions of apocalyptic literature, including symbolism, crisis imagery, and visions.

- The Letter to the Hebrews presents a Christology that draws on the tradition of the ancient Israelite priesthood.

- The pastoral epistles, which are attributed to Paul, and the catholic epistles address the various needs and situations of the early Christians.

In addition to demonstrating understanding of these four main concepts of the unit, your final performance task must also contain or demonstrate the following:

- In-depth, substantial content appropriate for an upper-level high-school religious studies course

- Responsible and accurate use of Scripture

- Substantive content that creatively and accurately engages with and interprets the material of this unit

- Proper grammar, spelling, and diction

- A neat and well-organized presentation

Option 1: An Exegetical Paper

Choose one passage, approximately five to fifteen verses in length, from any of the late first-century New Testament writings that you have studied in this unit. Ask your teacher to approve the passage that you select. Then, research and write a four- to five-page exegetical paper in which you interpret that passage. Use one of the exegetical methods you studied in unit 2, and consult at least three sources of information other than your student book. Your paper should follow this structure:

- an introduction that situates the passage you have chosen within the broad context of the literary, historical, and theological emphases of the book in which it appears

- an overview of the major topics or questions regarding the selected passage that your paper will explore

- an explanation of the methodology you will use to interpret the passage—that is, literary, sociohistorical, or ideological

- at least three substantive body paragraphs in which you analyze the passage using the methodology you have chosen and present your interpretation

- a conclusion in which you apply your interpretation of the passage to some aspect of the world today: for example, a concern that many young people face, a problem that your school is encountering, or a pressing matter of national or international justice

- a bibliography

Option 2: A Catholic Radio Talk Show

Write and produce a 5- to 8-minute episode of a Catholic radio talk show titled *Misunderstood Books of the Bible*. The focus of this episode will be misunderstood books of the New Testament, especially those late first-century writings that are difficult for modern-day audiences to read and interpret because of their literary genre, sociohistorical context, or theological perspective. Your show may include interviews with biblical scholars, appearances by time-traveling authors of one or more of these books, or phone calls from listeners who offer comments or questions. On the due date, submit a written transcript of your program, as well as an audio file of the program itself.

Option 3: A Bible Game Show

Develop a Bible game show in which contestants demonstrate the extent and depth of their knowledge of late first-century New Testament writings. You may model your show on one with which you are already familiar (like *Jeopardy* or *Knowledge Bowl*), or you may develop your own. Be sure that the bank of questions you generate for your show covers not only the basic factual information of this unit but also more complex and in-depth analysis and understanding. On the due date, submit your show in either paper or electronic format, as well as a list of all of your questions and answers. We may play part of your show in class, with your classmates as the contestants.

Rubric for Final Performance Tasks for Unit 8

Criteria	4	3	2	1
Assignment includes all items requested in the instructions.	Assignment includes all items requested, and they are completed above expectations.	Assignment includes all items requested.	Assignment includes over half of the items requested.	Assignment includes less than half of the items requested.
Assignment shows understanding of the following concept: *The Book of Revelation was written at a time in which the early Christian communities faced persecution.*	Assignment shows unusually insightful understanding of this concept.	Assignment shows good understanding of this concept.	Assignment shows adequate understanding of this concept.	Assignment shows little understanding of this concept.
Assignment shows understanding of the following concept: *The Book of Revelation uses the conventions of apocalyptic literature, including symbolism, crisis imagery, and visions.*	Assignment shows unusually insightful understanding of this concept.	Assignment shows good understanding of this concept.	Assignment shows adequate understanding of this concept.	Assignment shows little understanding of this concept.
Assignment shows understanding of the following concept: *The Letter to the Hebrews presents a Christology that draws on the tradition of the ancient Israelite priesthood.*	Assignment shows unusually insightful understanding of this concept.	Assignment shows good understanding of this concept.	Assignment shows adequate understanding of this concept.	Assignment shows little understanding of this concept.
Assignment shows understanding of the following concept: *The pastoral epistles, which are attributed to Paul, and the catholic epistles address the various needs and situations of the early Christians.*	Assignment shows unusually insightful understanding of this concept.	Assignment shows good understanding of this concept.	Assignment shows adequate understanding of this concept.	Assignment shows little understanding of this concept.
Assignment uses proper grammar, spelling, and diction.	Assignment has no grammar or spelling errors.	Assignment has one grammar or spelling error.	Assignment has two grammar or spelling errors.	Assignment has more than two grammar or spelling errors.
Assignment uses its assigned or chosen media effectively.	Assignment uses its assigned or chosen media in a way that greatly enhances it.	Assignment uses its assigned or chosen media effectively.	Assignment uses its assigned or chosen media somewhat effectively.	Assignment uses its assigned or chosen media ineffectively.
Assignment is neatly done.	Assignment not only is neat but is exceptionally creative.	Assignment is neatly done.	Assignment is neat for the most part.	Assignment is not neat.

Vocabulary for Unit 8

apocalyptic literature: A literary form that uses highly dramatic and symbolic language to offer hope to a people in crisis.

apostate: A person who was a believer but has abandoned his or her faith.

crisis imagery: A common literary feature of apocalyptic writing that includes images or visions of widespread chaos and cataclysmic destruction.

Dispersion (Diaspora): Refers to the Israelites' living outside of Palestine after the Babylonian Exile; *Diaspora* means "dispersion" or "the scattered ones."

end times: In apocalyptic literature, refers to the end of the persecution that the intended audience is presently enduring. Often misinterpreted as referring to the end of the world.

expiation: The act of atoning for sin or wrongdoing.

Holy of Holies: The most holy place in the Tabernacle, which at one time contained the Ark of the Covenant. Only the High Priest could enter, and he only once a year.

Levitical priests: The priests of ancient Israel, who offered sacrifice on behalf of the people at the Temple in Jerusalem. They were all members of the tribe of Levi, descendants of Aaron.

martyr: A person who suffers death because of his or her beliefs. The Church has canonized many martyrs as saints.

New Jerusalem: In the Book of Revelation, a symbol of a renewed society in which God dwells; a symbol of the Church, the "holy city," the assembly of the People of God called together from "the ends of the earth"; also, in other settings, a symbol of Heaven.

prophet: A person God chooses to speak his message of salvation. In the Bible, primarily a communicator of a divine message of repentance to the Chosen People, not necessarily a person who predicted the future.

salvation: From the Latin *salvare,* meaning "to save," referring to the forgiveness of sins and the restoration of friendship with God, attained for us through the Paschal Mystery—Christ's work of redemption accomplished through his Passion, death, Resurrection, and Ascension. Only at the time of judgment can a person be certain of salvation, which is a gift of God.

Septuagint: A Greek translation of the Old Testament begun about 250 BC. The Septuagint included the forty-six books of the Old Testament. It is often referred to by the Roman number LXX, which means seventy, in honor of the legendary seventy rabbis who translated the Hebrew text into Greek in supposedly seventy days.

vision: A revelation given by God to an individual or group that evokes the imagination and stirs strong emotions. In apocalyptic literature, these often include symbolism and allegory.

© 2012 by Saint Mary's Press
Living in Christ Series

Document #: TX002315

Literary Features of Apocalyptic Writing

1. Circle the chapters in Revelation that your group has been assigned:

4–5

6–7

12–13

16–17

20–21

2. Read through the following list of common literary features of apocalyptic writing. Then examine your assigned chapters in the Book of Revelation, seeking instances of that feature in those chapters. Note these instances (chapter and verse, with a brief description) in the space allotted in the right-hand column. You will not find every feature in your chapters; simply find as many as you can.

Literary Feature	Examples in the Book of Revelation
angels or heavenly messengers: Beings who impart information or visions from God to the writer	
crisis imagery: Images or visions of widespread chaos and cataclysmic destruction	
end times: The end of the persecution that the intended audience is presently enduring; sometimes misinterpreted as referring to the end of the world	
good vs. evil: A cosmic battle in which good will ultimately triumph	
judgment: The reward of the just and the punishment or demise of the unjust	
Old Testament references: Not necessarily direct quotes but rather literary allusions or references evocative of the Old Testament (*Note:* This literary feature does not apply to the Book of Daniel, an apocalyptic text that itself appears in the Old Testament.)	

renewal of Heaven or earth: The creation of a new world order, in which good triumphs over evil	
sealed book: Secret knowledge is placed in a sealed book that can be opened only during the end times.	
suffering: Descriptions of suffering that the target audience is currently enduring, such as famine, war, conquest, plagues, natural disasters, and death	
symbolism: Words, colors, and numbers used to suggest a deeper meaning	
visions: Granted by God to the person receiving secret knowledge; often contain symbolic or allegorical elements	

New Testament Christologies

Mark	A human, suffering Messiah
Luke	A universal Savior who extends love and mercy to all
Matthew	The New Moses
John	The Divine Son of God
Acts	The one who appears to Paul on the road to Damascus
Corinthians	The one who dwells in every member of the Church
Romans	The one who was "raised from the dead by the glory of the Father, so that we too might walk in newness of life" (6:4)
Hebrews	The great High Priest in the tradition of the ancient Israelite priesthood
Revelation	The Lamb who was slain, who now reigns in Heaven, and who will one day reign on earth as well

Living in Christ Series

Document #: TX002317

Priests and Levites

Martin C. Albl, PhD

In modern times, we think of a priest or a minister as a person who has a special calling or vocation to serve God and God's people. In ancient Judaism, however, the priesthood was hereditary—the tribe of Levi was set aside to serve as priests.

Aaron, Moses' brother, a member of the tribe of Levi, was the first priest, and all his male descendants were priests (see Ex 28:1). The entire tribe of Levi was set apart to oversee the worship of God, at first in the dwelling that contained the Ark of the Covenant, and later in the Temple (see Nm 1:47–54, 8:5–26; 1 Chr 24). Male members of the tribe who were not sons of Aaron were known as Levites. They acted primarily as assistants to the priests in conducting the worship of the Lord (see Nm 18:1–5).

Because they had been set aside for this special task, members of the tribe of Levi did not inherit a portion of the land of Israel, nor were they to work the land. Priests and Levites were supported directly through activities of worship. Portions of the sacrifices provided food for the priests, and the Levites were supported by tithes (see vv. 8–21). These tithes were essentially on crops; the Levites in turn were to give a tenth of their tithes to the priests (see vv. 21–32).

Within the priestly families, Zadokite priests (descendants of Zadok, a priest who had anointed and supported King Solomon against his rivals [see 1 Kgs 1:38–39]) held a special position. After the return from the Babylonian Exile, the high priests in Jerusalem were Zadokites and remained so until the time of the Maccabean revolt. After that time, members of the Maccabean family (also known as Hasmoneans), who were non-Zadokites, served as high priests (see 1 Mc 10:18–20). Supporters of the Zadokites objected to this change. One Zadokite priest and his followers fled to Egypt and established a temple there. Another priestly group supporting the Zadokites established their own community in the desert at Qumran. The name Sadducee most likely derives from Zadok—so this Jewish group was probably connected with the Zadokite priesthood too.

Work in the Temple

Priests and Levites were divided into twenty-four divisions (sometimes called courses), meaning that they worked in the Temple for one week out of every twenty-four (see Lk 1:5–10; John the Baptist's father Zechariah belonged to the priestly division of Abijah).

The primary work of the priests at the Temple involved offering sacrifices. They had to inspect the animals for blemishes, slaughter the animals, skin them, and cut them up for distribution. They would also hear the confessions when a person brought a sin offering. Other tasks included offering incense (see Lk 1:9).

The Levites assisted the priests. Among their tasks were bringing in wood for the sacrifices, slaughtering the animals, and guarding the gates to the Temple. Levites also sang the Psalms during the Temple worship service. Names of some Levitical singers (see 1 Chr 6:16–33) are attached to various Psalms: Asaph (see Ps 50, 73–83), "the sons of Korah" (see 42–49, 84–85, 87–88), Heman (see 88), and Ethan (see 89).

© 2012 by Saint Mary's Press
Living in Christ Series

Document #: TX002318

Priests wore special clothes made from linen, not cotton (see Ez 44:17), including undergarments, a tunic, a sash, and a turban (or miter). They most likely worked barefoot.

The high priest wore additional garments, including a type of vest called an *ephod*, a "breastplate," and a crown (see Ex, ch. 28; Lv 8:1–13; Sir 45:8–13). These vestments were made of gold thread, and violet, purple, and scarlet yarn. In two precious stones on the straps of the *ephod* were carved the names of the twelve Tribes of Israel; twelve precious stones also decorated the breastplate. Small golden bells were sewn to the bottom of his tunic.

Priests maintained a higher degree of purity for their work in the Temple; for example, they had special restrictions on coming into contact with a dead body (Lv 21:1–8). Because physical wholeness was closely related to purity and holiness, priests were to have no physical defects (see vv. 16–23).

Only the high priest could enter the Holy of Holies in the Temple, and he could do so only once a year, on the Day of Atonement, Yom Kippur (see Lv 16:1–19).

Work Outside of the Temple

The high priest was not a religious leader only; he was also considered a leader of the whole community of Israel. After the Exile in Babylon, the governor of the community in Jerusalem, Zerubbabel, and Joshua, the high priest, are both mentioned as leaders (see Hg 1:1; see also 2 Chr 19:11). Later the Hasmonean rulers were political and military leaders as well as high priests (see 1 Mc 10:19–20).

The title chief priest does not refer to an official position in ancient Judaism; rather, it refers to a group of priests who, due to the fact that they belonged to a few aristocratic, high priestly families, were closely allied with the high priest.

Priests and Levites also served as judges (see Dt 21:5, 2 Chr 19:8–11, Ez 44:24), teachers of the Torah (see Neh 8:5-8, Sir 45:17), and scribes (in the sense of copying texts or writing up legal documents, and also in the sense of teaching the Torah).

Josephus thus says that the priests, led by the high priest and his colleagues, governed Israel by their tasks as interpreters of the Torah, judges, and punishers of wrongdoers.

In the time of Roman rule, the high priest and his council had the primary responsibility for keeping order. If they kept order and made sure that tribute was paid to the Romans, the Romans generally allowed the chief priests a fair amount of freedom to rule. It is likely that the high priest and his council regarded Jesus (with his claims to be the Messiah) as a threat to the Roman rule as well as to their own authority, and thus had him executed.

Sanhedrin

In the Gospel accounts of Jesus' trial, a group known as the Sanhedrin plays a key role. "As soon as morning came, the chief priests with the elders and the scribes, that is, the whole Sanhedrin, held a council" (Mk 15:1). With the urging of the high priest, they condemn Jesus to death (see Mt 26:59, Mk 14:64).

Scholars debate on the exact make-up of the Jerusalem Sanhedrin and the extent of its powers. The Mishna describes the Sanhedrin as composed of seventy-one leaders who met on the Temple Mount to make various judicial and religious decisions.

The name Sanhedrin is derived from the Greek *synedrion,* which is a general word for any gathering or meeting: meetings of city leaders were known as *synedrions.* The Sanhedrin mentioned in the Gospels

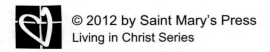

was most likely the primary council in Jerusalem, led by the high priest and composed of the chief priests and scribes along with non-priestly community leaders.

Scribes

The word *scribe* has a broad range of meanings in the Bible. The general sense of *scribe* is an educated person who knows how to write—similar to the English word *secretary.* The scribe was often a mid-level government official in both ancient Jewish and Hellenistic societies. In the villages, scribes would draw up legal documents (such as marriage agreements or business contracts).

The word *scribe* can also have the sense of one trained in interpreting the law. Ezra, leader of the Jewish community after their return from exile in Babylon, is described as "a scribe, well-versed in the law of Moses" (Ezr 7:6). Ezra was also a priest, which shows that the two roles could overlap.

In the Gospels, the scribes are often associated with Jerusalem and the chief priests (see Mk 14:1), as well as with the Pharisees (see Mt 23:2, Mk 7:1). They have a reputation as teachers of the Law (see Mk 1:22, 9:11).

Related Passages

- **Priests and Levites as descendants of Aaron:** Ex 28:1; Nm 1:47–54, 8:5–26, 18:1–5; 1 Chr, ch. 24

- **Assistant role of Levites:** Nm 18:1–7

- **Support of priests and Levites through tithes:** Nm 18:8–32

- **Vestments of the high priest:** Ex, ch. 28; Sir 45:8–13

- **Special purity laws for priests:** Lv, ch. 21

- **High priest and the Holy of Holies:** Lv 16:1–19

- **Priests as judges and teachers:** Dt 21:5, Sir 45:17

- **Sanhedrin:** Mk 14:53–64

- **Scribes:** Ezr 7:6; Mk 1:22, 7:1, 9:11, 14:1

This handout is excerpted from *Saint Mary's Press® Essential Guide to Biblical Life and Times*, by Martin Albl (Winona, MN: Saint Mary's Press, 2009), pages 96–98. Copyright © 2009 by Saint Mary's Press. All rights reserved.

The Tradition of the Ancient Israelite Priesthood and the Letter to the Hebrews

Traditions of the Ancient Israelite Priesthood	Description and Definition	Application and Interpretation in Hebrews
Expiation		2:14–18
High Priest		4:14—5:10
Levitical priesthood		7:23–28
Tabernacle		9:1–5,23–28

Traditions of the Ancient Israelite Priesthood	Description and Definition	Application and Interpretation in Hebrews
Holy of Holies		9:6–12
Covenant		9:13–22
Sacrifice		10:1–10

After you have completed the chart, discuss the following question with your partner and write a brief response: What important information about Jesus' life, identity, and saving mission emerges from the unique Christology of the Letter to the Hebrews?

The Pastoral and Catholic Epistles

With your group, discuss questions A through D and complete the column corresponding to your group. During the class discussion, use the other columns to take notes on the findings that the other groups report.

	Group 1: 1 Timothy	Group 2: 2 Timothy & Titus	Group 3: James & Jude	Group 4: 1 & 2 Peter	Group 5: 1, 2, & 3 John
A. What is one way in which this selection is similar to one or more of the Pauline Letters—for example, in content, format, or tone?					
B. What is one way in which this selection is different from the Pauline Letters?					

Document #: TX002320

C. What is one problem or issue in the early Christian community to which the author or authors of this selection are responding? What solution or advice regarding this problem is offered?					
D. What is one quote from this selection that you believe to be particularly relevant to our lives of faith today?					

Document #: TX002320

Unit 8 Test

Part 1: True or False

Write *true* or *false* in the space next to each statement.

1. _____ The Book of Revelation foretells the end of the world.

2. _____ The Letter to the Hebrews portrays Jesus as a modern-day priest.

3. _____ The Book of Revelation was written in code.

4. _____ The catholic epistles are addressed only to Roman Catholics.

5. _____ Conventions of apocalyptic literature include symbolism, crisis imagery, and visions.

6. _____ The books of the New Testament present a variety of Christologies.

7. _____ At the time in which the Book of Revelation was written, the early Christians were being persecuted by the Greeks.

8. _____ In the Book of Revelation, the Lamb who was slain is a symbol for Jesus.

9. _____ The author of the Letter to the Hebrews compares the sacrifice of Jesus' death with the sacrifices offered by the Levitical priests at the Temple in Jerusalem.

10. _____ The pastoral epistles are Jude, Hebrews, and 1 John.

Part 2: Matching

Match each term in column 1 with a statement from column 2. Write the letter that corresponds to your choice in the space provided.

Column 1

1. _____ exhortations

2. _____ apocalyptic literature

3. _____ crisis imagery

4. _____ Melchizedek

5. _____ pastoral

6. _____ Diaspora

7. _____ Revelation

8. _____ expiation

9. _____ Domitian

10. _____ Holy of Holies

11. _____ vision

12. _____ martyr

13. _____ New Jerusalem

14. _____ Levitical priests

Column 2

A. the Israelites' living outside of Palestine after the Babylonian Exile

B. foreshadows Jesus the high priest

C. parts of the Letter to the Hebrews that encourage the early Christians to remain faithful

D. Roman emperor who persecuted the Christians

E. type of epistle in the New Testament that was directed to leaders of the early Church

F. a literary form that uses dramatic elements and symbolism to offer hope to people in crisis

G. the last book in the Bible

H. a revelation given by God that evokes the imagination and stirs strong emotions

I. symbol of a renewed society in which God dwells

J. a person who suffers death because of his or her beliefs

K. the priests of ancient Israel

L. the most holy place in the Tabernacle, containing the Ark of the Covenant

M. the means of atoning or making reparation for sin or wrongdoing

N. a common feature of apocalyptic writing, which includes visions of chaos and destruction

Document #: TX002321

Part 3: Essay

Respond to the following with at least two substantial paragraphs.

1. In what sociohistorical context was the Book of Revelation written? How does knowing this context help us to understand and interpret this book accurately?

2. In what ways does the Book of Revelation follow the literary conventions of apocalyptic literature? How does this information help us to understand and interpret this book accurately?

3. What is the Christology of the Letter to the Hebrews?

4. Choose any one of the pastoral epistles or catholic epistles. Explain how the author of this epistle attempted to support the early Christian community by responding to its concrete needs, problems, and concerns. What is one specific way in which the message of this epistle may be relevant to our lives of faith today?

Unit 8 Test Answer Key

Part 1: True or False

1. false
2. false
3. true
4. false

5. true
6. true
7. false
8. true

9. true
10. false

Part 2: Matching

1. C
2. F
3. N
4. B
5. E

6. A
7. G
8. M
9. D
10. L

11. H
12. J
13. I
14. K

Part 3: Essay

1. The Book of Revelation was written during a time in which the early Christians faced persecution from the Romans because, among other reasons, they would not participate in the imperial cult that worshipped the emperor as a deity. Persecution of Christians was sporadic and often limited to particular cities or regions during the first three centuries of Christianity. However, when it occurred, it brought severe penalties, including torture and death.

Biblical scholars believe that the Book of Revelation was written during the reign of the Emperor Domitian (AD 81–96). Domitian has been described as a tyrant who ruthlessly persecuted not only Christians but also his political enemies. He even ordered the execution of some of his own family members.

Because of this context of persecution, the early Christians needed a way to communicate with one another that they could understand, but that their Roman oppressors could not. The Book of Revelation is, therefore, a prime example of a message to a persecuted community that is written in symbolic language. The early Christians would be able to determine the meaning of the various numbers, colors, and symbols in the book; the Romans would not.

Awareness of this sociohistorical context of persecution can help us to understand and interpret the Book of Revelation accurately. Images from the book that seem disturbing or fanciful make sense when we take the time to learn the symbolic language in which they were written and, in that process, to decipher the message of hope this book offered to a struggling, suffering Christian community.

2. The Book of Revelation is an example of apocalyptic literature, that is, writing that uses dramatic elements and highly symbolic language to offer hope to people in a crisis. As such it uses many of the typical literary features of this genre. For example, the author receives information and visions from an angel. These highly symbolic and allegorical visions include crisis imagery, that is, images of widespread chaos and cataclysmic destruction. The knowledge the author receives from the angel is placed in a sealed book, which can be opened only at the end times. Contrary to popular belief, the *end times* does not refer to the end of the world; rather, it refers to the end of the suffering or persecution being endured by the audience to whom the book was directed. In the cosmic battle between good and evil that leads up to these end times, good ultimately triumphs, the just are rewarded, evildoers are punished, and a new world order (presented as "a new heaven and a new earth") is established.

Understanding the ways in which the Book of Revelation follows the conventions of apocalyptic literature helps us to understand and interpret it accurately. First, it enables us to refute the popular misconception that the Book of Revelation foretells the end of the world. Second, it enables us to understand more clearly parts of the book that seem obscure, strange, or even disturbing. Third, it helps us to discern the deeper truths that the Book of Revelation can offer us, even though we live in a different cultural and sociohistorical situation than the people to whom this book was originally directed. These truths include that Jesus Christ is our Savior and our Judge—the one who has triumphed over sin, evil, and death and who offers us eternal life.

3. The Christology of the Letter to the Hebrews draws on the traditions of the ancient Israelite priesthood in presenting Jesus as a great High Priest. The work of the Levitical priests, centered in the Temple in Jerusalem, consisted of offering sacrifices on behalf of the people, as directed by the laws in the Torah. These priests—all members of the tribe of Levi, descendants of Aaron—were led by the high priest. Once a year, on the Day of Atonement (Yom Kippur), the high priest would enter the Holy of Holies, the most sacred part of the Tabernacle.

The author of the Letter to the Hebrews interprets the life, ministry, and saving death of Jesus using language and concepts associated with the ancient Israelite priesthood. For example, he presents Jesus' death as a sacrifice for sin, which, unlike the sacrifices offered daily in the Temple in Jerusalem, will never need to be repeated. Moreover, unlike the power of the Levitical priests, whose priesthood ended with their deaths, Jesus' power to save us endures forever. The author also compares Jesus' entrance into the heavenly sanctuary with the high priest's annual entrance into the Holy of Holies. Finally, although the worship and sacrifice offered by the priests of ancient Israel was a manifestation of the first covenant God made with humanity, Jesus is the mediator of a second covenant, a new covenant. Through his life, death, and Resurrection, Jesus offers us redemption, the forgiveness of our sin, and eternal life.

4. Answers will vary. Students will choose to write about 1 Timothy, 2 Timothy, Titus, James, Jude, 1 Peter, 2 Peter, 1 John, 2 John, or 3 John.

Appendix

Additional Resources
"Learning about Learning" (Document #: TX001159)
"Semester-Long Project Overview" (Document #: TX002229)
"Semester-Long Project: A Portfolio of Exegetical Papers" (Document #: TX002230)
"Course Synthesis Overview" (Document #: TX002231)
"Course Synthesis" (Document #: TX002232)

Learning about Learning

We can understand ourselves better by taking the time to review the process of learning the material in a unit.

Respond by using the scale below. Put a mark where you think your understanding falls. Then write your answers to the other questions below.

Unit Number and Name _____

Knew none of this material before	**Knew everything already**

What was your favorite learning experience in this unit and why? Do you usually enjoy this type of learning experience?

What was your least favorite learning experience and why? Do you usually find this type of learning experience challenging?

How did your understanding of the unit's subject matter change throughout the unit?

Was anything you learned particularly interesting? Why?

Write any other observations you have.

Document #: TX001159

Semester-Long Project Overview

Through this semester-long project option, the students develop expertise in all three of the exegetical methods presented in this course: literary criticism, sociohistorical criticism, and ideological criticism. In addition, the students reflect on their developing knowledge of the New Testament, articulate implications of that knowledge for their personal life of faith and for social justice, and consider the ways in which their exegetical skills may prove useful in other arenas.

To complete this project successfully, the students will choose an exegetical paper for their final performance task for any four of the units of this course. In these four papers, they must employ each of the three exegetical methods at least once. The completed portfolio consists of the following:

- the original copies of these four papers (with the grade and your comments)

- a four- or five-page reflective synthesis, as explained in the handout "Semester-Long Project: A Portfolio of Exegetical Papers" (Document #: TX002230).

Although the instructions on the handout indicate that the reflective synthesis should be a written paper, you could instead, at your discretion, offer students the option of presenting their synthesis in another format, such as a PowerPoint presentation, podcast, creative writing piece, or video. Ensure that students who choose an alternative format still address all of the questions listed on the handout "Semester-Long Project: A Portfolio of Exegetical Papers" (Document #: TX002230).

This portfolio may serve as the culminating project of the course in place of a traditional final exam. If you choose this option, you may wish to require that the students present their reflective syntheses orally to the class. Alternatively, you may facilitate an in-class sharing process in which the students share their reflective syntheses with a small group of their classmates.

Semester-Long Project: A Portfolio of Exegetical Papers

To complete this project successfully, you must choose the exegetical paper option for your final performance task for any four of the units of this course. In these four papers, you must employ each of the exegetical methods (literary criticism, sociohistorical criticism, and ideological criticism) in at least one paper. Your completed portfolio will consist of the original copies of these four papers (with your grade and teacher's comments), as well as a four- or five-page reflective synthesis.

In your reflective synthesis, provide thoughtful answers to the following questions as you consider all that you have learned throughout the semester, especially what you have learned from the process of writing your exegetical papers. Rather than simply summarizing your knowledge, a synthesis invites you to step back, look at the big picture, and notice associations, connections, relationships, and common themes in what you have been learning. Therefore, you may wish to articulate connections among elements of this project, the course content you have been studying all semester, and your personal experience. Do not number the questions and your responses; rather, use these questions to develop your reflective synthesis as an essay.

- Examine your four papers carefully, noting the order in which you wrote them. How did your skills in research and exegesis grow over the course of writing four papers? Did your approach to exegesis shift over the course of the semester? If so, how?

- If you were going to write a fifth paper now, how would you approach it? What would you do differently from what you did in the first four papers? What particular skills in research and exegesis do you feel you have mastered and can employ readily?

- Which of the three methods of exegesis most piqued your curiosity, intrigued you, or enabled you to engage with the text in a creative way? Why?

- Which of the three methods of exegesis was most difficult or challenging for you? Why?

- How might you use these exegetical skills in other academic disciplines, in your college studies, in other reading, or in other aspects of your life?

- How has your understanding of the New Testament grown, changed, or deepened through the process of writing these papers?

- In considering the passages on which your papers were focused, what theme or pattern do you notice that could inform your approach to or view of some important issue of social justice facing our Church or world?

- How has your close study of the New Testament—and especially your careful exegesis of selected passages from it—helped you to grow in faith? What have you learned about the essential role that the New Testament must play in a life of discipleship?

- What further questions do you have about the New Testament? What have your studies this semester made you still curious about? How will you satisfy that curiosity?

© 2012 by Saint Mary's Press
Living in Christ Series

Document #: TX002230

Compile your four exegetical papers and your reflective synthesis into a portfolio. The first page of the portfolio must be a table of contents. Submit the portfolio on the designated due date. Your teacher may also ask you to do an oral presentation of your reflective synthesis.

Course Synthesis Overview

In this learning experience, the students will synthesize the knowledge of the New Testament they have gained in this course and propose concrete ideas for applying this deep understanding of Scripture in their daily lives.

1. **Prepare** by downloading and printing the handout "Course Synthesis" (Document #: TX002232), one for each student. Ask the students to bring *all* of their completed copies of the handout "Learning about Learning" (Document #: TX001159), one for each unit they have studied in this course.

2. **Begin** by telling the students that this final learning experience will give them an opportunity to identify the knowledge they have gained about the New Testament during this course and to reflect on the significance of this knowledge for their lives of faith.

3. **Organize** the class into groups of four or five students. Distribute copies of the handout "Course Synthesis" (Document # TX002232). Ask the students to use the column labeled "What?" to list significant information they have gained about the New Testament during this course. Explain that referring to their accumulated copies of the handout "Learning about Learning" will help to refresh their memories. Ask them to list at least one concept for each unit they have studied. If they seem overwhelmed by the amount of information, they may find it helpful to focus on the person of Jesus: what have they learned from the various New Testament presentations of and reflections on the life, ministry, and saving work of Jesus? Allow about 15 minutes for the students to work.

4. **Direct** the students to turn their attention to the "So What?" column on the handout. Have them consider *who they are called to be* as a result of what they have learned about the New Testament:

   ▶ Who does the New Testament call you to be? Why does knowledge of the New Testament matter?

   ▶ For example, if we have learned that Jesus extended compassion to the poor, the sick, and the forgotten, then we are called to be compassionate and merciful in the circumstances of our own daily lives.

   ▶ If we have learned that Jesus was a real human being who experienced both happiness and sorrow, then we are called to view all of the events of our lives—whether joyful or difficult—through the eyes of faith.

Allow about 10 minutes for the students to list their responses in this column.

5. **Direct** the students to work on the "Now What?" column on the handout. Have them review the first two columns and reflect on *what they are called to do* as a result of what they have learned about the New Testament.

   ▶ How can our knowledge of the New Testament shape our decisions, priorities, and actions?

   ▶ For example, if we have learned that the New Testament cannot be legitimately used to support anti-Semitism, then perhaps we are called to work cooperatively with our Jewish sisters and brothers on interfaith projects of service and justice.

   ▶ If we have learned that Jesus focused his ministry on the marginalized people of his day and age, then we are called to seek out the marginalized of our own time—to welcome them, serve them, and advocate for their needs.

Allow about 10 minutes for the students to list their responses in this column.

6. **Draw** the class back together, and invite the groups to share their work, beginning with "What" they have learned, moving to "So What," and ending with "Now What." Affirm the students' depth of understanding and reflection as they seek to synthesize an entire semester's worth of material. In addition, challenge them to commit themselves to one "So What" and one "Now What": that is, to choose one item from each of those columns that they will personally work on in the coming weeks and months. Help the students to recognize that true understanding of the New Testament cannot be reduced simply to factual knowledge. Rather, true understanding must take deep root in our minds, hearts, and spirits; be expressed in our words and actions; and transform us more and more into the image of Christ.

7. **Conclude** this learning experience with prayer.

- Call the students to quiet, perhaps by lighting a candle or incense or by playing soft music.

- Direct a student to read Luke 4:16–21 aloud.

- Invite the students to recall that, as disciples, we share in the mission of Jesus to "bring glad tidings to the poor. / . . . to proclaim liberty to captives / and recovery of sight to the blind, / to let the oppressed go free, / and to proclaim a year acceptable to the Lord" (Luke 4:18–19). Through our Baptism, we have been commissioned to partner with God in continuing to bring this ancient promise of Scripture to fulfillment.

- If your students are willing, ask each person to mention aloud one of the items from the "So What" or "Now What" columns to which she or he is willing to commit herself or himself.

- Conclude by praying the Lord's Prayer together and then listening to a suitable song or hymn, such as "I Have Been Anointed," by Steven C. Warner, available on the CD *God Is My Rock: Songs of Strength and Mercy* (World Library Publications, 2004).

Teacher Note

If you have adequate time left in the semester, one of the "Now What" items could easily be developed into a service-learning project that your students can coordinate with your guidance. There would be no more powerful and appropriate way to end a course on the New Testament than to engage in concrete action on behalf of those in need. Even if time does not permit this, encourage the students to act on these items in other venues, perhaps as a project for another class or as a way to fulfill your school's community service requirement.

Course Synthesis

What?	So What?	Now What?

Document #: TX002232

Appendix 2

Student Book/Teacher Guide Correlation

Section 1: The Word of God

Section 2: The Synoptic Gospels and the Acts of the Apostles

Section 3: The Johannine Writings

Section 4: The Letters of Paul

Part 2: The Letter to the Hebrews

Part 3: The Catholic Epistles

Acknowledgments

Scripture texts used in this work are taken from the *New American Bible, revised edition* © 2010, 1991, 1986, 1970 Confraternity of Christian Doctrine, Inc., Washington, DC. All Rights Reserved. No part of this work may be reproduced or transmitted in any form or by any means, electronic or mechanical, including photocopying, recording, or by any information storage and retrieval system, without permission in writing from the copyright owner.

Some of the Scripture texts in this book are paraphrased and are not to be interpreted or used as official translations of the Bible.

The list of what makes up a mature understanding on page 13 is from *Understanding by Design*, expanded 2nd edition, by Grant Wiggins and Jay McTighe (Upper Saddle River, NJ: Pearson Education, 2006), page 84. Copyright © 2005 by ASCD. Used with permission of ASCD.

The quotation on page 28 is from *The Documents of Vatican II,* Walter Abbott, general editor; Very Rev. Msgr. Joseph Gallagher, translation editor (New York: Guild Press, American Press, Association Press), page 715. Copyright © 1966 by the America Press.

The quotations on pages 29–30 and on the handout "Unit 1 Test Answer Key" (Document #: TX002207) from *Dogmatic Constitution on Divine Revelation (Dei Verbum*, 1965), numbers 10, 4, and 16; and page 33 from *Constitution on the Sacred Liturgy (Sacrosanctum Concilium*, 1963), number 35, are in *Vatican Council II: Volume 1: the Conciliar and Postconciliar Documents*, New Revised Edition, Austin Flannery, general editor (Northport, NY: Costello Publishing, 1996). Copyright © 1975, 1986, 1992, 1996 by Reverend Austin Flannery.

The quotations on page 36 and on the handout "Gospel Reflection Questions" (Document #: TX002205), and the excerpts on the handout "Reflections on the Liturgical Year" (Document #: TX002204) are from *The Liturgical Year*, by Joan Chittister (Nashville, TN: Thomas Nelson, 2009), pages 13, 11, 6, 10–11, and 13, respectively. Copyright © 2009 by Joan Chittister. Used with permission of Thomas Nelson, Inc., Nashville, TN. All rights reserved.

The excerpts on the handout "Vocabulary for Unit 1" (Document #: TX002196) and on page 84 are from the English translation of the *Catechism of the Catholic Church* for use in the United States of America, second edition, numbers 125 and 110. Copyright © 1994 by the United States Catholic Conference, Inc.—Libreria Editrice Vaticana (LEV). English translation of the *Catechism of the Catholic Church: Modifications from the Editio Typica* copyright © 1997 by the United States Catholic Conference, Inc.—LEV.

The excerpts on page 89 and on the handout "Priests and Levites" (Document #: TX002318) are from *Saint Mary's Press® Essential Guide to Biblical Life and Times*, by Martin Albl (Winona, MN: Saint Mary's Press, 2009), pages 42–43 and 96–98. Copyright © 2009 by Saint Mary's Press. All rights reserved.

Endnote Cited in a Quotation from the *Catechism of the Catholic Church,* Second Edition
Unit 2
1. *Dei Verbum* 12 § 2.